# ROYALS

## BEYOND INHUMAN

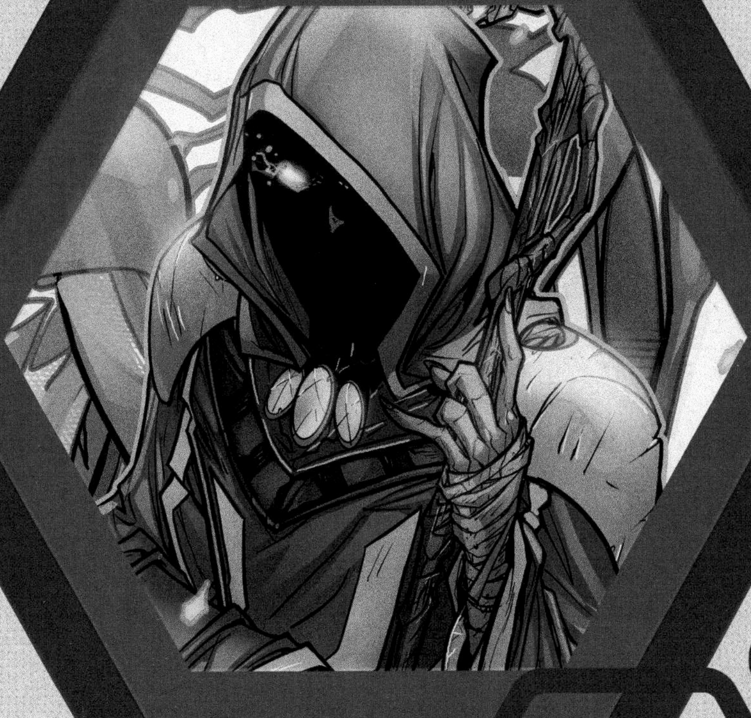

# EONS AGO,

THE ALIEN RACE KNOWN AS THE KREE EXPERIMENTED UPON EARLY MAN, IMBUING SOME OF THEM WITH HEIGHTENED PHYSICAL AND MENTAL POWER — AND THE POTENTIAL TO MANIFEST AMAZING ABILITIES. THESE HUMANS BECAME THE INHUMANS. AFTER THE KREE ABANDONED THEM AS A FAILED EXPERIMENT, THEY DISCOVERED A WAY TO UNLOCK THOSE ABILITIES — USING THE MYSTERY ELEMENT TERRIGEN.

MILLENNIA PASSED. IN THE MODERN DAY, THE INHUMANS — RULED BY THEIR KING, BLACK BOLT, AND QUEEN, MEDUSA — ESTABLISHED A HOME FOR THEMSELVES OUTSIDE MANHATTAN CALLED NEW ATTILAN.

BUT AFTER TERRIGEN WAS RELEASED INTO THE ATMOSPHERE, THE INHUMANS LEARNED IT WAS LETHAL TO MUTANTS, AND SO MEDUSA MADE THE DECISION TO DESTROY THE TERRIGEN, MEANING THERE WILL NOW BE NO MORE NEW INHUMANS. AS A RESULT, SHE ABDICATED THE THRONE — LEAVING THE INHUMANS WITHOUT THEIR ROYALS.

BUT IF THE ROYAL FAMILY CAN NO LONGER RULE INHUMANITY…THEY CAN STILL SAVE IT.

## BLACK BOLT
HUSBAND OF MEDUSA. HIS SLIGHTEST WORD WILL SHATTER MOUNTAINS.

## MARVEL BOY
KREE EXPLORER FROM ANOTHER DIMENSION. ENGINEERED WITH INSECT TRAITS FOR COMBAT SUPERIORITY.

## CRYSTAL
SISTER OF MEDUSA. SHE HAS TOTAL CONTROL OVER AIR, EARTH, FIRE, AND WATER.

## MEDUSA
WIFE OF BLACK BOLT. HER HAIR IS STRONGER THAN STEEL — AND ENTIRELY UNDER HER CONTROL.

## GORGON
COUSIN OF BLACK BOLT. ONE STOMP OF HIS HOOVES MAKES THE EARTH TREMBLE.

## SWAIN
A NEW INHUMAN. SHE CAN PUSH EMOTIONS AND OPINIONS IN HER FAVOR.

## FLINT
A NEW INHUMAN. ROCK AND STONE OBEYS HIS THOUGHTS — THE BIGGER, THE BETTER.

**ROYALS VOL. 1: BEYOND INHUMAN.** Contains material originally published in magazine form as ROYALS #1-5 and INHUMANS PRIME #1. First printing 2017. ISBN# 978-1-302-90694-8. Published by MARVEL WORLDWIDE, INC., a subsidiary of MARVEL ENTERTAINMENT, LLC. OFFICE OF PUBLICATION: 135 West 50th Street, New York, NY 10020. Copyright © 2017 MARVEL No similarity between any of the names, characters, persons, and/or institutions in this magazine with those of any living or dead person or institution is intended, and any such similarity which may exist is purely coincidental. **Printed in the U.S.A.** DAN BUCKLEY, President, Marvel Entertainment; JOE QUESADA, Chief Creative Officer; TOM BREVOORT, SVP of Publishing; DAVID BOGART, SVP of Business Affairs & Operations, Publishing & Partnership; C.B. CEBULSKI, VP of Brand Management & Development, Asia; DAVID GABRIEL, SVP of Sales & Marketing, Publishing; JEFF YOUNGQUIST, VP of Production & Special Projects; DAN CARR, Executive Director of Publishing Technology; ALEX MORALES, Director of Publishing Operations; SUSAN CRESPI, Production Manager; STAN LEE, Chairman Emeritus. For information regarding advertising in Marvel Comics or on Marvel.com, please contact Vit DeBellis, Integrated Sales Manager, at vdebellis@marvel.com. For Marvel subscription inquiries, please call 888-511-5480. **Manufactured between 8/11/2017 and 9/11/2017 by QUAD/GRAPHICS WASECA, WASECA, MN, USA.**

10 9 8 7 6 5 4 3 2 1

# ROYALS

## BEYOND INHUMAN

WRITER:
**AL EWING**

### INHUMANS PRIME #1

PENCILERS: **RYAN SOOK**
WITH **CHRIS ALLEN**

INKERS: **RYAN SOOK**, **WALDEN WONG**
& **KEITH CHAMPAGNE**

COLOR ARTIST: **PAUL MOUNTS**

COVER ART: **JONBOY MEYERS**

### ROYALS #1-5

ARTISTS: **JONBOY MEYERS** (#1-2)
& **THONY SILAS** (#2-5)
WITH **WILL ROBSON** (#3)

COLOR ARTISTS: **RYAN KINNAIRD** (#1-2)
& **JIM CHARALAMPIDIS** (#2-5)
WITH **JOSÉ VILLARRUBIA** (#5)

COVER ART:
**JONBOY MEYERS** (#1, #3-4),
**JONBOY MEYERS**
& **DAVID CURIEL** (#2)
AND **KRIS ANKA** (#5)

LETTERER:
**VC's CLAYTON COWLES**

ASSISTANT EDITOR:
**CHARLES BEACHAM**

ASSOCIATE EDITOR:
**SARAH BRUNSTAD**

EDITOR:
**WIL MOSS**

INHUMANS CREATED BY
**STAN LEE** & **JACK KIRBY**

COLLECTION EDITOR: **JENNIFER GRÜNWALD** | ASSISTANT EDITOR: **CAITLIN O'CONNELL**
ASSOCIATE MANAGING EDITOR: **KATERI WOODY** | EDITOR, SPECIAL PROJECTS: **MARK D. BEAZLEY**
VP PRODUCTION & SPECIAL PROJECTS: **JEFF YOUNGQUIST** | SVP PRINT, SALES & MARKETING: **DAVID GABRIEL**
BOOK DESIGNER: **JAY BOWEN**

EDITOR IN CHIEF: **AXEL ALONSO** | CHIEF CREATIVE OFFICER: **JOE QUESADA**
PRESIDENT: **DAN BUCKLEY** | EXECUTIVE PRODUCER: **ALAN FINE**

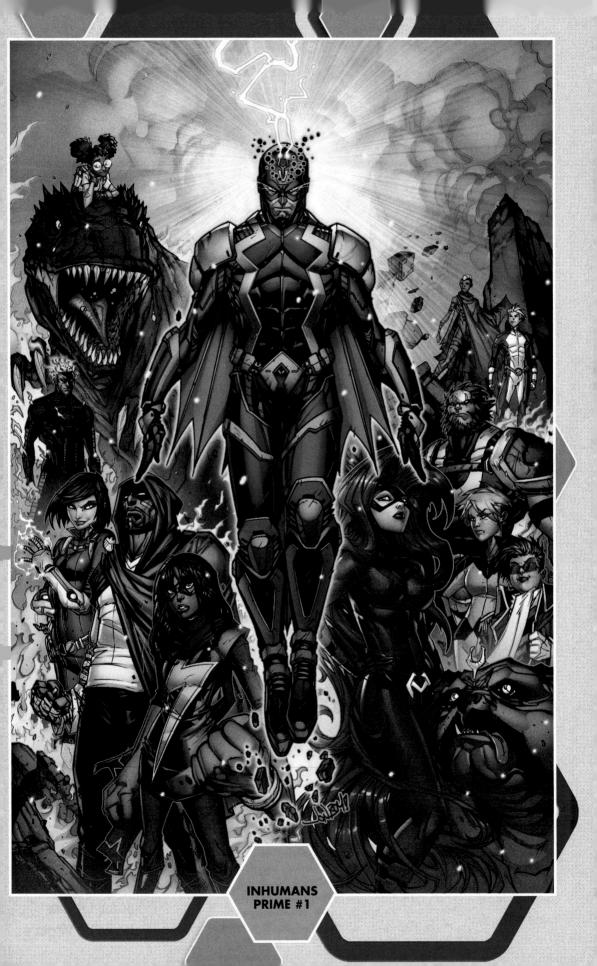

INHUMANS
PRIME #1

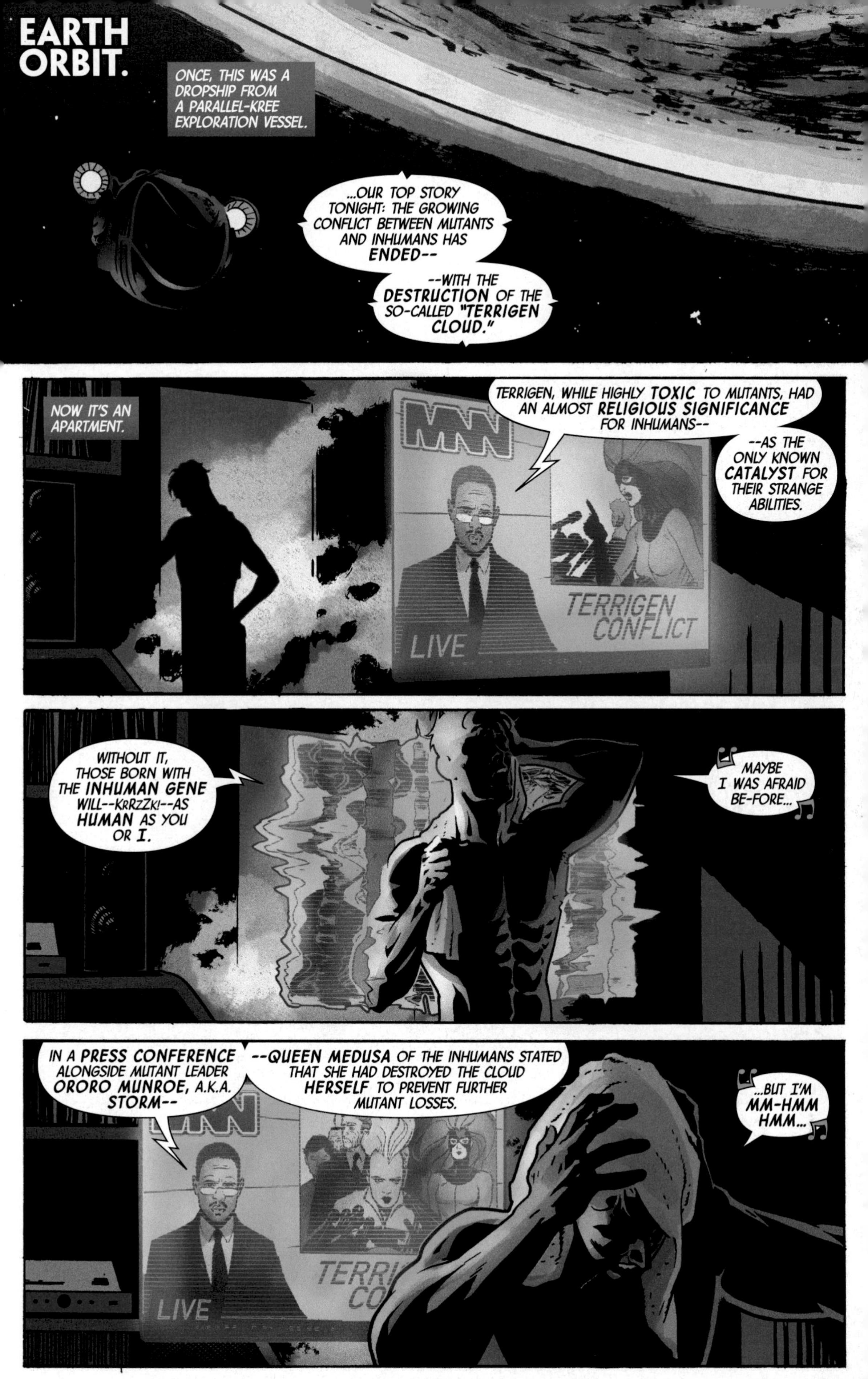
EARTH ORBIT.
ONCE, THIS WAS A DROPSHIP FROM A PARALLEL-KREE EXPLORATION VESSEL.
...OUR TOP STORY TONIGHT: THE GROWING CONFLICT BETWEEN MUTANTS AND INHUMANS HAS ENDED--
--WITH THE DESTRUCTION OF THE SO-CALLED "TERRIGEN CLOUD."
NOW IT'S AN APARTMENT.
MNN
TERRIGEN, WHILE HIGHLY TOXIC TO MUTANTS, HAD AN ALMOST RELIGIOUS SIGNIFICANCE FOR INHUMANS--
--AS THE ONLY KNOWN CATALYST FOR THEIR STRANGE ABILITIES.
TERRIGEN CONFLICT
LIVE
WITHOUT IT, THOSE BORN WITH THE INHUMAN GENE WILL--KRRZZK!--AS HUMAN AS YOU OR I.
MAYBE I WAS AFRAID BE-FORE...
IN A PRESS CONFERENCE ALONGSIDE MUTANT LEADER ORORO MUNROE, A.K.A. STORM--
--QUEEN MEDUSA OF THE INHUMANS STATED THAT SHE HAD DESTROYED THE CLOUD HERSELF TO PREVENT FURTHER MUTANT LOSSES.
...BUT I'M MM-HMM HMM...
LIVE

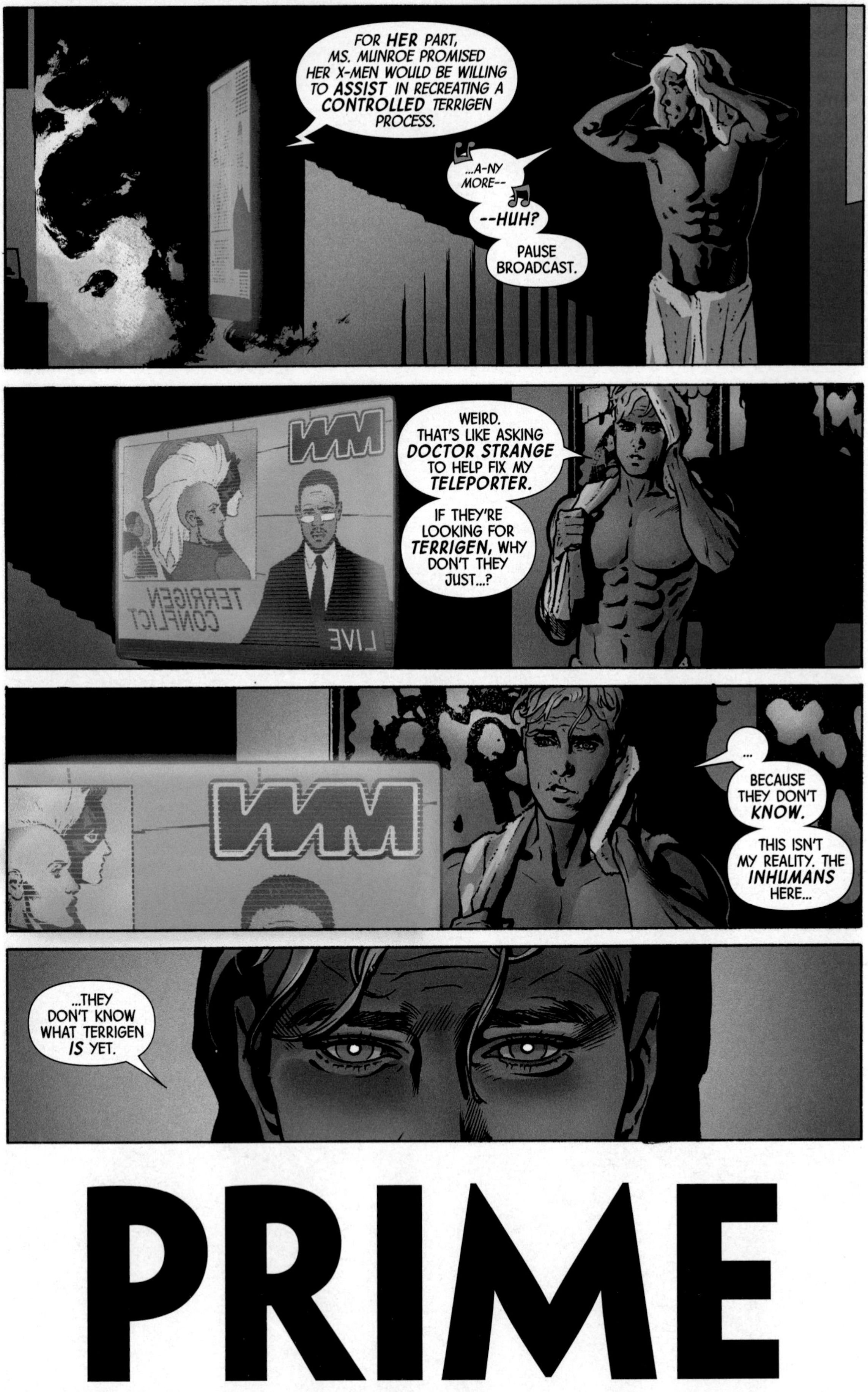
FOR HER PART, MS. MUNROE PROMISED HER X-MEN WOULD BE WILLING TO ASSIST IN RECREATING A CONTROLLED TERRIGEN PROCESS.
...A-NY MORE--
--HUH?
PAUSE BROADCAST.
WEIRD. THAT'S LIKE ASKING DOCTOR STRANGE TO HELP FIX MY TELEPORTER.
IF THEY'RE LOOKING FOR TERRIGEN, WHY DON'T THEY JUST...?
...
BECAUSE THEY DON'T KNOW.
THIS ISN'T MY REALITY. THE INHUMANS HERE...
...THEY DON'T KNOW WHAT TERRIGEN IS YET.

# PRIME

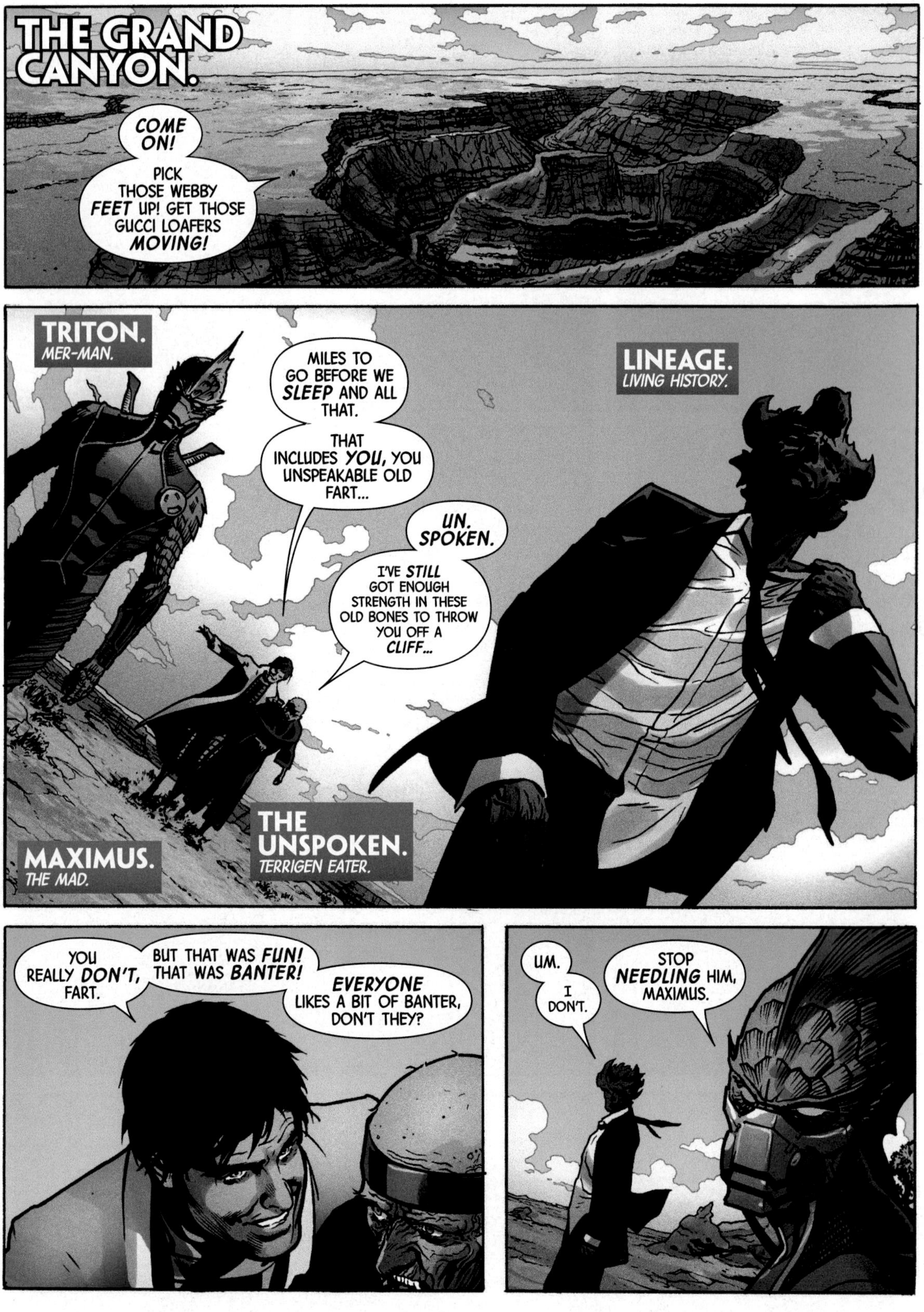
THE GRAND CANYON.
COME ON!
PICK THOSE WEBBY FEET UP! GET THOSE GUCCI LOAFERS MOVING!
TRITON. MER-MAN.
MILES TO GO BEFORE WE SLEEP AND ALL THAT.
THAT INCLUDES YOU, YOU UNSPEAKABLE OLD FART...
UN. SPOKEN.
I'VE STILL GOT ENOUGH STRENGTH IN THESE OLD BONES TO THROW YOU OFF A CLIFF...
LINEAGE. LIVING HISTORY.
MAXIMUS. THE MAD.
THE UNSPOKEN. TERRIGEN EATER.
YOU REALLY DON'T, FART.
BUT THAT WAS FUN! THAT WAS BANTER!
EVERYONE LIKES A BIT OF BANTER, DON'T THEY?
UM.
I DON'T.
STOP NEEDLING HIM, MAXIMUS.

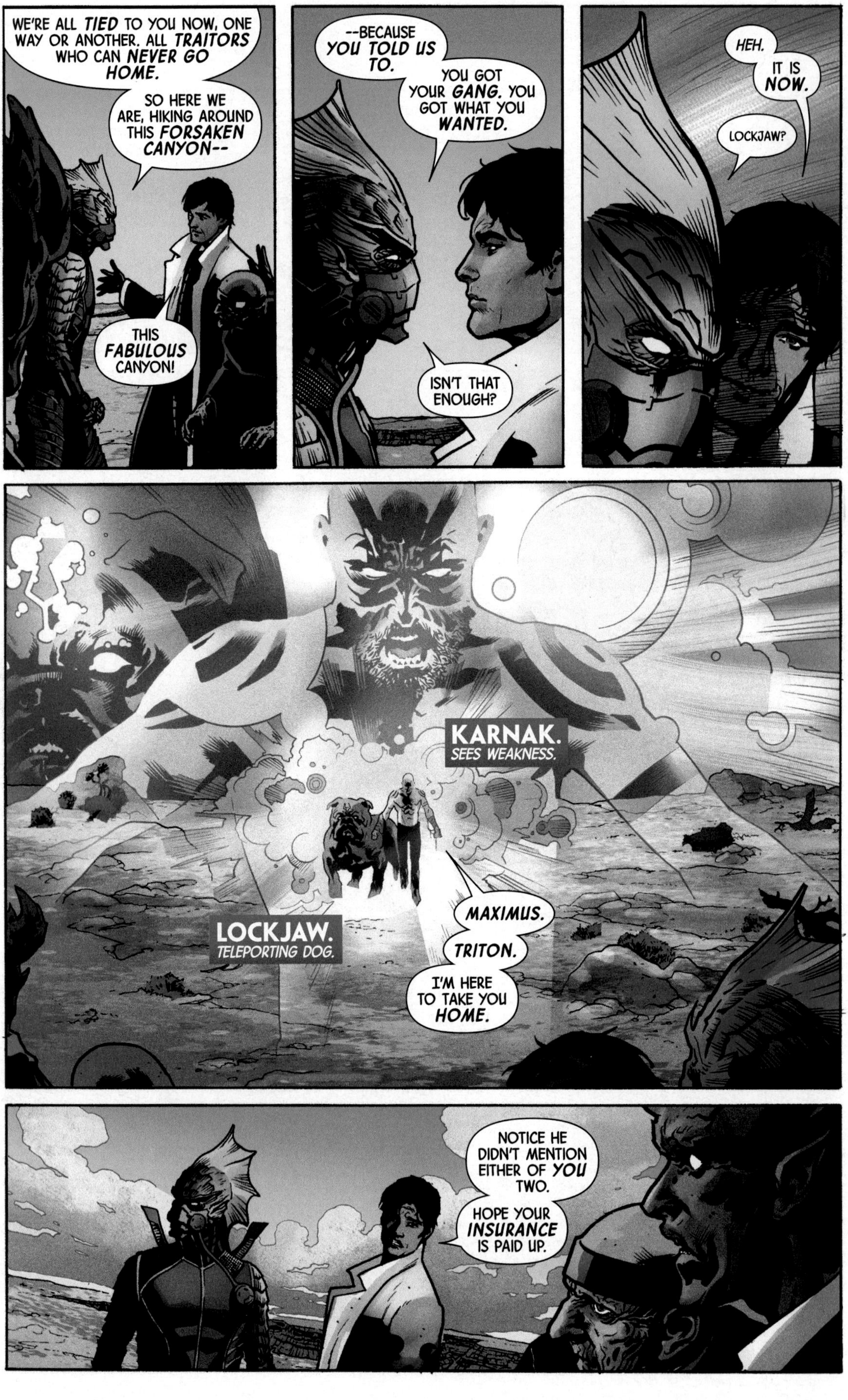
WE'RE ALL TIED TO YOU NOW, ONE WAY OR ANOTHER. ALL TRAITORS WHO CAN NEVER GO HOME.
SO HERE WE ARE, HIKING AROUND THIS FORSAKEN CANYON--
THIS FABULOUS CANYON!
--BECAUSE YOU TOLD US TO.
YOU GOT YOUR GANG. YOU GOT WHAT YOU WANTED.
ISN'T THAT ENOUGH?
HEH.
IT IS NOW.
LOCKJAW?
KARNAK. SEES WEAKNESS.
LOCKJAW. TELEPORTING DOG.
MAXIMUS.
TRITON.
I'M HERE TO TAKE YOU HOME.
NOTICE HE DIDN'T MENTION EITHER OF YOU TWO.
HOPE YOUR INSURANCE IS PAID UP.

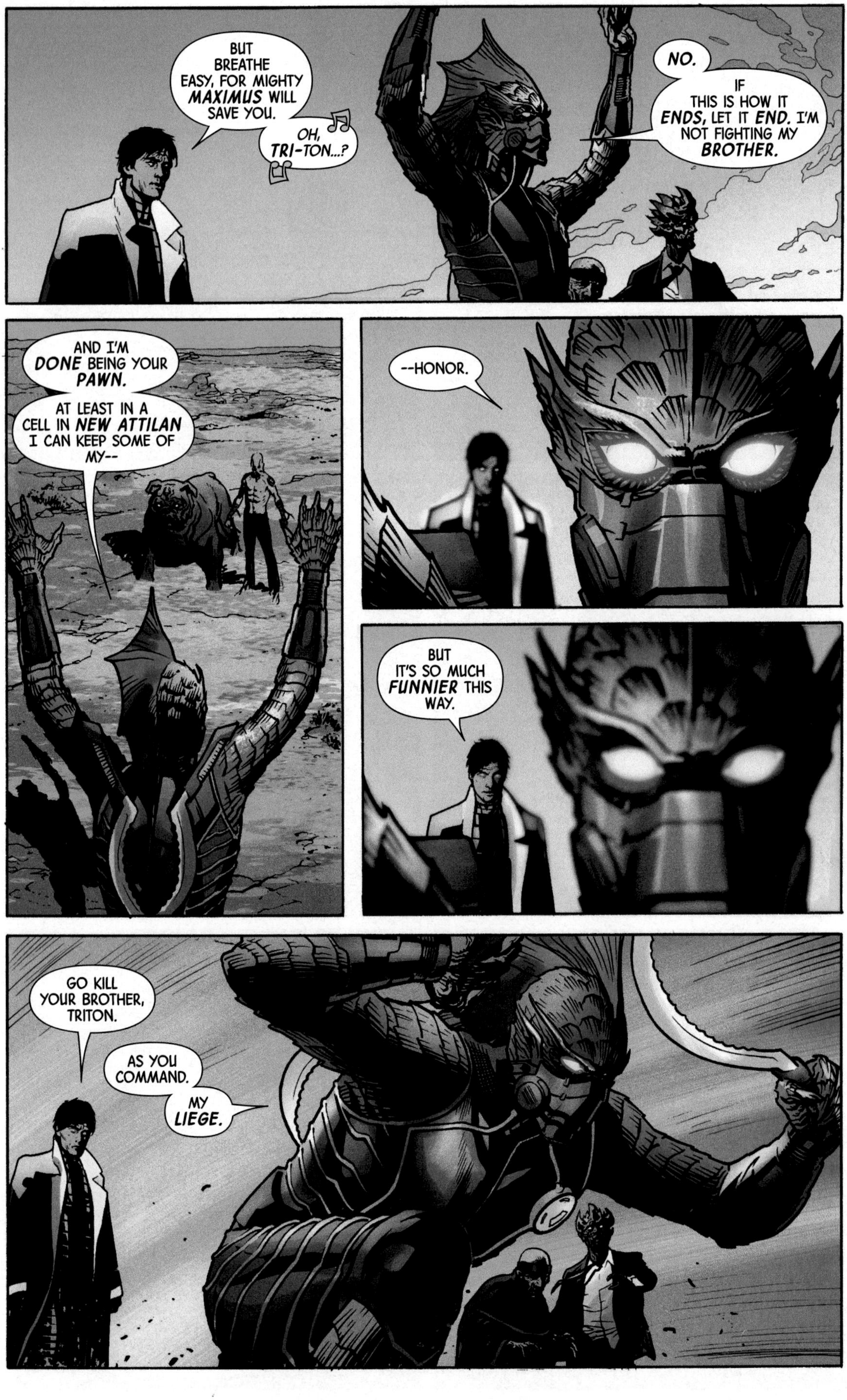

BUT BREATHE EASY, FOR MIGHTY MAXIMUS WILL SAVE YOU.
OH, TRI-TON...?
NO.
IF THIS IS HOW IT ENDS, LET IT END. I'M NOT FIGHTING MY BROTHER.
AND I'M DONE BEING YOUR PAWN.
AT LEAST IN A CELL IN NEW ATTILAN I CAN KEEP SOME OF MY--
--HONOR.
BUT IT'S SO MUCH FUNNIER THIS WAY.
GO KILL YOUR BROTHER, TRITON.
AS YOU COMMAND.
MY LIEGE.

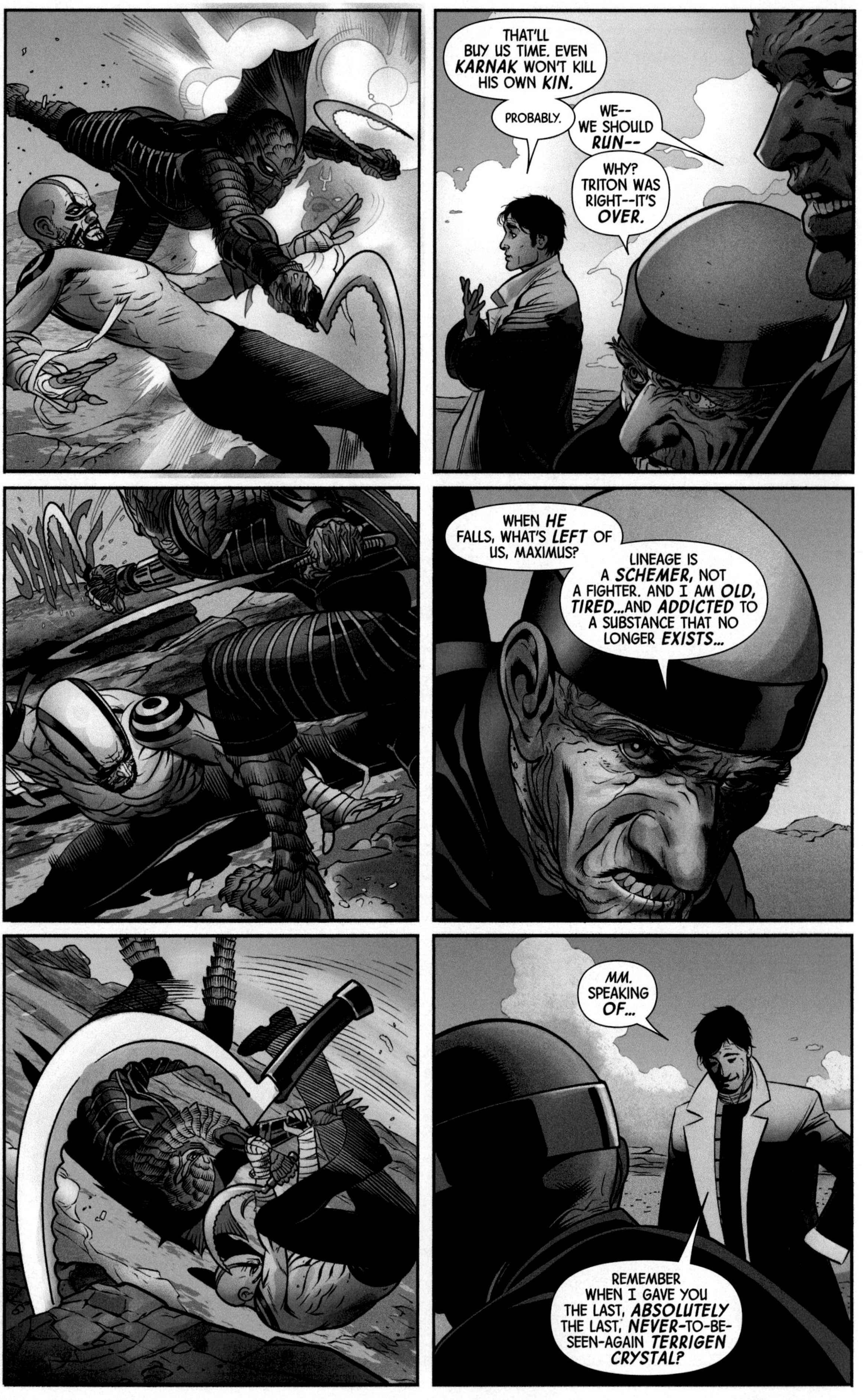
THAT'LL BUY US TIME. EVEN KARNAK WON'T KILL HIS OWN KIN.
PROBABLY.
WE-- WE SHOULD RUN--
WHY? TRITON WAS RIGHT--IT'S OVER.
SHING
WHEN HE FALLS, WHAT'S LEFT OF US, MAXIMUS?
LINEAGE IS A SCHEMER, NOT A FIGHTER. AND I AM OLD, TIRED...AND ADDICTED TO A SUBSTANCE THAT NO LONGER EXISTS...
MM. SPEAKING OF...
REMEMBER WHEN I GAVE YOU THE LAST, ABSOLUTELY THE LAST, NEVER-TO-BE-SEEN-AGAIN TERRIGEN CRYSTAL?

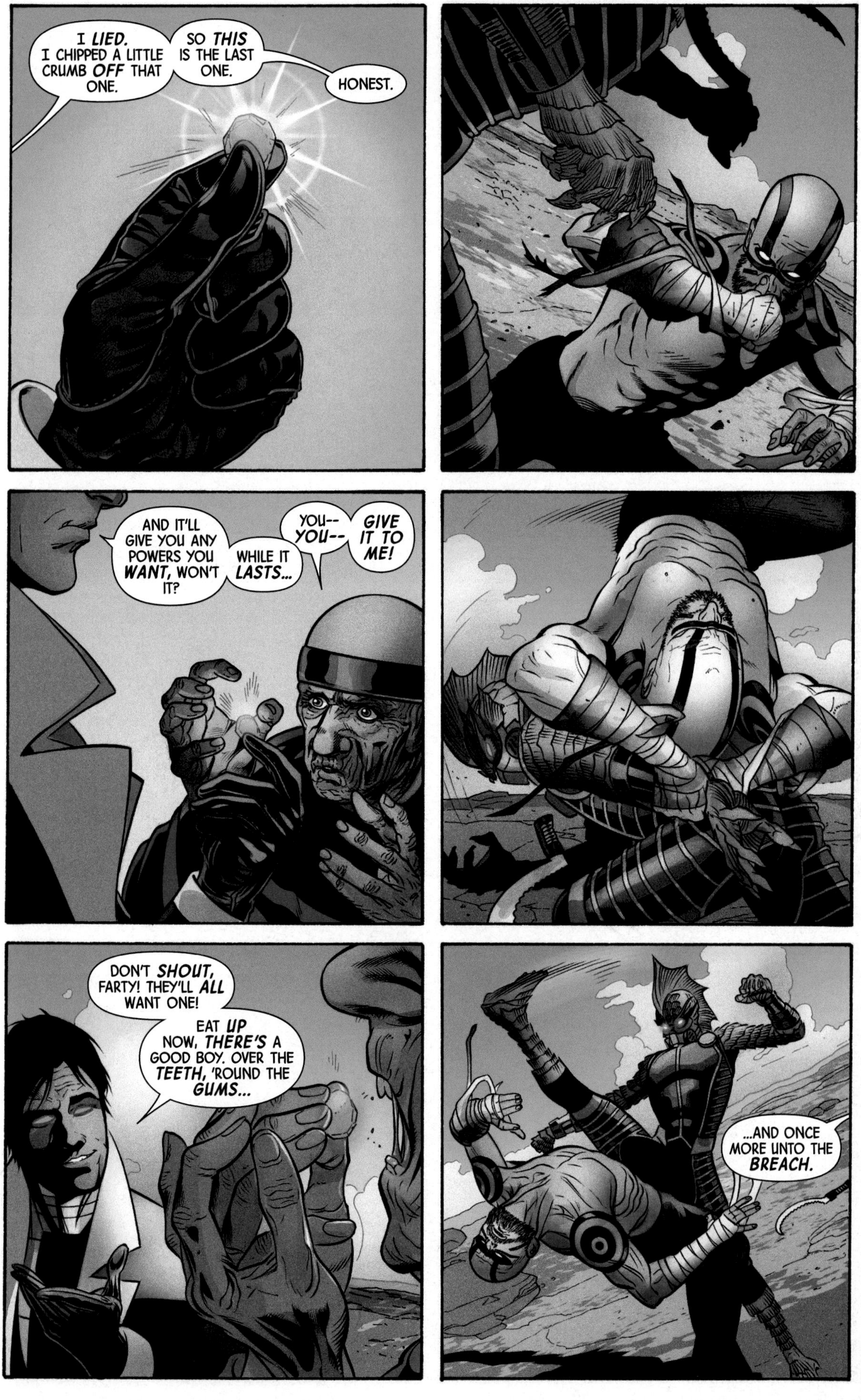
I LIED. I CHIPPED A LITTLE CRUMB OFF THAT ONE.
SO THIS IS THE LAST ONE.
HONEST.
AND IT'LL GIVE YOU ANY POWERS YOU WANT, WON'T IT?
WHILE IT LASTS...
YOU-- YOU--
GIVE IT TO ME!
DON'T SHOUT, FARTY! THEY'LL ALL WANT ONE!
EAT UP NOW, THERE'S A GOOD BOY. OVER THE TEETH, 'ROUND THE GUMS...
...AND ONCE MORE UNTO THE BREACH.

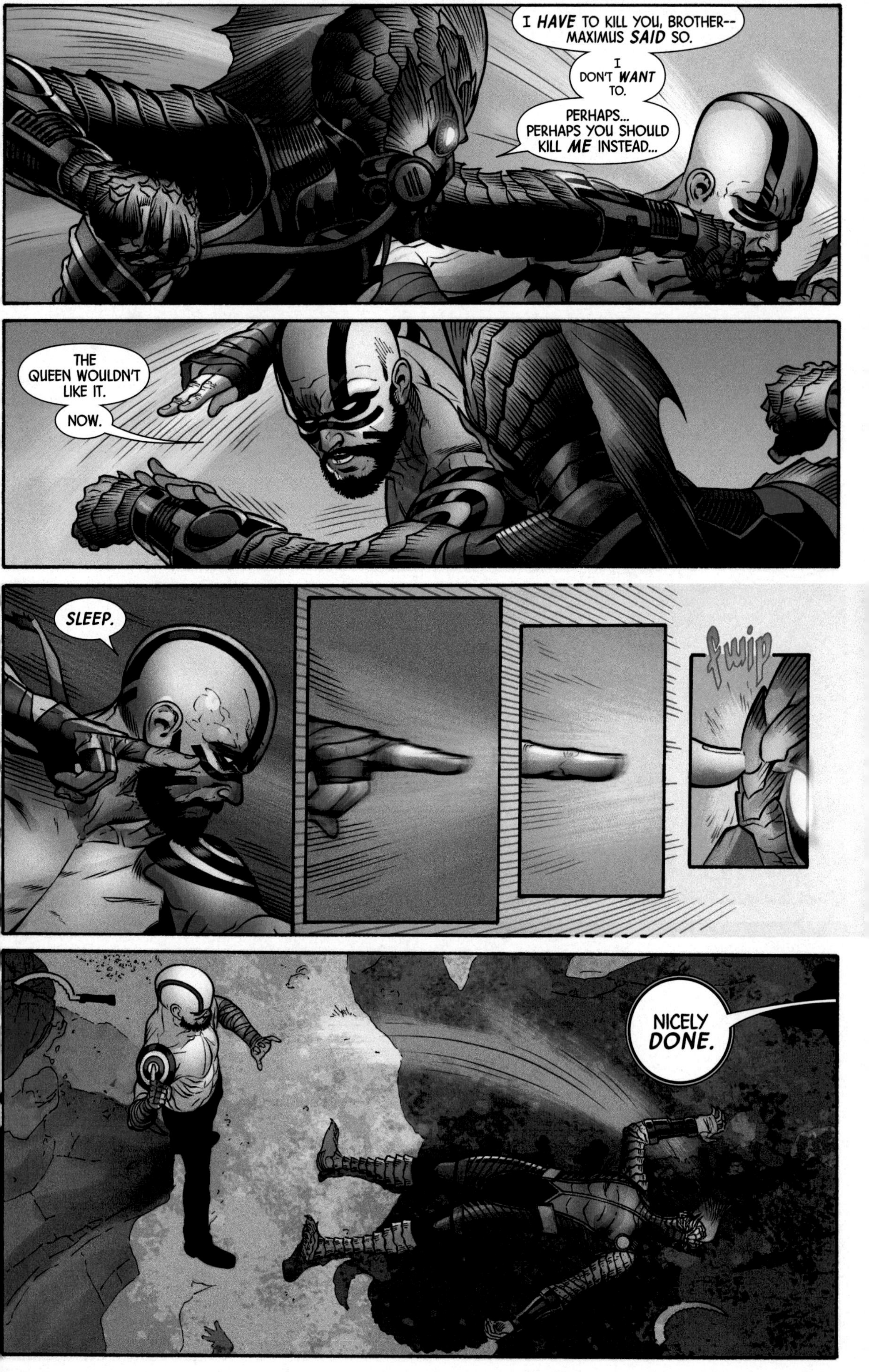
I HAVE TO KILL YOU, BROTHER-- MAXIMUS SAID SO.
I DON'T WANT TO.
PERHAPS... PERHAPS YOU SHOULD KILL ME INSTEAD...
THE QUEEN WOULDN'T LIKE IT.
NOW.
SLEEP.
fwip
NICELY DONE.

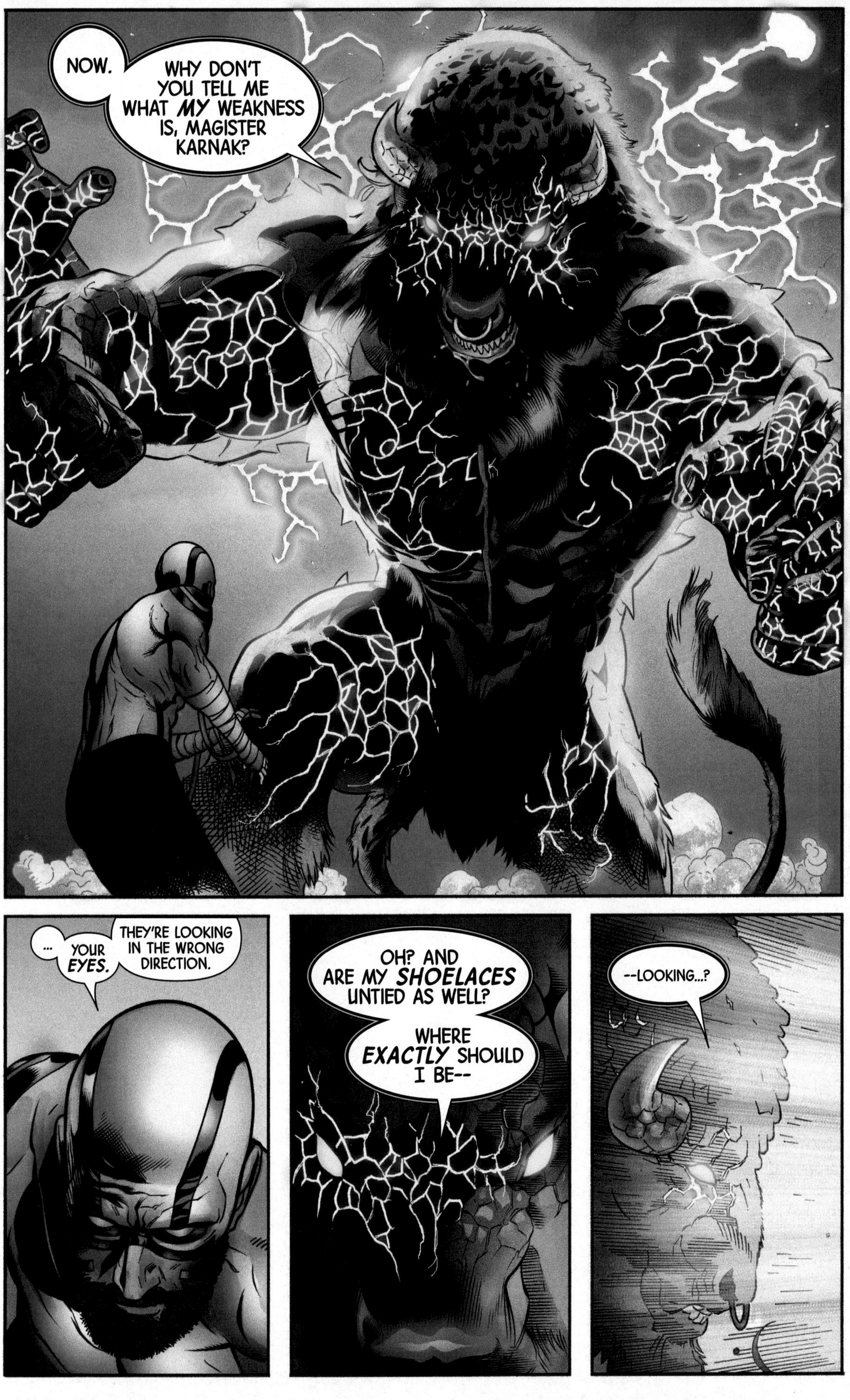
NOW.
WHY DON'T YOU TELL ME WHAT MY WEAKNESS IS, MAGISTER KARNAK?
... YOUR EYES.
THEY'RE LOOKING IN THE WRONG DIRECTION.
OH? AND ARE MY SHOELACES UNTIED AS WELL?
WHERE EXACTLY SHOULD I BE--
--LOOKING...?

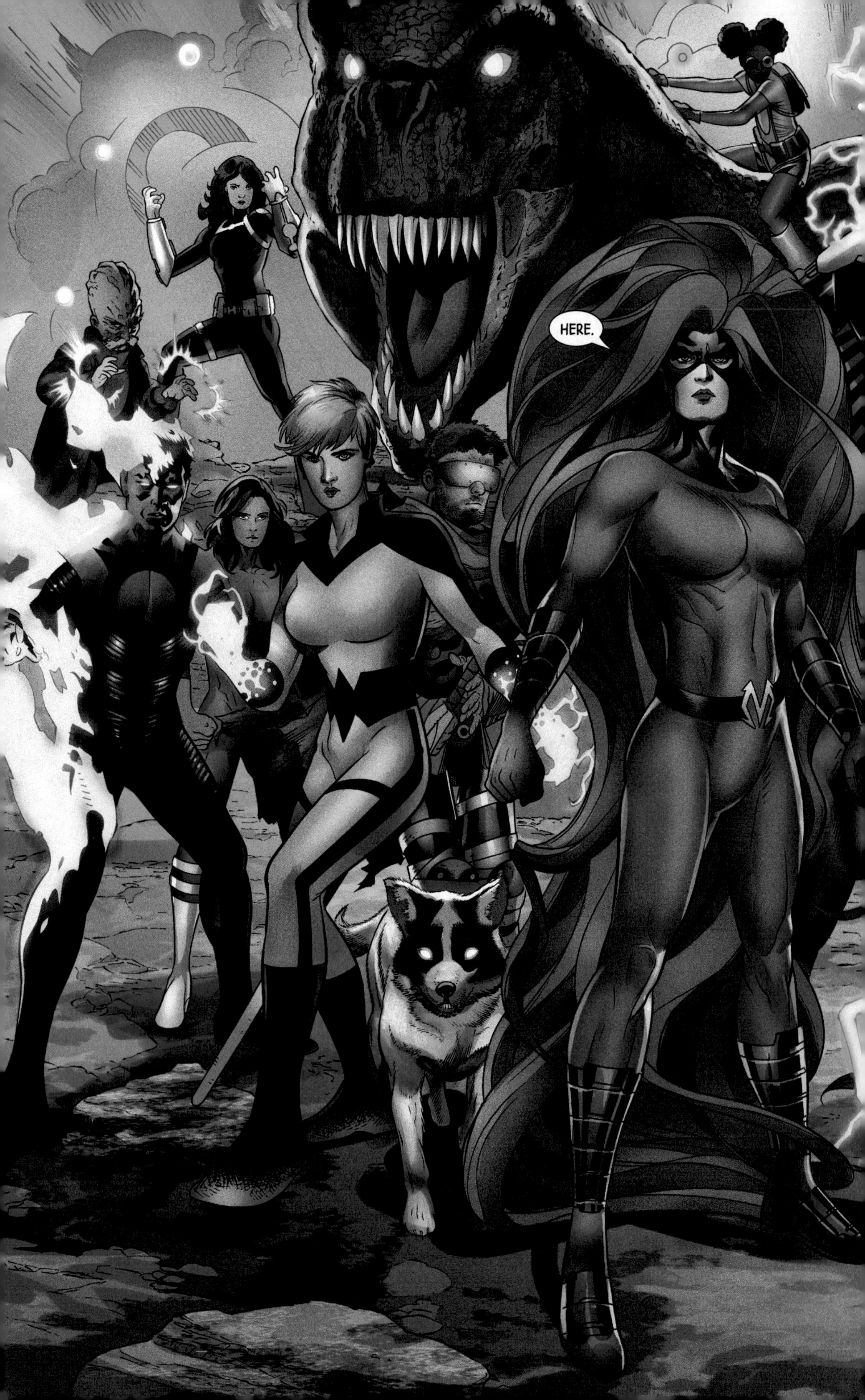
HERE.

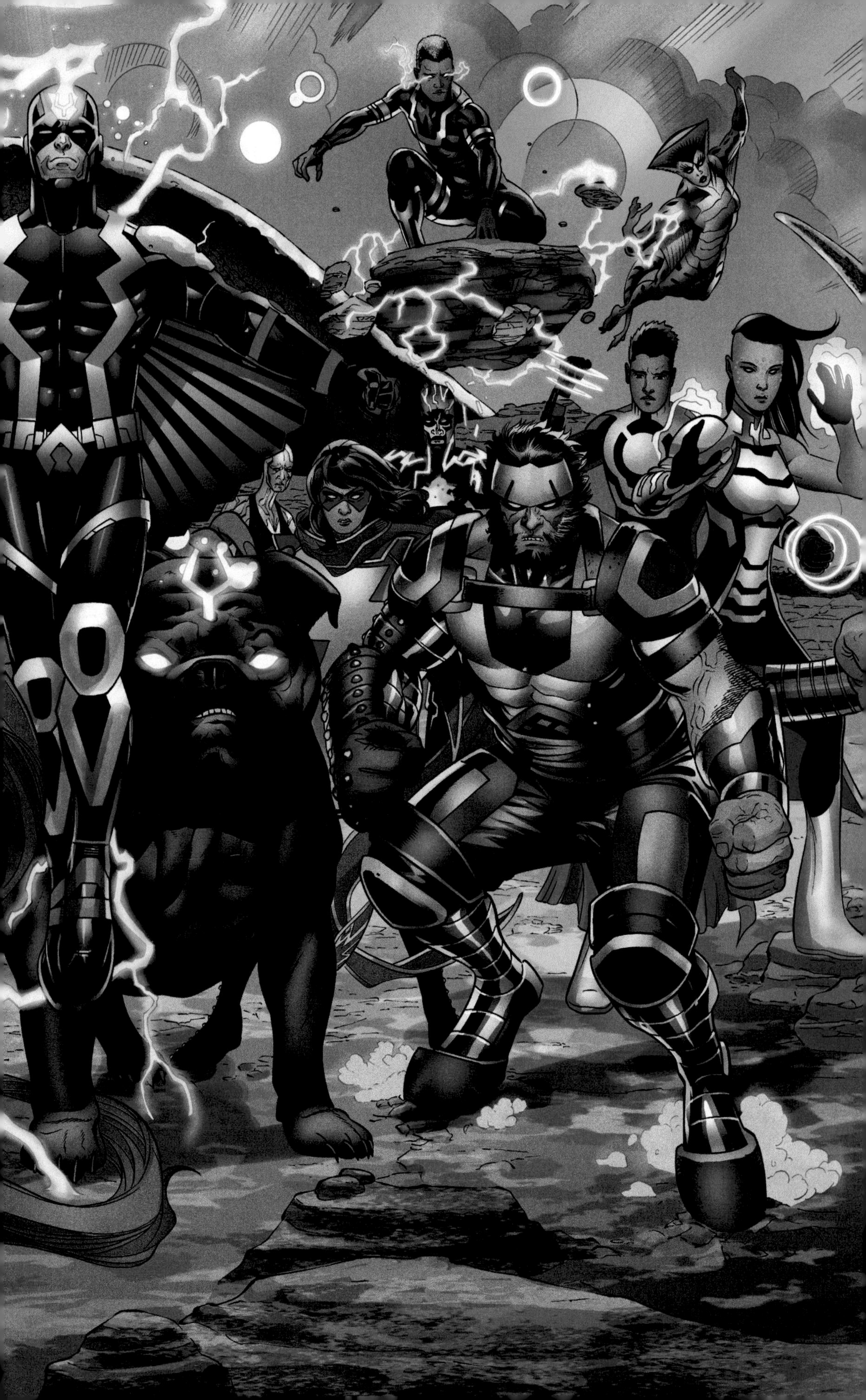

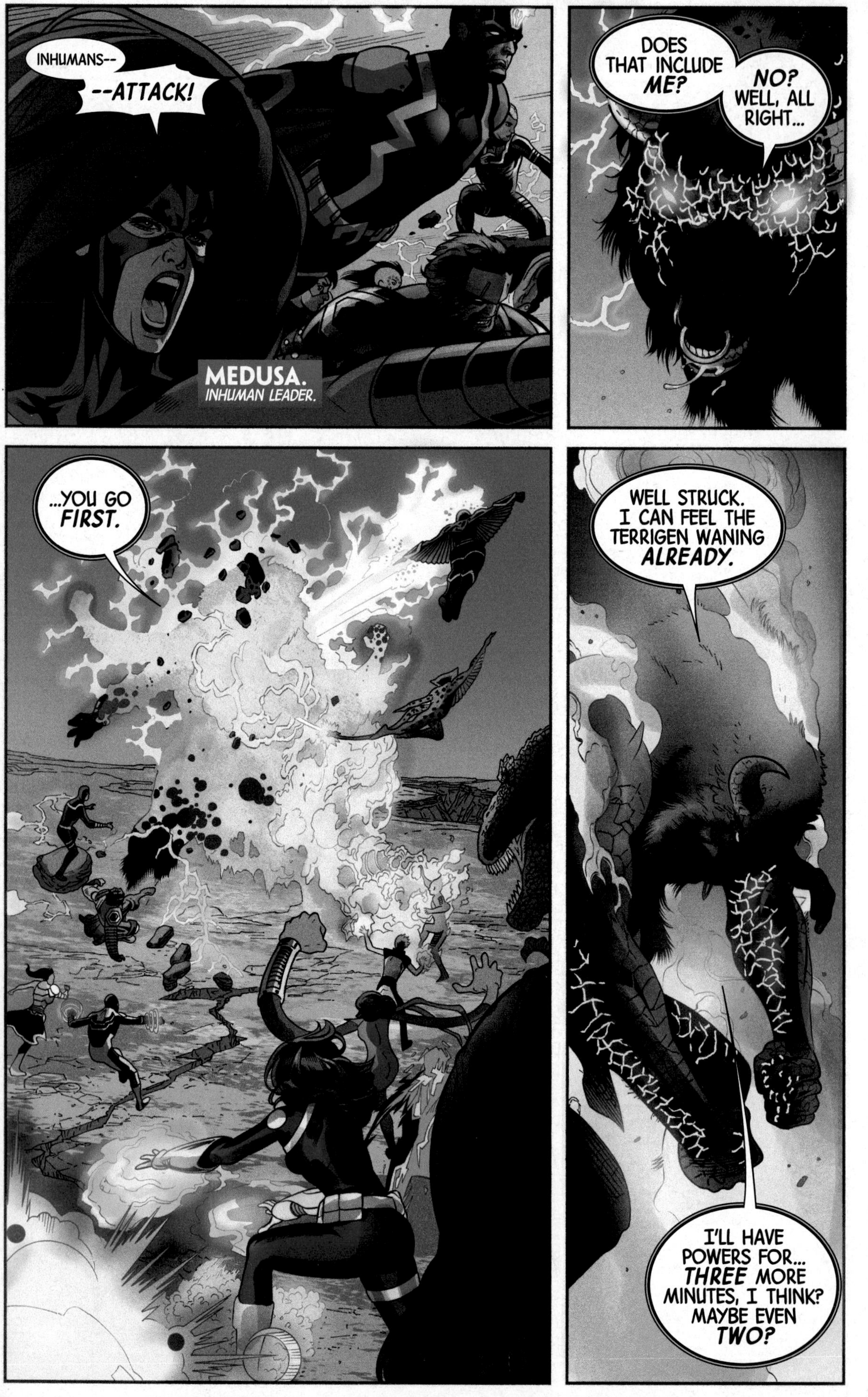
INHUMANS--
--ATTACK!
MEDUSA.
INHUMAN LEADER.
DOES THAT INCLUDE ME?
NO? WELL, ALL RIGHT...
...YOU GO FIRST.
WELL STRUCK. I CAN FEEL THE TERRIGEN WANING ALREADY.
I'LL HAVE POWERS FOR... THREE MORE MINUTES, I THINK? MAYBE EVEN TWO?

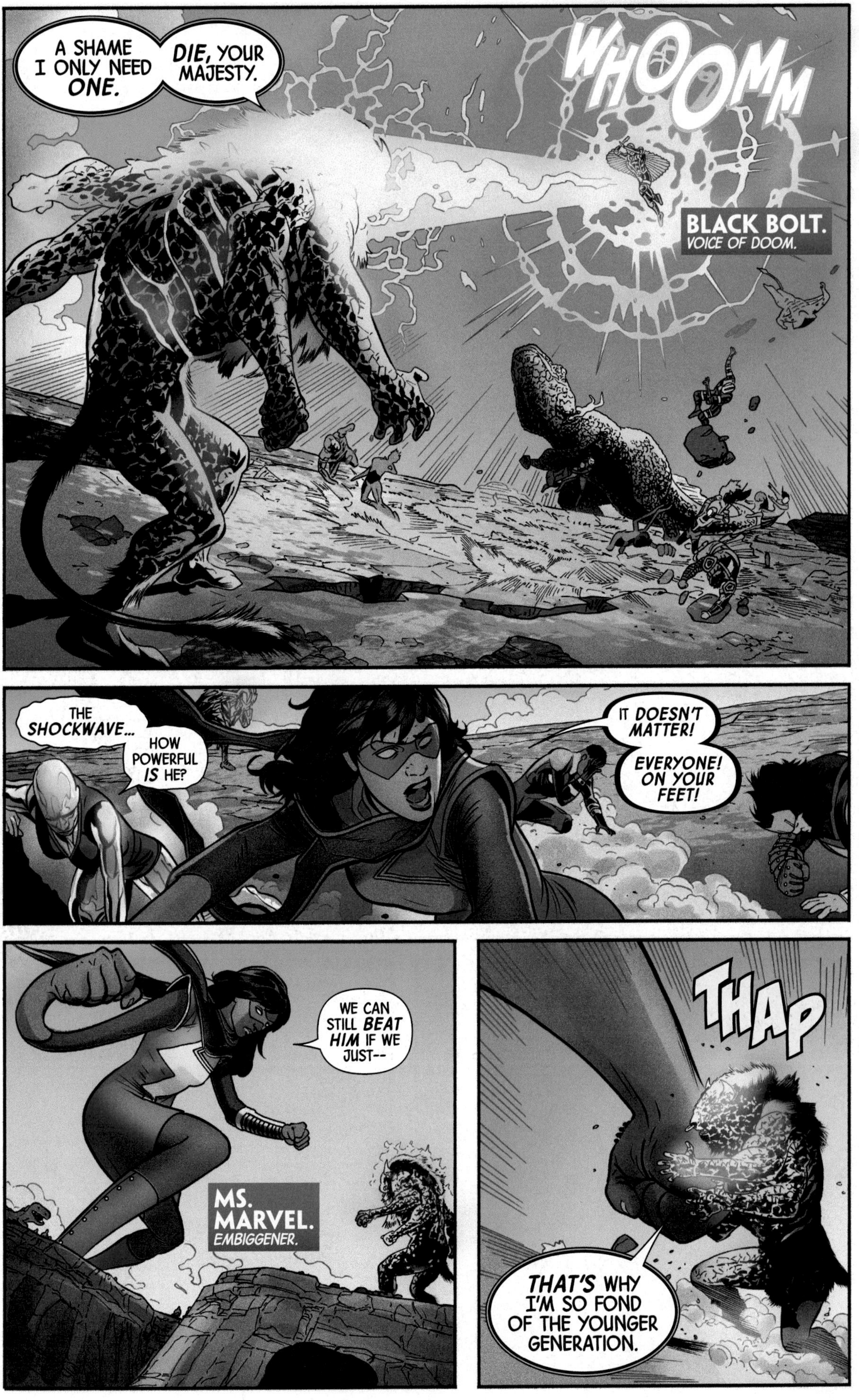

A SHAME I ONLY NEED ONE.
DIE, YOUR MAJESTY.
WHOOMM
BLACK BOLT. VOICE OF DOOM.
THE SHOCKWAVE...
HOW POWERFUL IS HE?
IT DOESN'T MATTER!
EVERYONE! ON YOUR FEET!
WE CAN STILL BEAT HIM IF WE JUST--
MS. MARVEL. EMBIGGENER.
THAP
THAT'S WHY I'M SO FOND OF THE YOUNGER GENERATION.

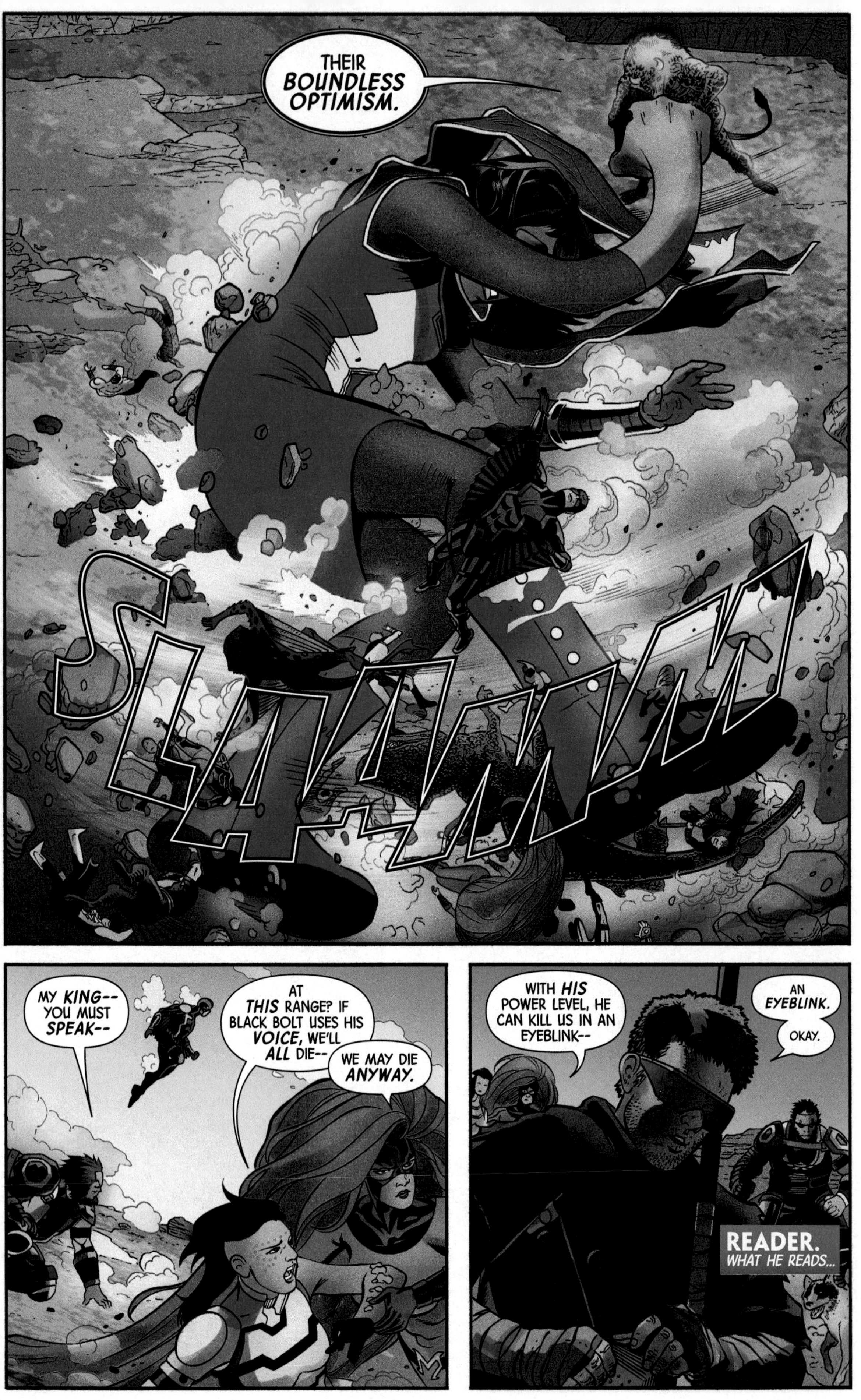
THEIR BOUNDLESS OPTIMISM.
SLAMM
MY KING-- YOU MUST SPEAK--
AT THIS RANGE? IF BLACK BOLT USES HIS VOICE, WE'LL ALL DIE--
WE MAY DIE ANYWAY.
WITH HIS POWER LEVEL, HE CAN KILL US IN AN EYEBLINK--
AN EYEBLINK.
OKAY.
READER.
WHAT HE READS...

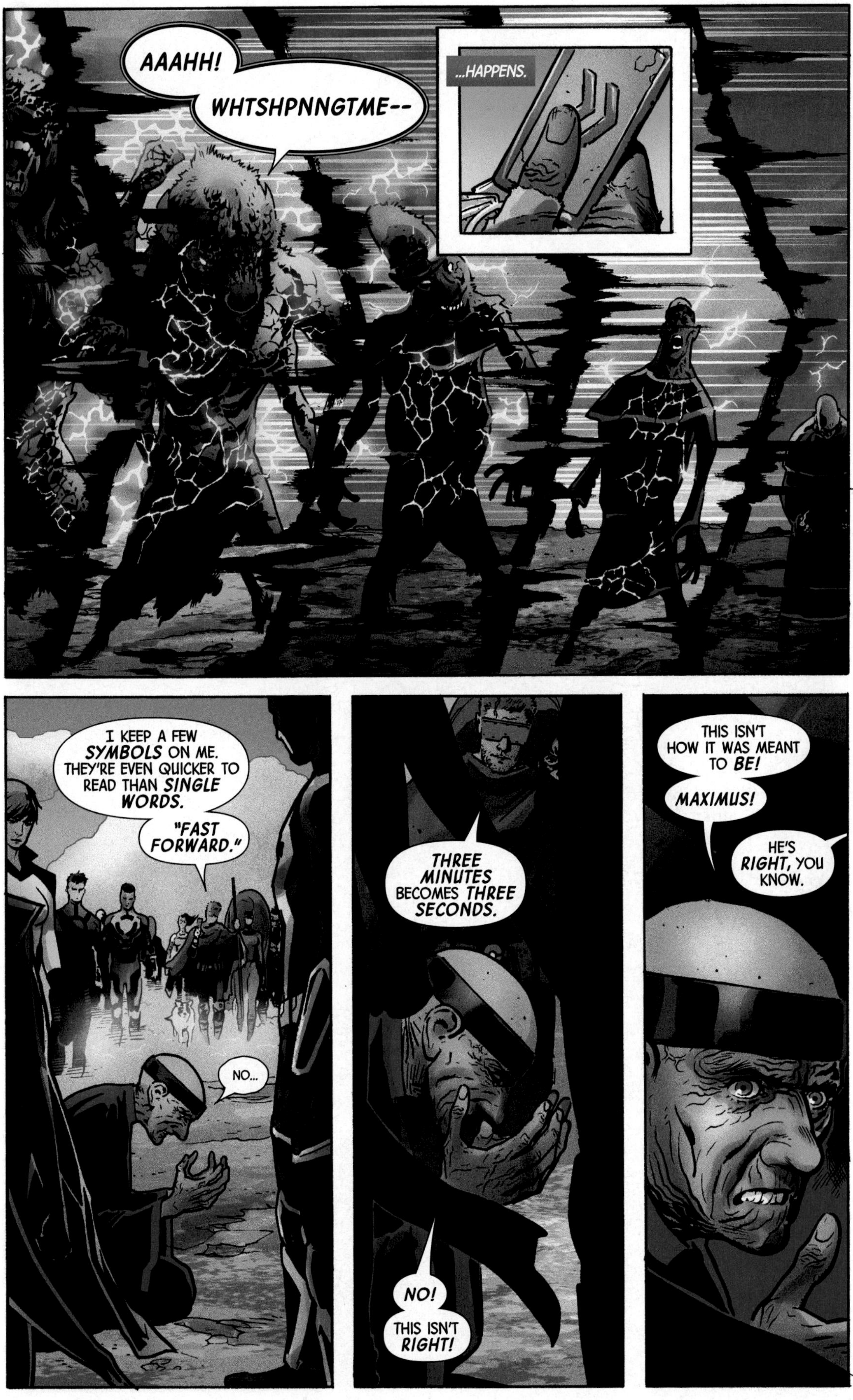

AAAHH!
WHTSHPNNGTME--
...HAPPENS.
I KEEP A FEW SYMBOLS ON ME. THEY'RE EVEN QUICKER TO READ THAN SINGLE WORDS.
"FAST FORWARD."
NO...
THREE MINUTES BECOMES THREE SECONDS.
NO!
THIS ISN'T RIGHT!
THIS ISN'T HOW IT WAS MEANT TO BE!
MAXIMUS!
HE'S RIGHT, YOU KNOW.

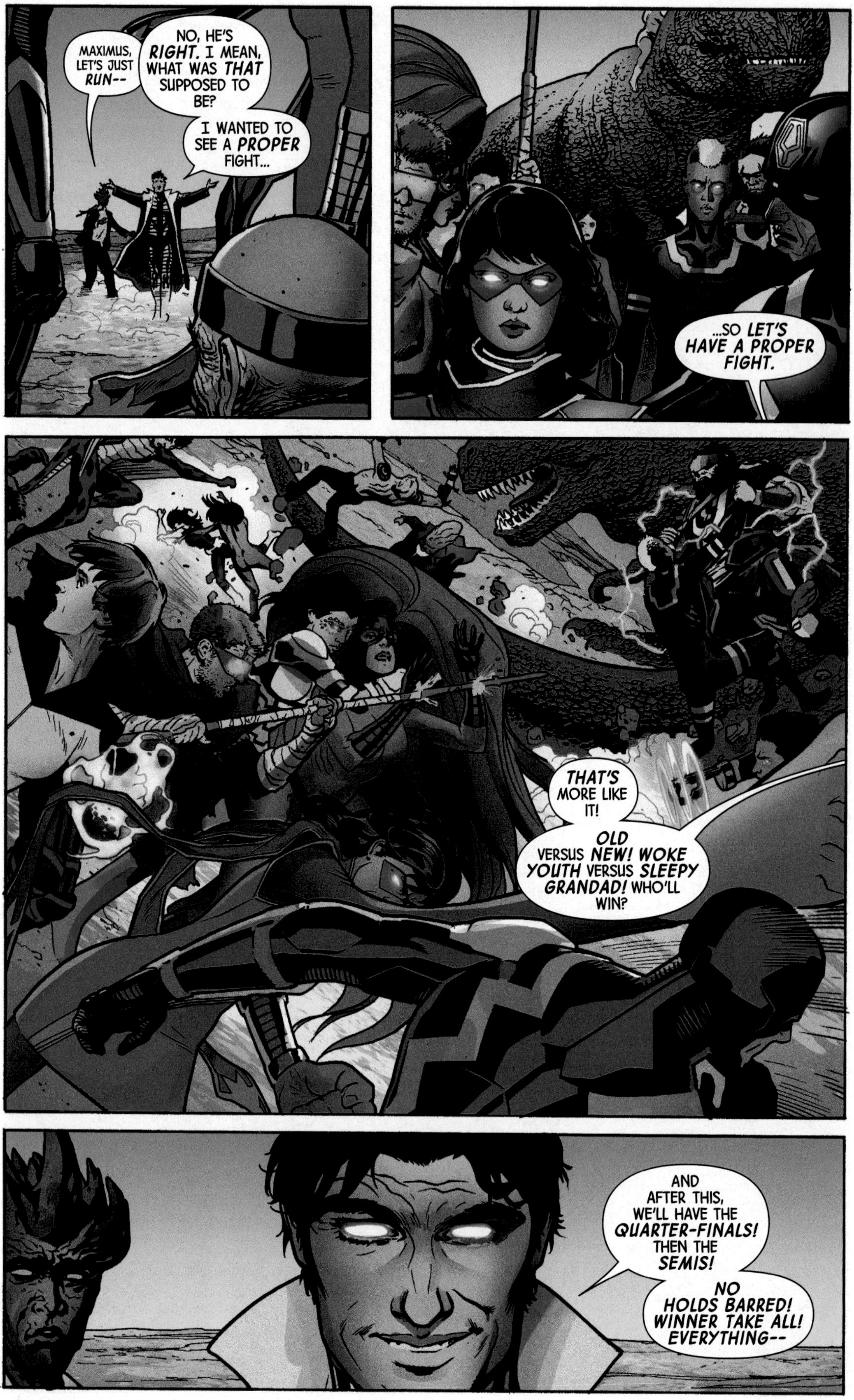

MAXIMUS, LET'S JUST RUN--
NO, HE'S RIGHT. I MEAN, WHAT WAS THAT SUPPOSED TO BE?
I WANTED TO SEE A PROPER FIGHT...
...SO LET'S HAVE A PROPER FIGHT.
THAT'S MORE LIKE IT!
OLD VERSUS NEW! WOKE YOUTH VERSUS SLEEPY GRANDAD! WHO'LL WIN?
AND AFTER THIS, WE'LL HAVE THE QUARTER-FINALS! THEN THE SEMIS!
NO HOLDS BARRED! WINNER TAKE ALL! EVERYTHING--

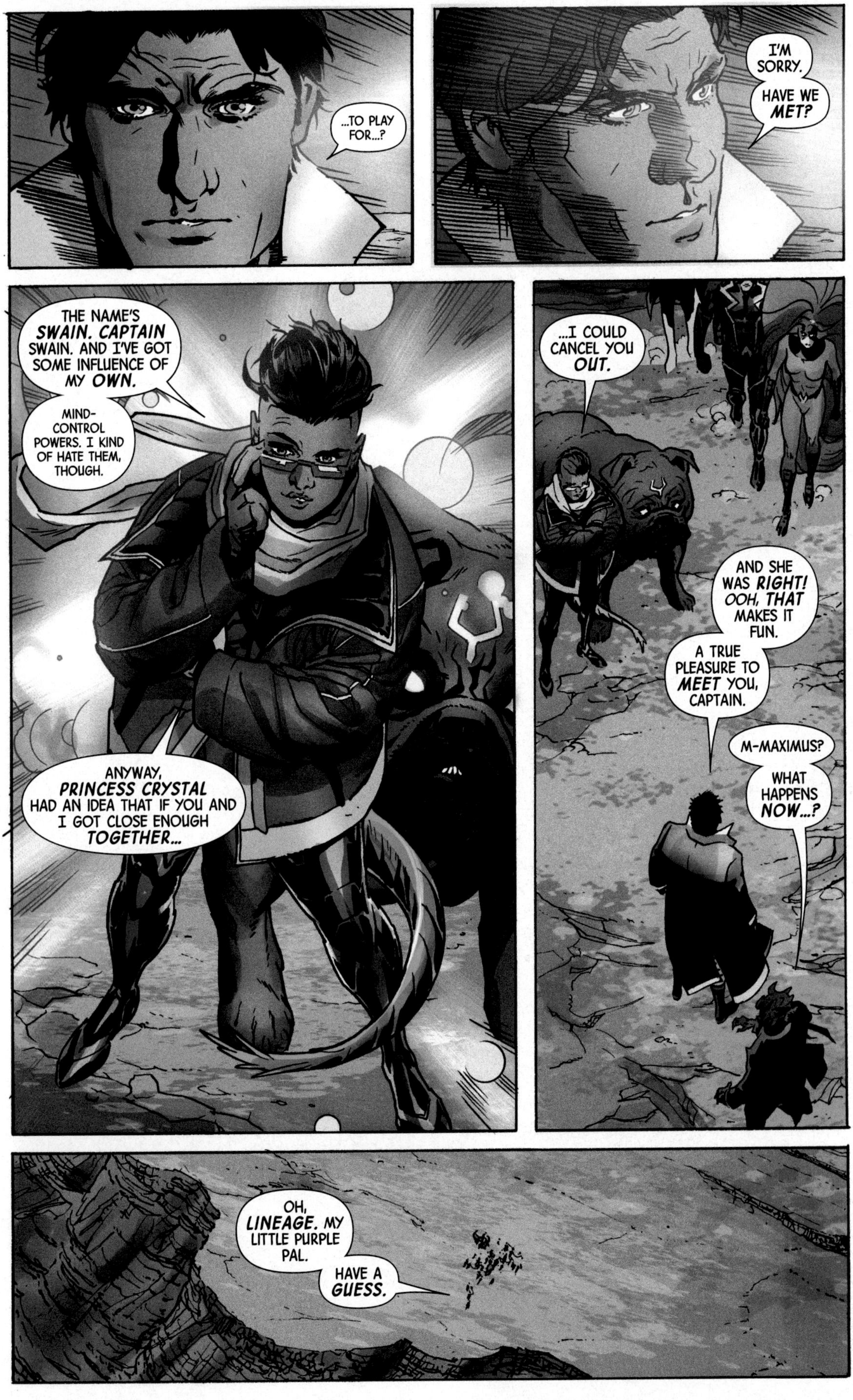

...TO PLAY FOR...?
I'M SORRY.
HAVE WE MET?
THE NAME'S SWAIN. CAPTAIN SWAIN. AND I'VE GOT SOME INFLUENCE OF MY OWN.
MIND-CONTROL POWERS. I KIND OF HATE THEM, THOUGH.
ANYWAY, PRINCESS CRYSTAL HAD AN IDEA THAT IF YOU AND I GOT CLOSE ENOUGH TOGETHER...
...I COULD CANCEL YOU OUT.
AND SHE WAS RIGHT! OOH, THAT MAKES IT FUN.
A TRUE PLEASURE TO MEET YOU, CAPTAIN.
M-MAXIMUS?
WHAT HAPPENS NOW...?
OH, LINEAGE. MY LITTLE PURPLE PAL.
HAVE A GUESS.

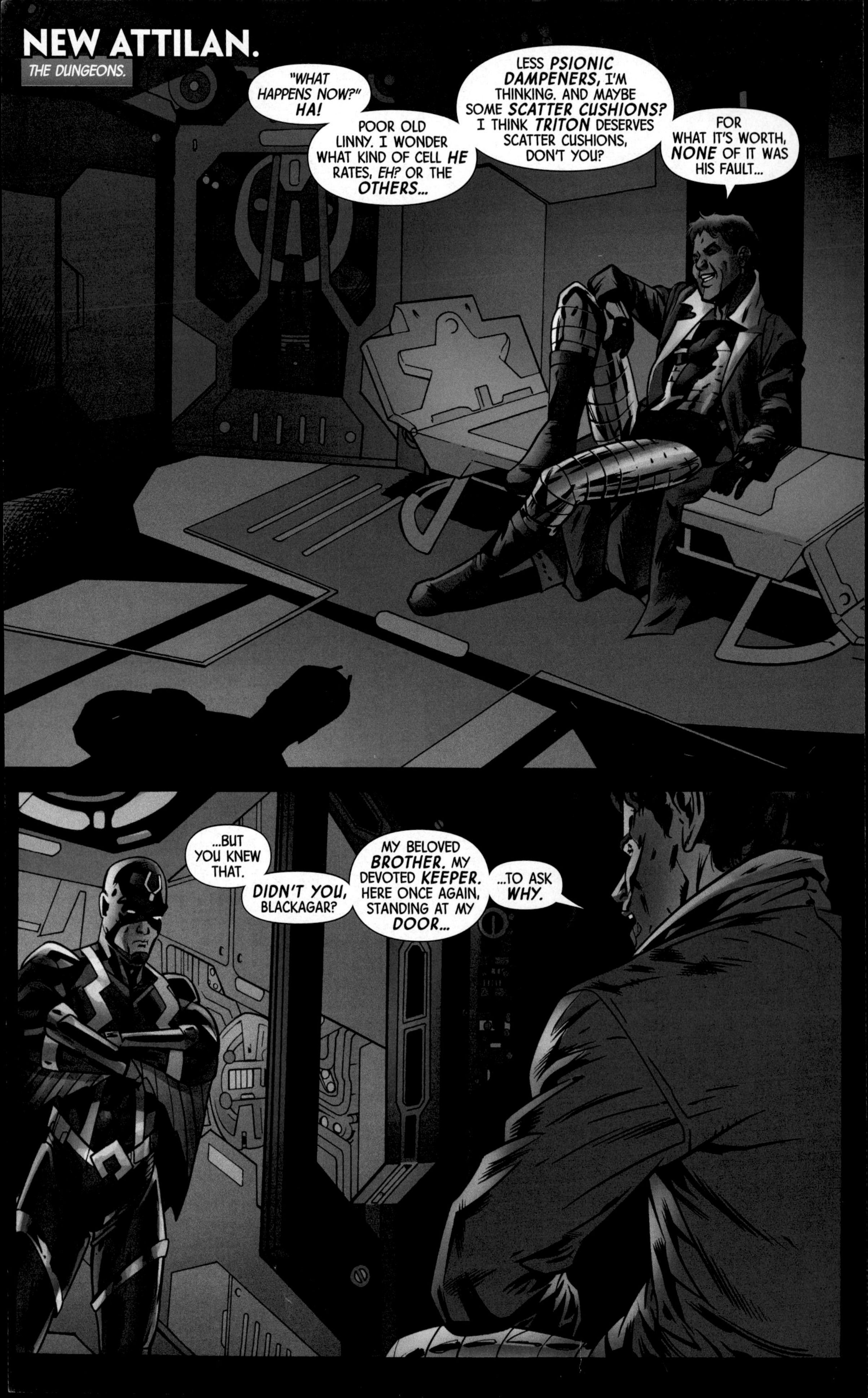
NEW ATTILAN.
THE DUNGEONS.
"WHAT HAPPENS NOW?" HA!
POOR OLD LINNY. I WONDER WHAT KIND OF CELL HE RATES, EH? OR THE OTHERS...
LESS PSIONIC DAMPENERS, I'M THINKING. AND MAYBE SOME SCATTER CUSHIONS? I THINK TRITON DESERVES SCATTER CUSHIONS, DON'T YOU?
FOR WHAT IT'S WORTH, NONE OF IT WAS HIS FAULT...
...BUT YOU KNEW THAT.
DIDN'T YOU, BLACKAGAR?
MY BELOVED BROTHER. MY DEVOTED KEEPER. HERE ONCE AGAIN, STANDING AT MY DOOR...
...TO ASK WHY.

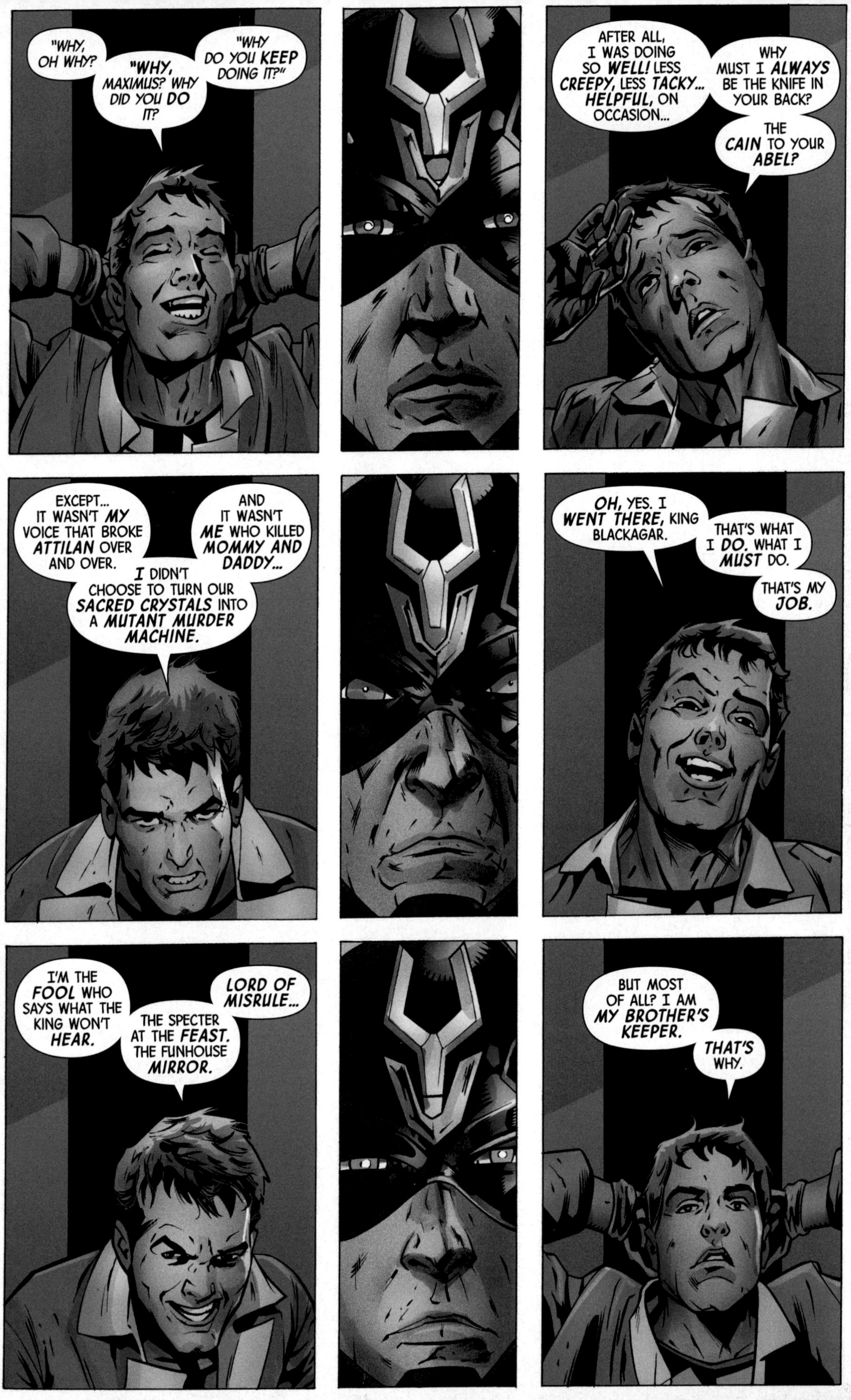
"WHY, OH WHY?
"WHY, MAXIMUS? WHY DID YOU DO IT?
"WHY DO YOU KEEP DOING IT?"
AFTER ALL, I WAS DOING SO WELL! LESS CREEPY, LESS TACKY... HELPFUL, ON OCCASION...
WHY MUST I ALWAYS BE THE KNIFE IN YOUR BACK?
THE CAIN TO YOUR ABEL?
EXCEPT... IT WASN'T MY VOICE THAT BROKE ATTILAN OVER AND OVER.
AND IT WASN'T ME WHO KILLED MOMMY AND DADDY...
I DIDN'T CHOOSE TO TURN OUR SACRED CRYSTALS INTO A MUTANT MURDER MACHINE.
OH, YES. I WENT THERE, KING BLACKAGAR.
THAT'S WHAT I DO. WHAT I MUST DO.
THAT'S MY JOB.
I'M THE FOOL WHO SAYS WHAT THE KING WON'T HEAR.
THE SPECTER AT THE FEAST. THE FUNHOUSE MIRROR.
LORD OF MISRULE...
BUT MOST OF ALL? I AM MY BROTHER'S KEEPER.
THAT'S WHY.

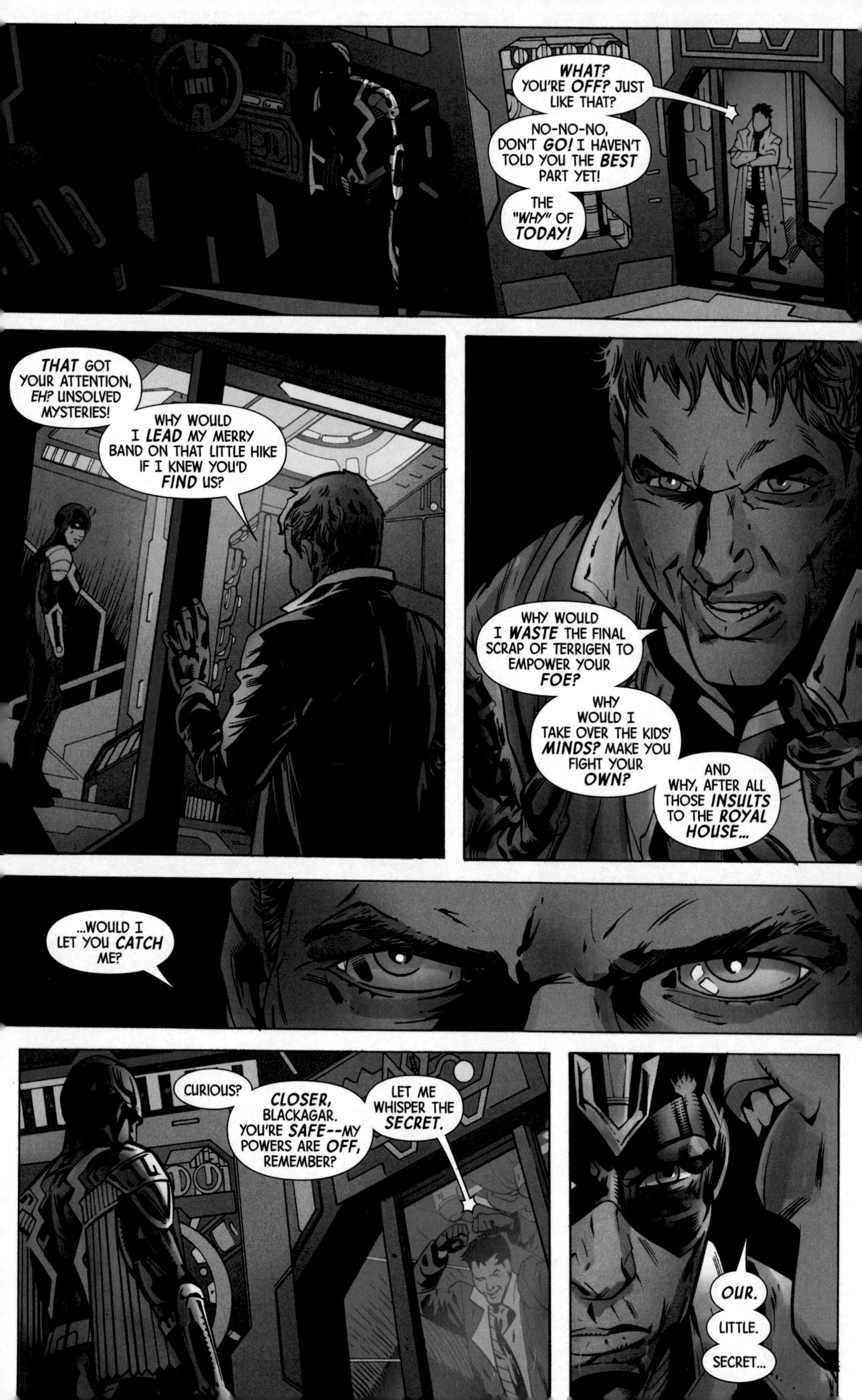
WHAT? YOU'RE OFF? JUST LIKE THAT?
NO-NO-NO, DON'T GO! I HAVEN'T TOLD YOU THE BEST PART YET!
THE "WHY" OF TODAY!
THAT GOT YOUR ATTENTION, EH? UNSOLVED MYSTERIES!
WHY WOULD I LEAD MY MERRY BAND ON THAT LITTLE HIKE IF I KNEW YOU'D FIND US?
WHY WOULD I WASTE THE FINAL SCRAP OF TERRIGEN TO EMPOWER YOUR FOE?
WHY WOULD I TAKE OVER THE KIDS' MINDS? MAKE YOU FIGHT YOUR OWN?
AND WHY, AFTER ALL THOSE INSULTS TO THE ROYAL HOUSE...
...WOULD I LET YOU CATCH ME?
CURIOUS?
CLOSER, BLACKAGAR. YOU'RE SAFE--MY POWERS ARE OFF, REMEMBER?
LET ME WHISPER THE SECRET.
OUR.
LITTLE.
SECRET...

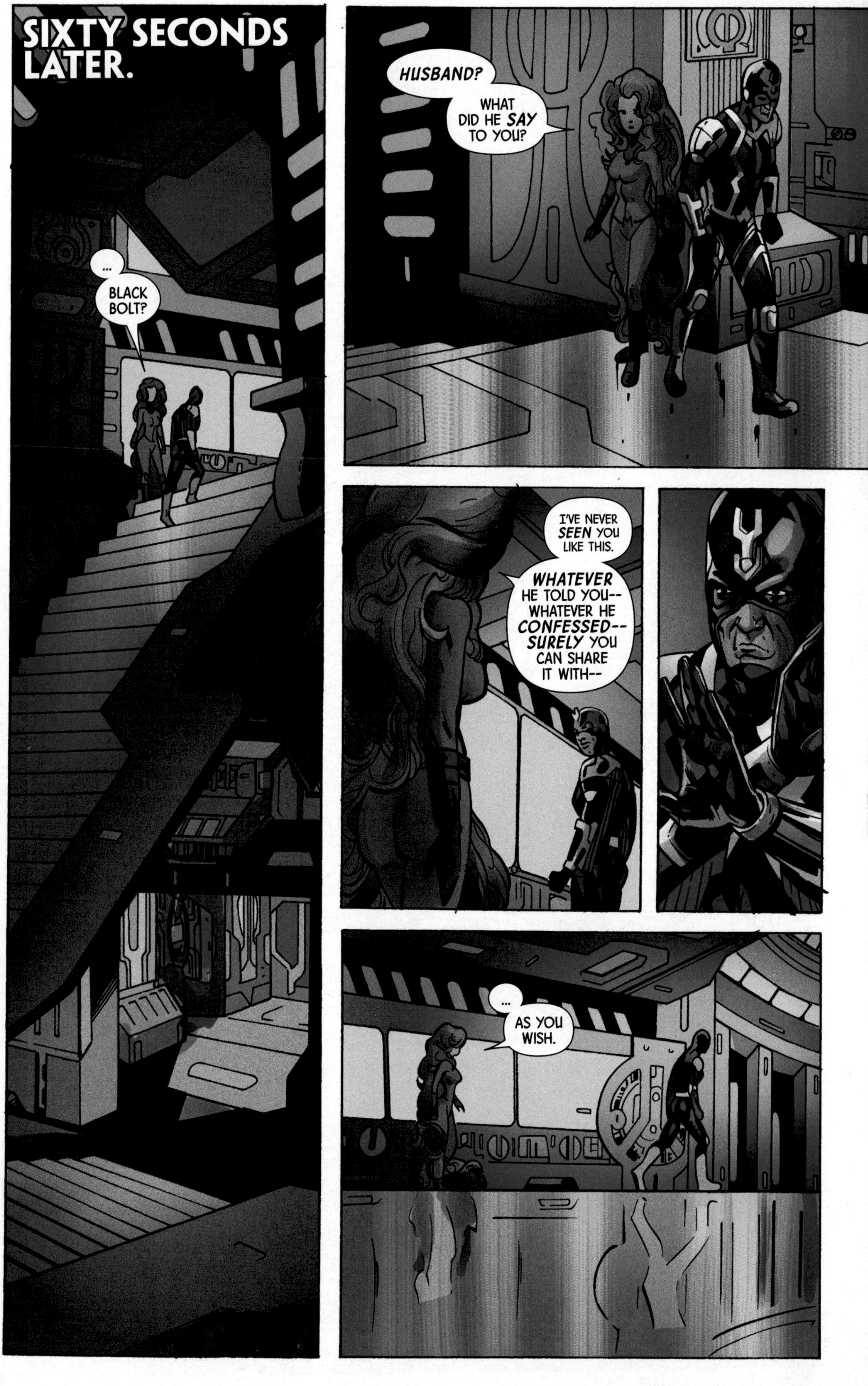
SIXTY SECONDS LATER.
... BLACK BOLT?
HUSBAND?
WHAT DID HE SAY TO YOU?
I'VE NEVER SEEN YOU LIKE THIS.
WHATEVER HE TOLD YOU-- WHATEVER HE CONFESSED-- SURELY YOU CAN SHARE IT WITH--
... AS YOU WISH.

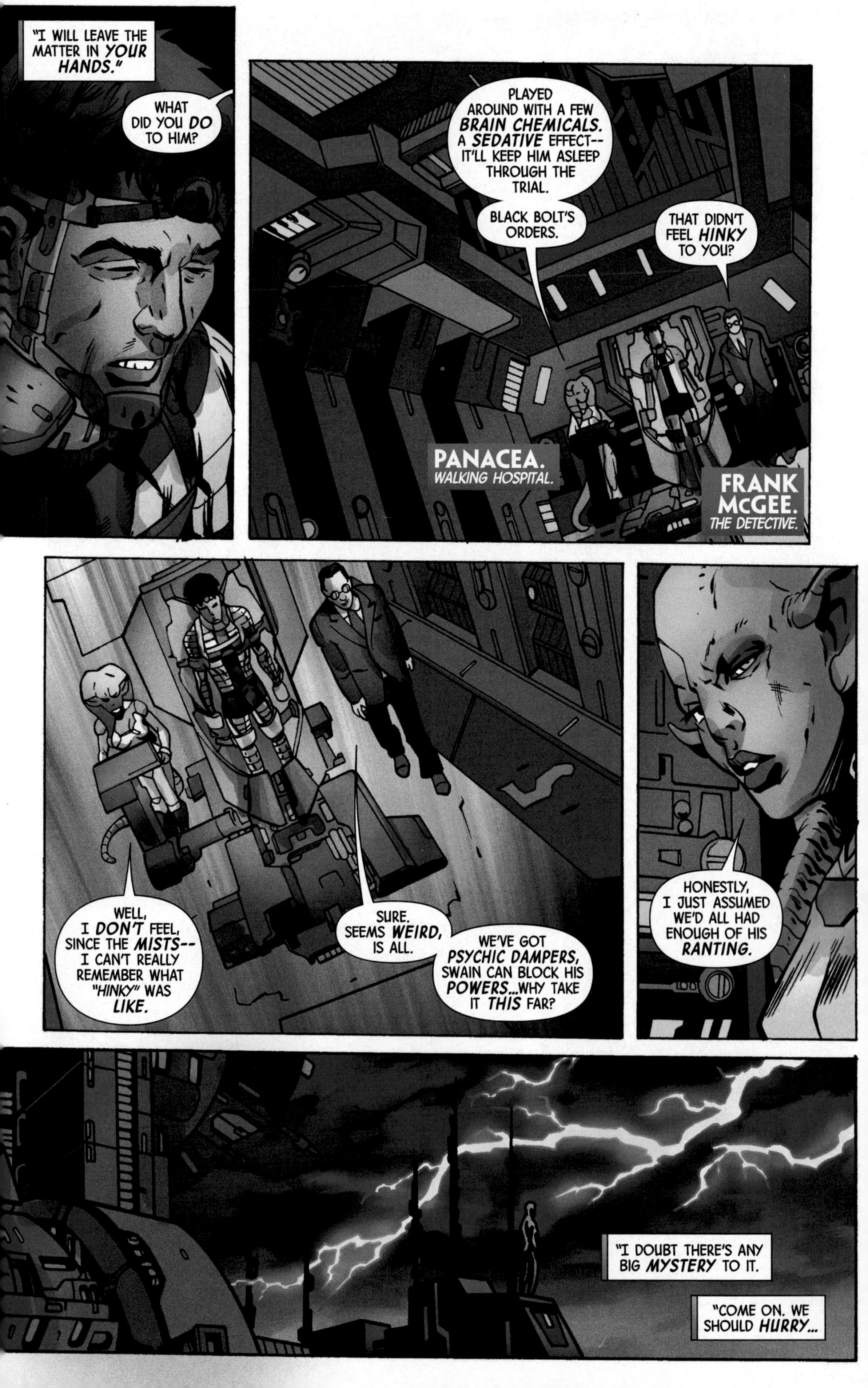
"I WILL LEAVE THE MATTER IN YOUR HANDS."
WHAT DID YOU DO TO HIM?
PLAYED AROUND WITH A FEW BRAIN CHEMICALS. A SEDATIVE EFFECT-- IT'LL KEEP HIM ASLEEP THROUGH THE TRIAL.
BLACK BOLT'S ORDERS.
THAT DIDN'T FEEL HINKY TO YOU?
PANACEA. WALKING HOSPITAL.
FRANK McGEE. THE DETECTIVE.
WELL, I DON'T FEEL, SINCE THE MISTS-- I CAN'T REALLY REMEMBER WHAT "HINKY" WAS LIKE.
SURE. SEEMS WEIRD, IS ALL.
WE'VE GOT PSYCHIC DAMPERS, SWAIN CAN BLOCK HIS POWERS...WHY TAKE IT THIS FAR?
HONESTLY, I JUST ASSUMED WE'D ALL HAD ENOUGH OF HIS RANTING.
"I DOUBT THERE'S ANY BIG MYSTERY TO IT.
"COME ON. WE SHOULD HURRY...

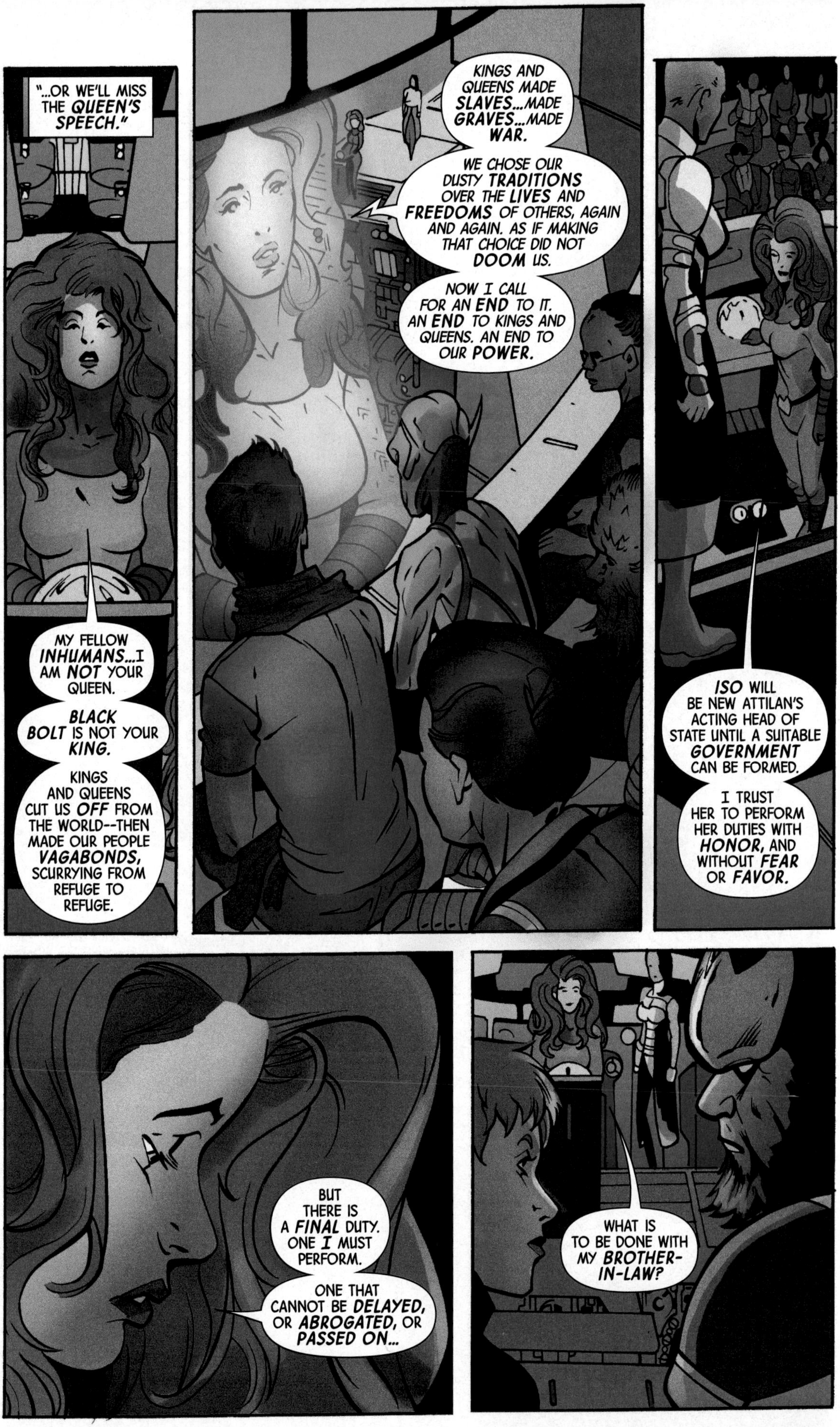
"...OR WE'LL MISS THE QUEEN'S SPEECH."
MY FELLOW INHUMANS...I AM NOT YOUR QUEEN.
BLACK BOLT IS NOT YOUR KING.
KINGS AND QUEENS CUT US OFF FROM THE WORLD--THEN MADE OUR PEOPLE VAGABONDS, SCURRYING FROM REFUGE TO REFUGE.
KINGS AND QUEENS MADE SLAVES...MADE GRAVES...MADE WAR.
WE CHOSE OUR DUSTY TRADITIONS OVER THE LIVES AND FREEDOMS OF OTHERS, AGAIN AND AGAIN. AS IF MAKING THAT CHOICE DID NOT DOOM US.
NOW I CALL FOR AN END TO IT. AN END TO KINGS AND QUEENS. AN END TO OUR POWER.
ISO WILL BE NEW ATTILAN'S ACTING HEAD OF STATE UNTIL A SUITABLE GOVERNMENT CAN BE FORMED.
I TRUST HER TO PERFORM HER DUTIES WITH HONOR, AND WITHOUT FEAR OR FAVOR.
BUT THERE IS A FINAL DUTY. ONE I MUST PERFORM.
ONE THAT CANNOT BE DELAYED, OR ABROGATED, OR PASSED ON...
WHAT IS TO BE DONE WITH MY BROTHER-IN-LAW?

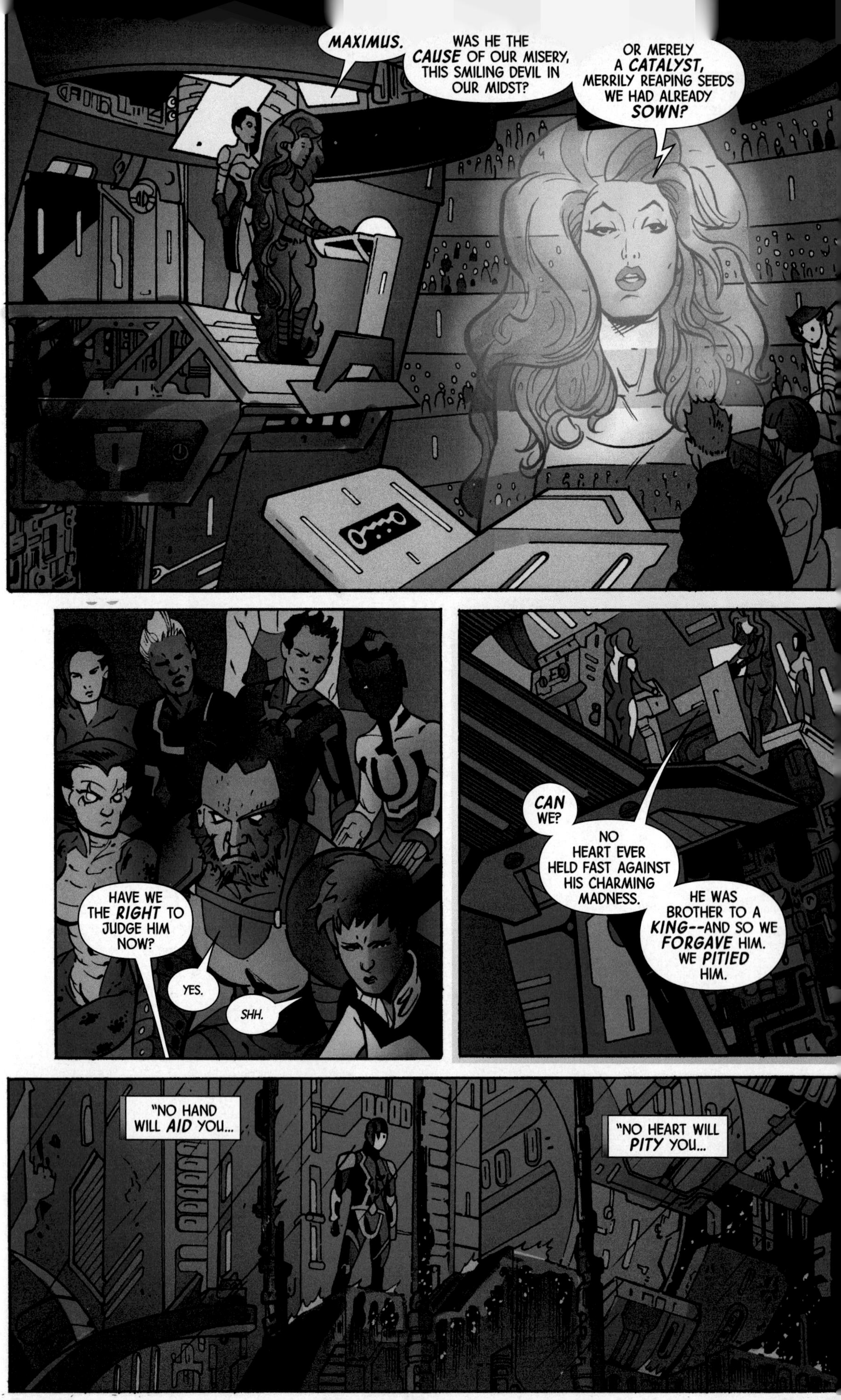
MAXIMUS.
WAS HE THE CAUSE OF OUR MISERY, THIS SMILING DEVIL IN OUR MIDST?
OR MERELY A CATALYST, MERRILY REAPING SEEDS WE HAD ALREADY SOWN?
HAVE WE THE RIGHT TO JUDGE HIM NOW?
YES.
SHH.
CAN WE?
NO HEART EVER HELD FAST AGAINST HIS CHARMING MADNESS.
HE WAS BROTHER TO A KING--AND SO WE FORGAVE HIM. WE PITIED HIM.
"NO HAND WILL AID YOU...
"NO HEART WILL PITY YOU...

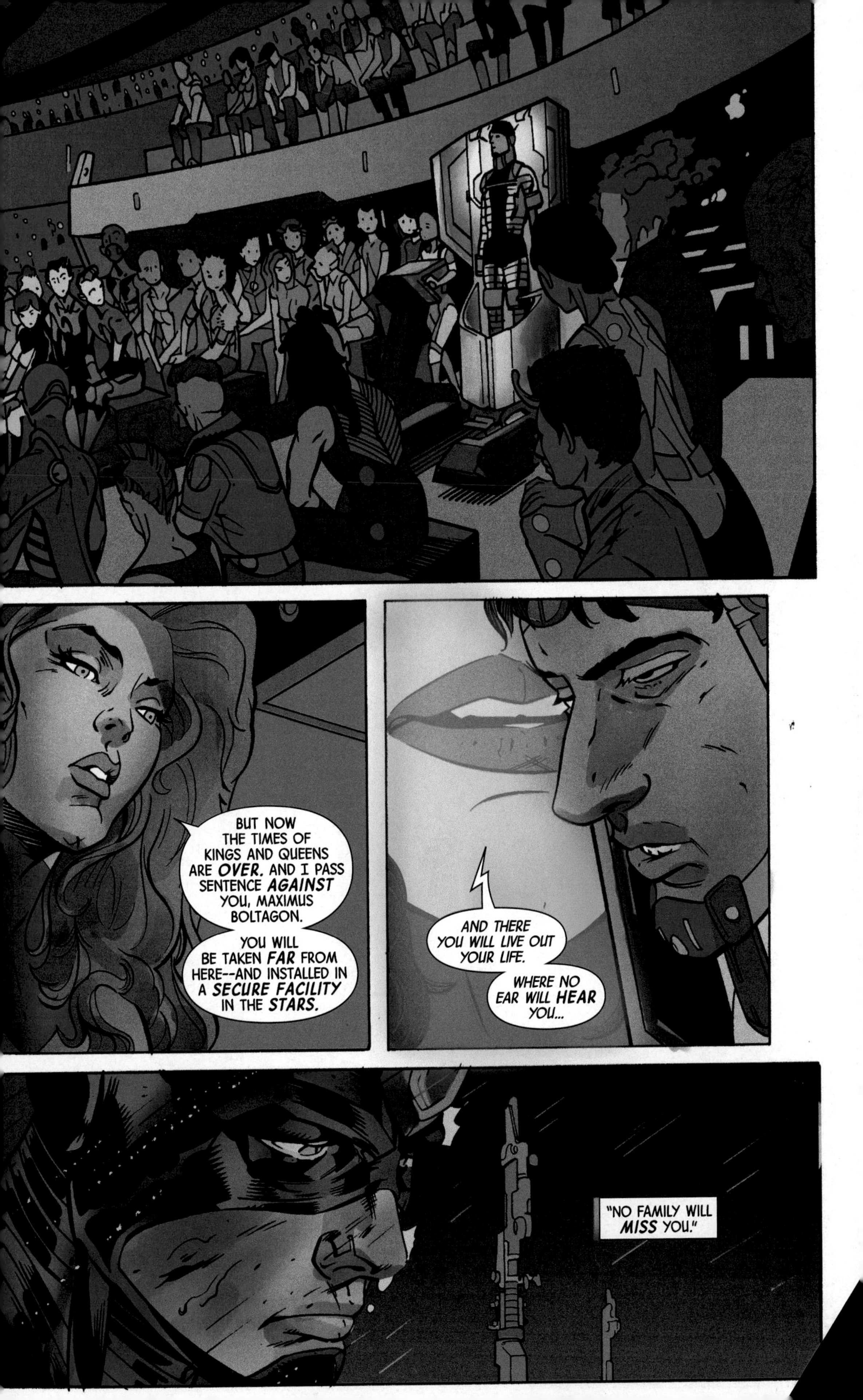
BUT NOW THE TIMES OF KINGS AND QUEENS ARE OVER. AND I PASS SENTENCE AGAINST YOU, MAXIMUS BOLTAGON.
YOU WILL BE TAKEN FAR FROM HERE--AND INSTALLED IN A SECURE FACILITY IN THE STARS.
AND THERE YOU WILL LIVE OUT YOUR LIFE.
WHERE NO EAR WILL HEAR YOU...
"NO FAMILY WILL MISS YOU."

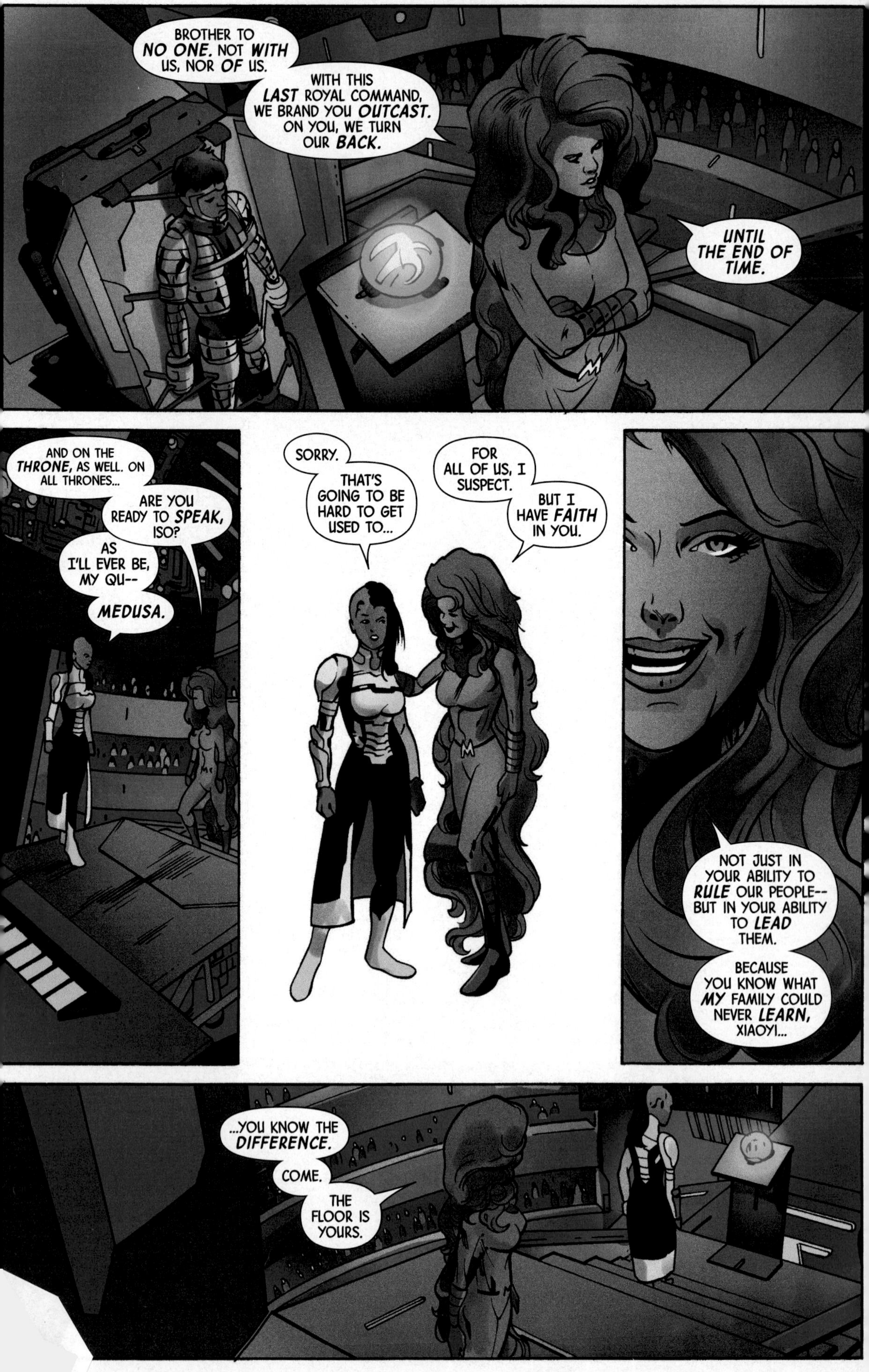
BROTHER TO NO ONE. NOT WITH US, NOR OF US.
WITH THIS LAST ROYAL COMMAND, WE BRAND YOU OUTCAST. ON YOU, WE TURN OUR BACK.
UNTIL THE END OF TIME.
AND ON THE THRONE, AS WELL. ON ALL THRONES...
ARE YOU READY TO SPEAK, ISO?
AS I'LL EVER BE, MY QU--
MEDUSA.
SORRY.
THAT'S GOING TO BE HARD TO GET USED TO...
FOR ALL OF US, I SUSPECT.
BUT I HAVE FAITH IN YOU.
NOT JUST IN YOUR ABILITY TO RULE OUR PEOPLE-- BUT IN YOUR ABILITY TO LEAD THEM.
BECAUSE YOU KNOW WHAT MY FAMILY COULD NEVER LEARN, XIAOYI...
...YOU KNOW THE DIFFERENCE.
COME.
THE FLOOR IS YOURS.

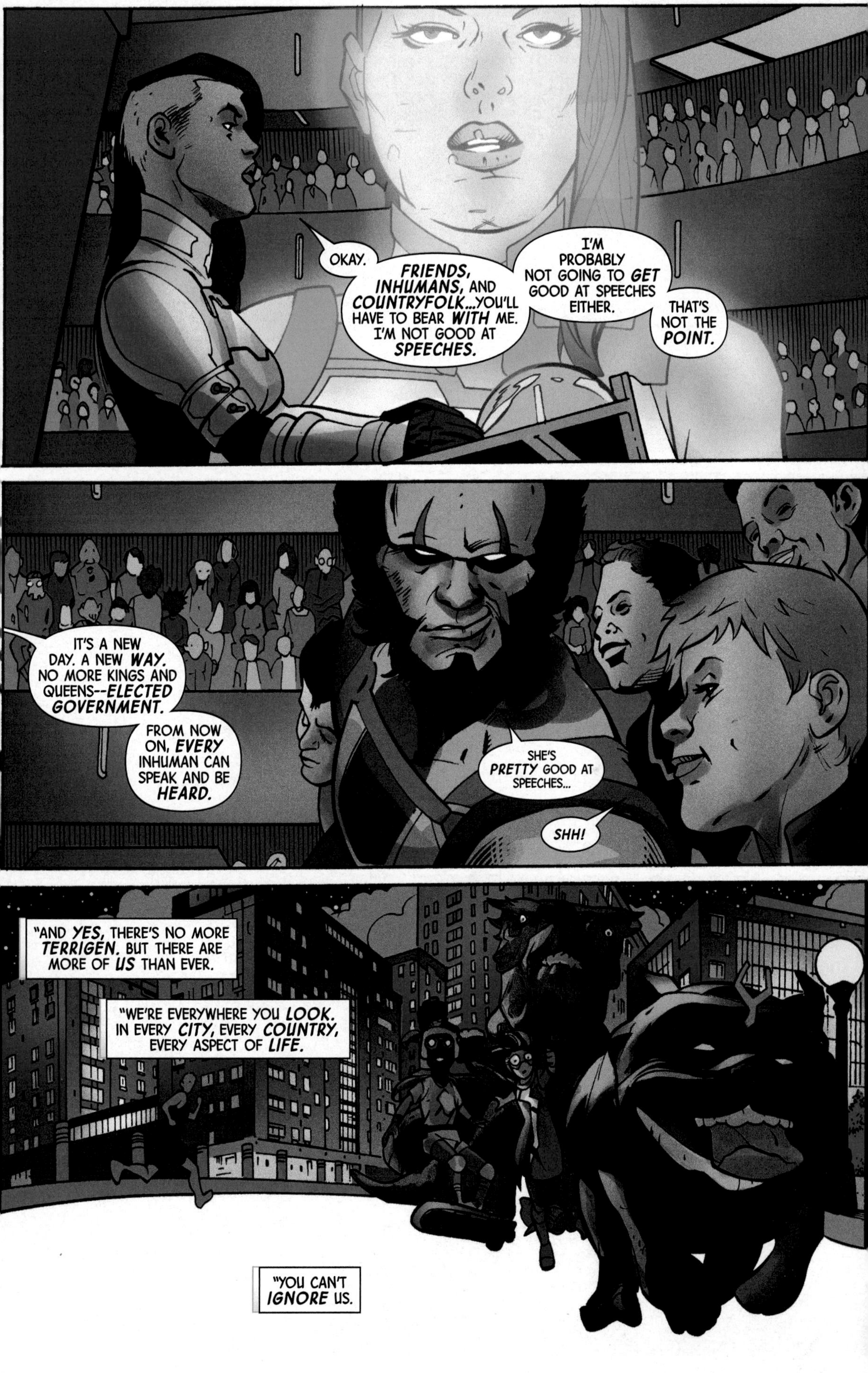
OKAY.
FRIENDS, INHUMANS, AND COUNTRYFOLK...YOU'LL HAVE TO BEAR WITH ME. I'M NOT GOOD AT SPEECHES.
I'M PROBABLY NOT GOING TO GET GOOD AT SPEECHES EITHER.
THAT'S NOT THE POINT.
IT'S A NEW DAY. A NEW WAY. NO MORE KINGS AND QUEENS--ELECTED GOVERNMENT.
FROM NOW ON, EVERY INHUMAN CAN SPEAK AND BE HEARD.
SHE'S PRETTY GOOD AT SPEECHES...
SHH!
"AND YES, THERE'S NO MORE TERRIGEN. BUT THERE ARE MORE OF US THAN EVER.
"WE'RE EVERYWHERE YOU LOOK. IN EVERY CITY, EVERY COUNTRY, EVERY ASPECT OF LIFE.
"YOU CAN'T IGNORE US.

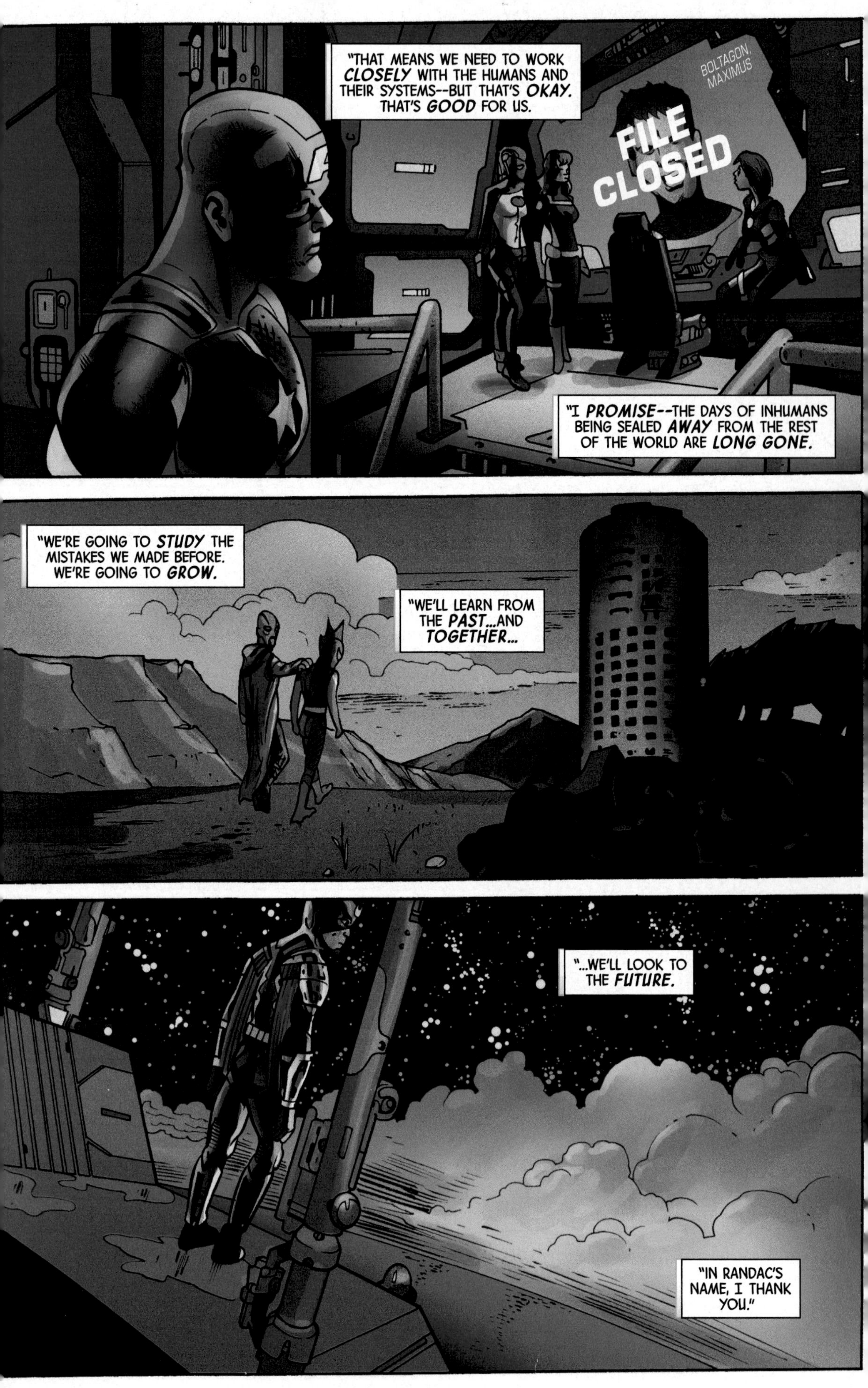
"THAT MEANS WE NEED TO WORK CLOSELY WITH THE HUMANS AND THEIR SYSTEMS--BUT THAT'S OKAY. THAT'S GOOD FOR US.
BOLTAGON, MAXIMUS
FILE CLOSED
"I PROMISE--THE DAYS OF INHUMANS BEING SEALED AWAY FROM THE REST OF THE WORLD ARE LONG GONE.
"WE'RE GOING TO STUDY THE MISTAKES WE MADE BEFORE. WE'RE GOING TO GROW.
"WE'LL LEARN FROM THE PAST...AND TOGETHER...
"...WE'LL LOOK TO THE FUTURE.
"IN RANDAC'S NAME, I THANK YOU."

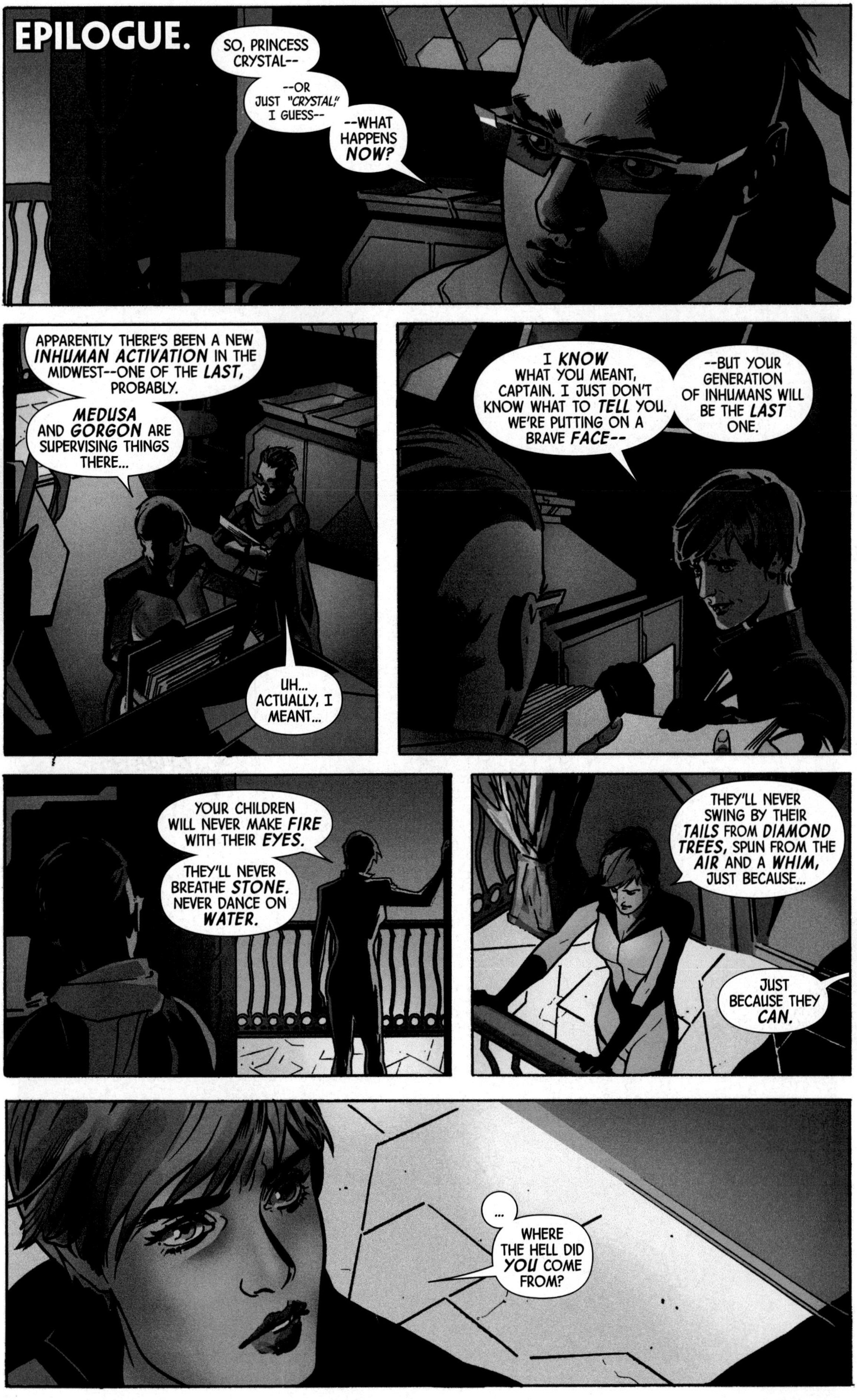
EPILOGUE.
SO, PRINCESS CRYSTAL--
--OR JUST "CRYSTAL," I GUESS--
--WHAT HAPPENS NOW?
APPARENTLY THERE'S BEEN A NEW INHUMAN ACTIVATION IN THE MIDWEST--ONE OF THE LAST, PROBABLY.
MEDUSA AND GORGON ARE SUPERVISING THINGS THERE...
UH... ACTUALLY, I MEANT...
I KNOW WHAT YOU MEANT, CAPTAIN. I JUST DON'T KNOW WHAT TO TELL YOU. WE'RE PUTTING ON A BRAVE FACE--
--BUT YOUR GENERATION OF INHUMANS WILL BE THE LAST ONE.
YOUR CHILDREN WILL NEVER MAKE FIRE WITH THEIR EYES.
THEY'LL NEVER BREATHE STONE. NEVER DANCE ON WATER.
THEY'LL NEVER SWING BY THEIR TAILS FROM DIAMOND TREES, SPUN FROM THE AIR AND A WHIM, JUST BECAUSE...
JUST BECAUSE THEY CAN.
...
WHERE THE HELL DID YOU COME FROM?

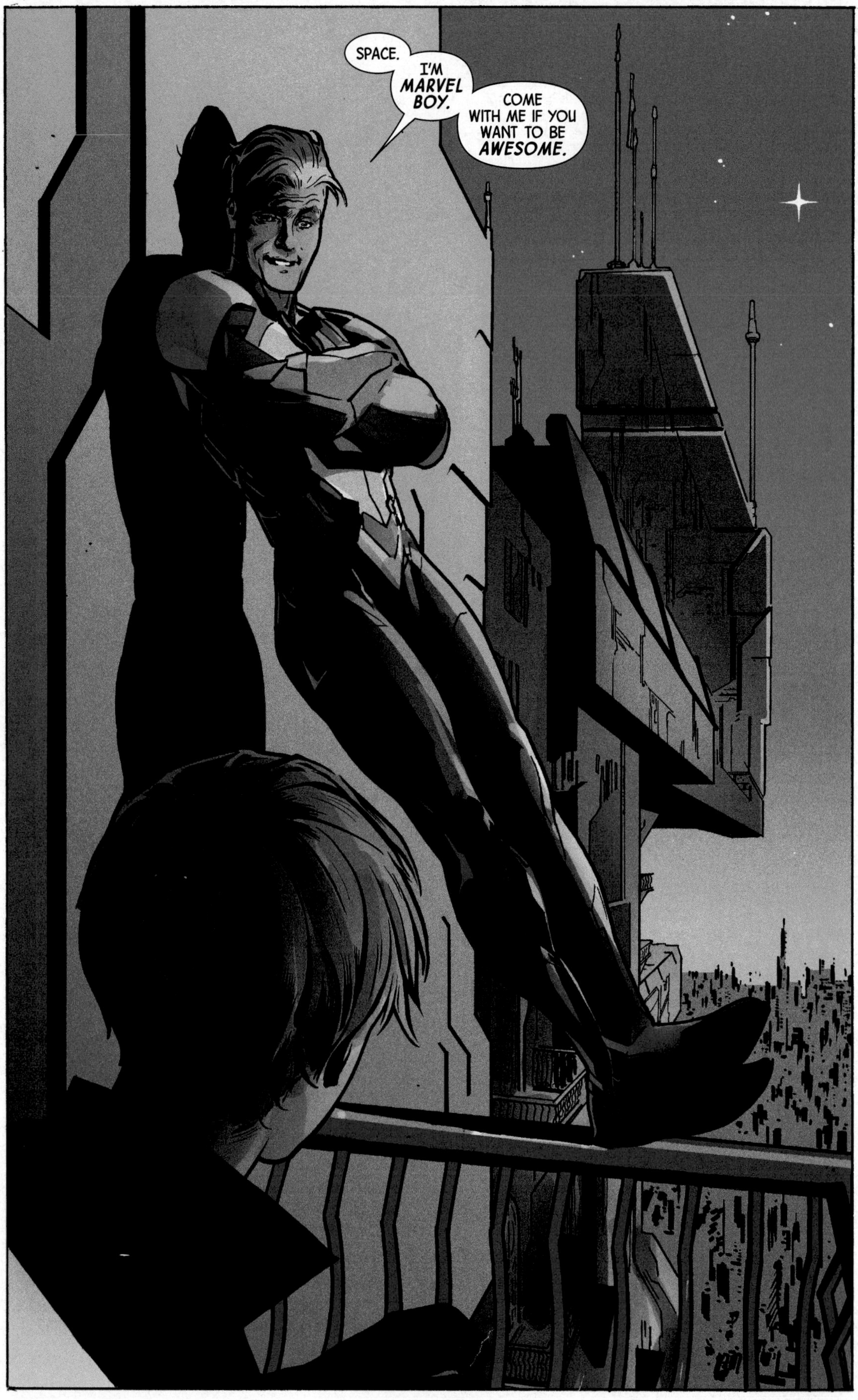
SPACE.
I'M *MARVEL BOY.*
COME WITH ME IF YOU WANT TO BE ***AWESOME.***

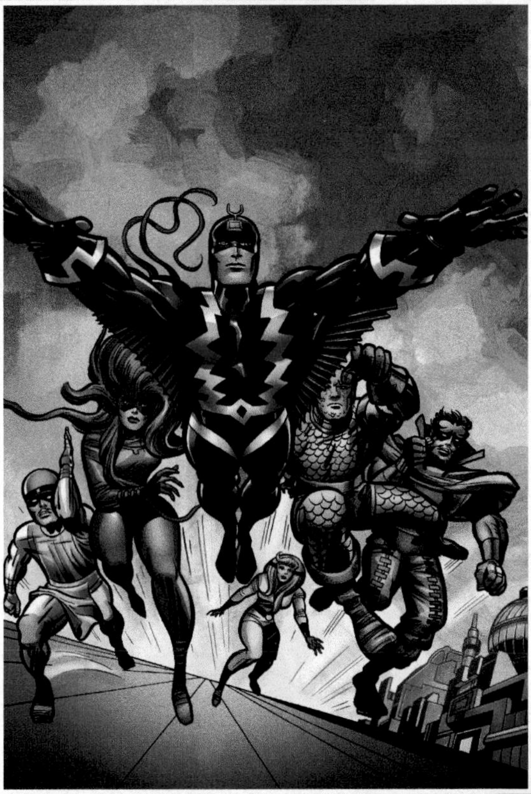

**INHUMANS PRIME #1 VARIANT**
BY JACK KIRBY & PAUL MOUNTS

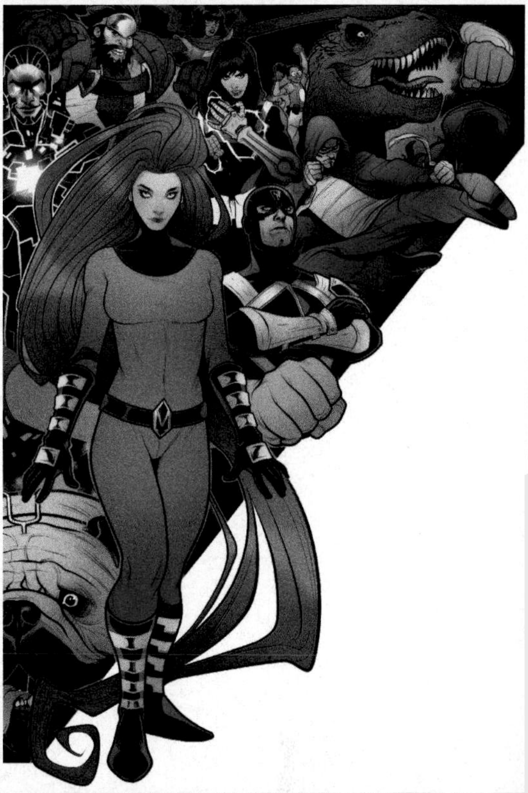

**INHUMANS PRIME #1 VARIANT**
BY ELIZABETH TORQUE

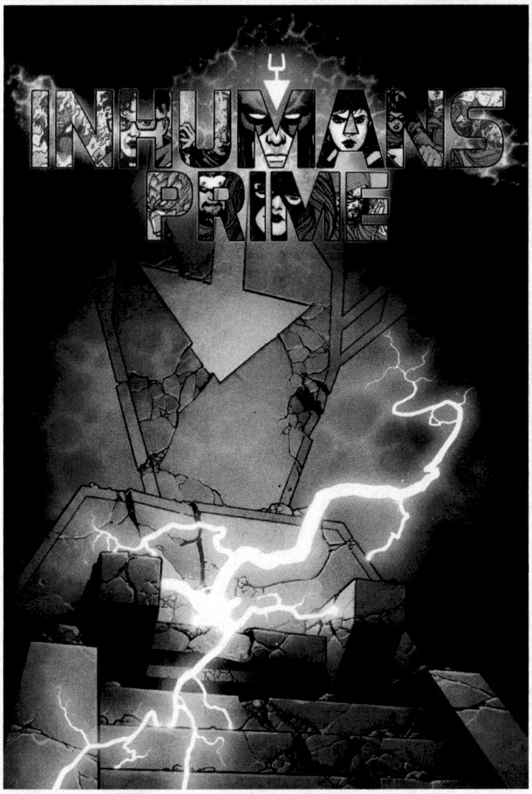
INHUMANS
PRIME

**INHUMANS PRIME #1 VARIANT**
BY RYAN SOOK

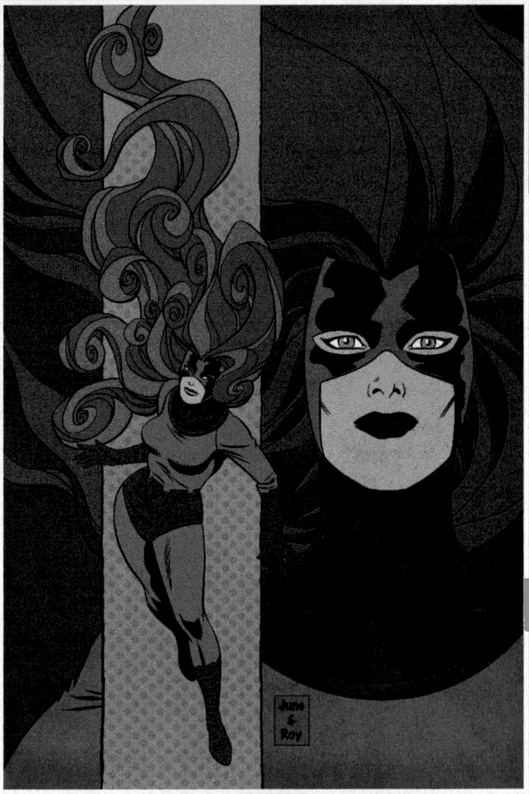
June & Roy

**INHUMANS PRIME #1 VARIANT**
BY JUNE BRIGMAN & ROY RICHARDSON

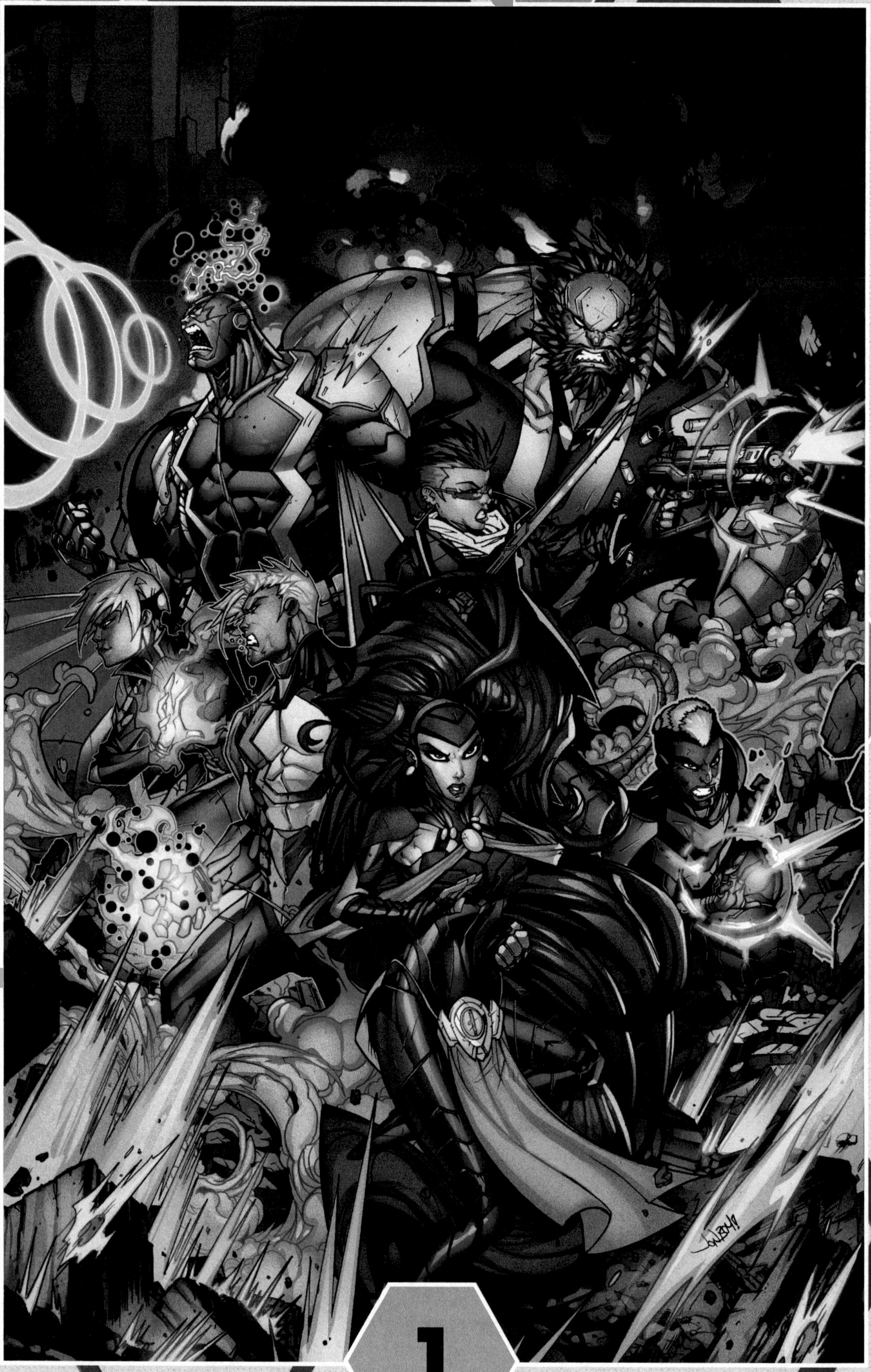

# 1

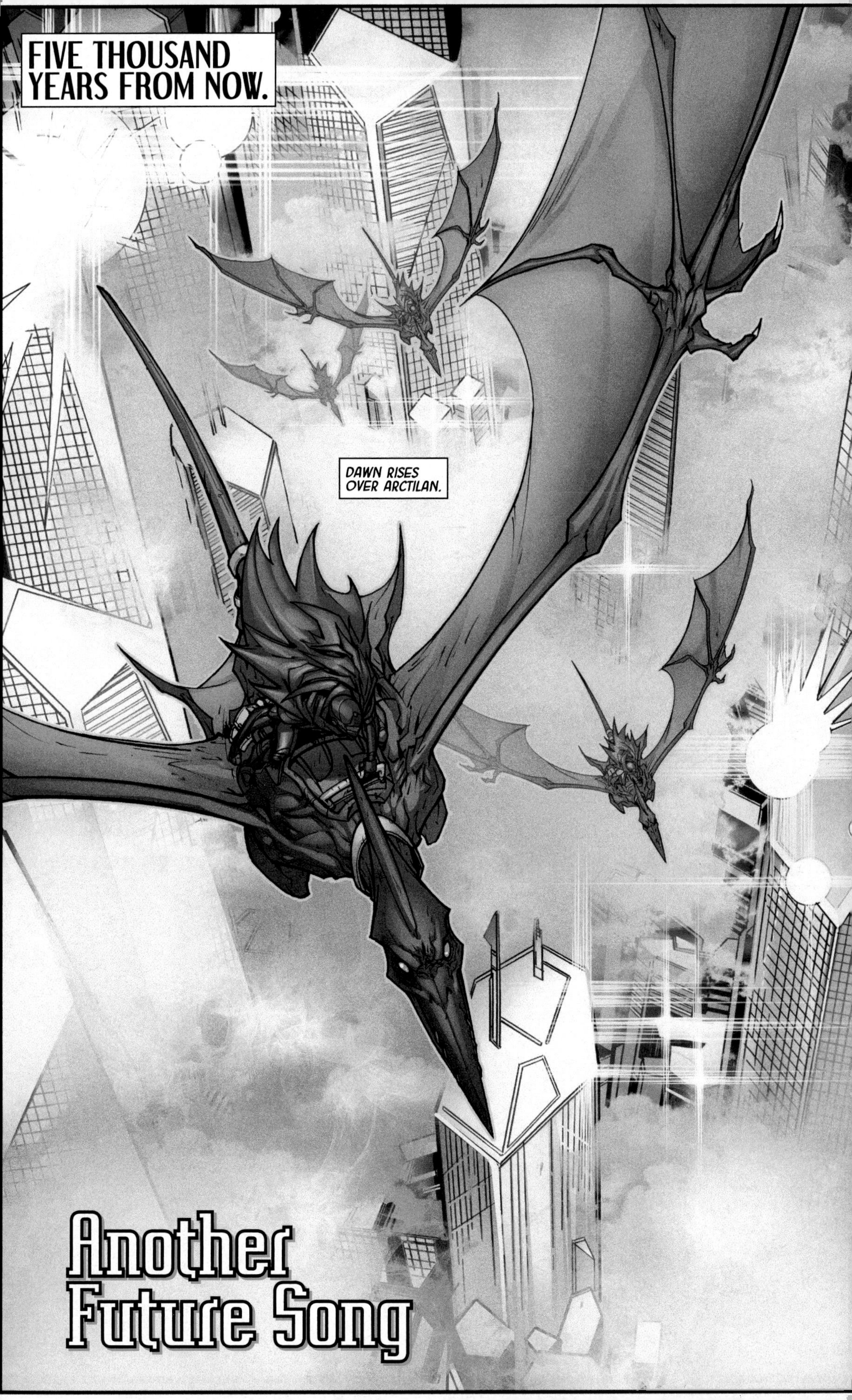
FIVE THOUSAND YEARS FROM NOW.
DAWN RISES OVER ARCTILAN.
Another Future Song

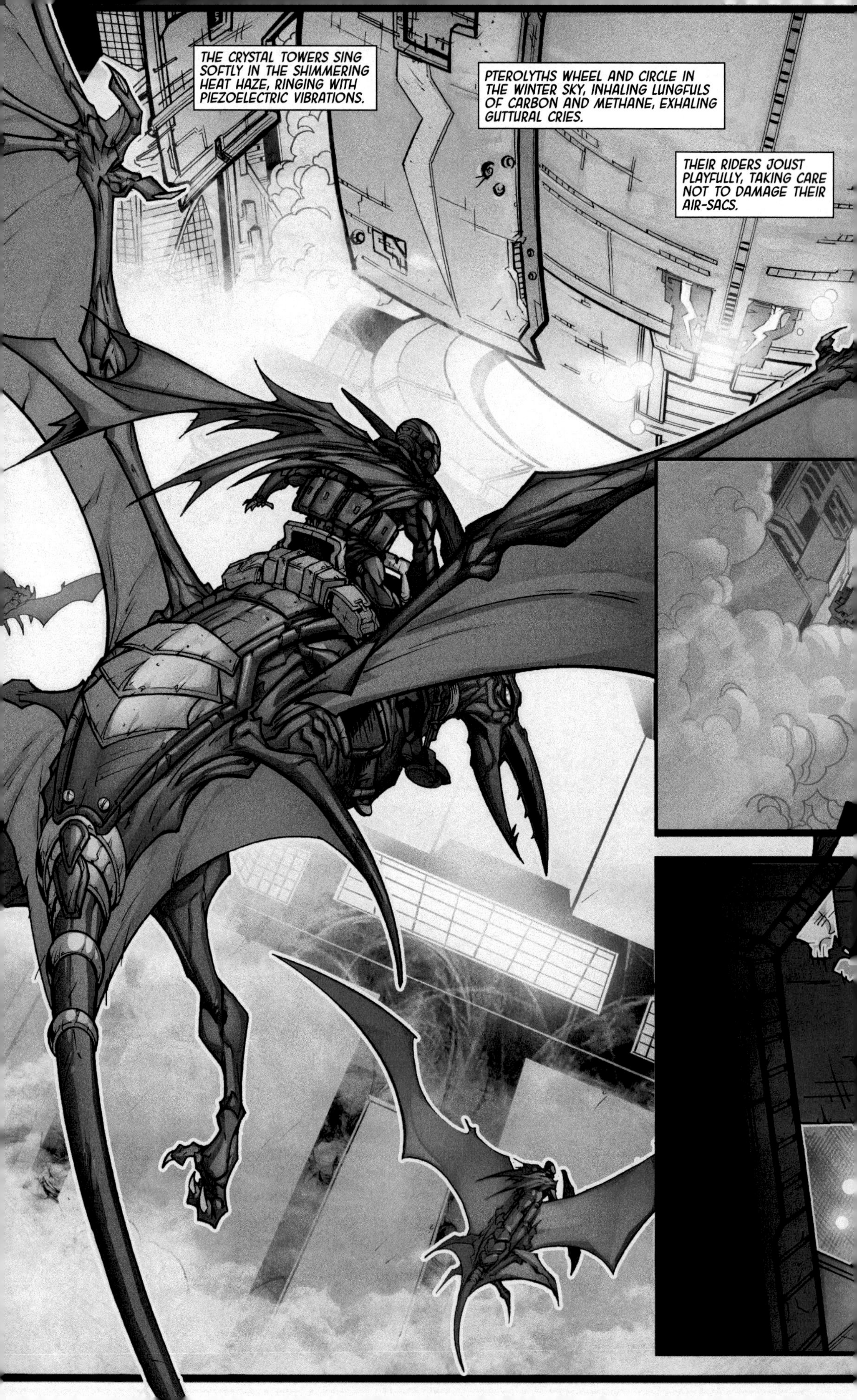
THE CRYSTAL TOWERS SING SOFTLY IN THE SHIMMERING HEAT HAZE, RINGING WITH PIEZOELECTRIC VIBRATIONS.
PTEROLYTHS WHEEL AND CIRCLE IN THE WINTER SKY, INHALING LUNGFULS OF CARBON AND METHANE, EXHALING GUTTURAL CRIES.
THEIR RIDERS JOUST PLAYFULLY, TAKING CARE NOT TO DAMAGE THEIR AIR-SACS.

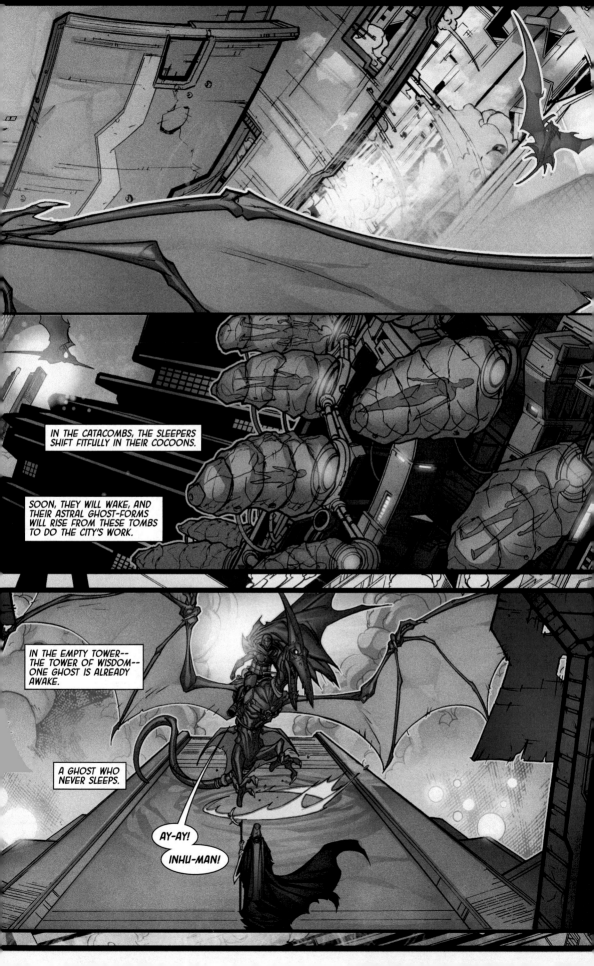

IN THE CATACOMBS, THE SLEEPERS SHIFT FITFULLY IN THEIR COCOONS.

SOON, THEY WILL WAKE, AND THEIR ASTRAL GHOST-FORMS WILL RISE FROM THESE TOMBS TO DO THE CITY'S WORK.

IN THE EMPTY TOWER-- THE TOWER OF WISDOM-- ONE GHOST IS ALREADY AWAKE.

A GHOST WHO NEVER SLEEPS.

AY-AY!

INHU-MAN!

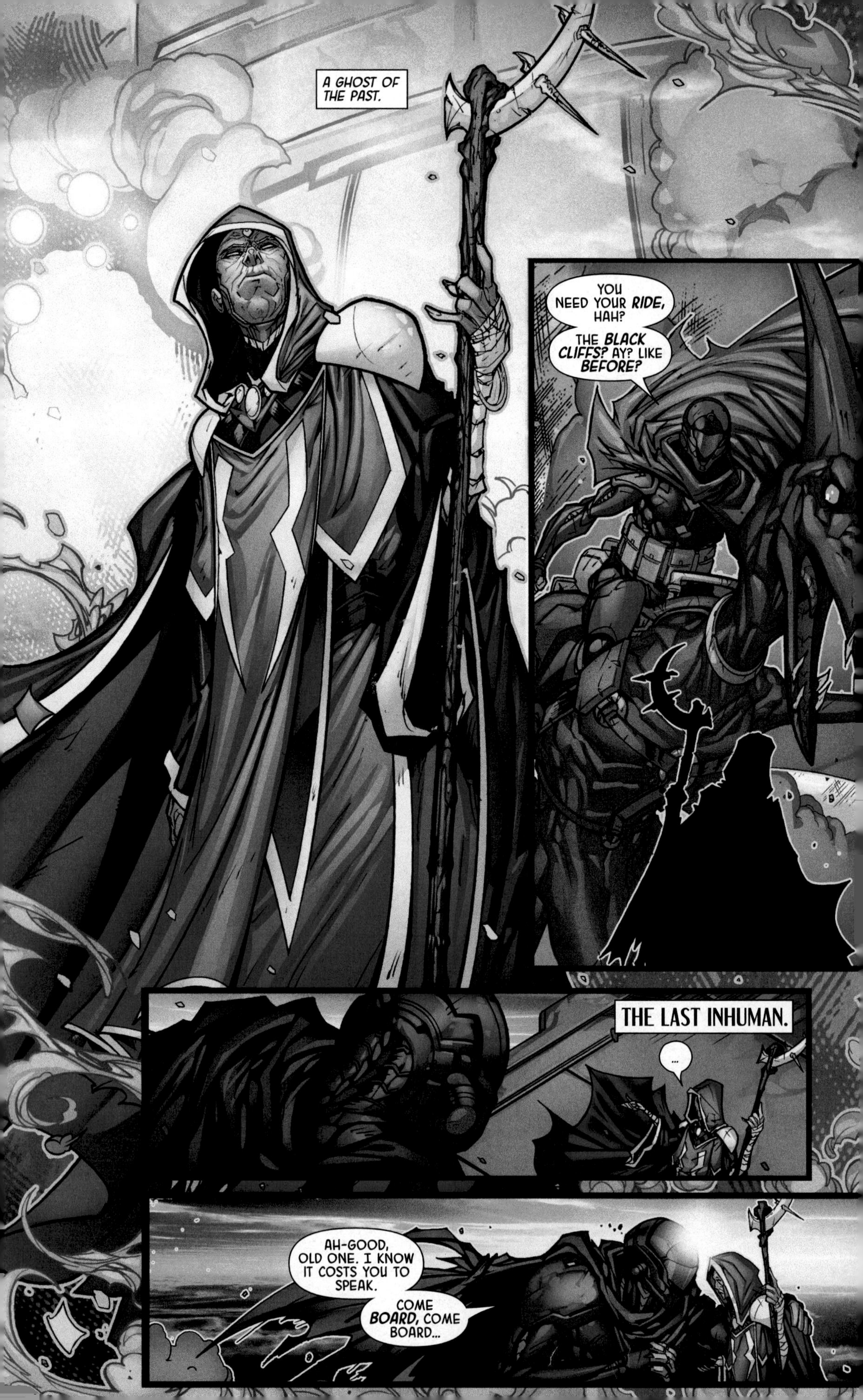
A GHOST OF THE PAST.
YOU NEED YOUR RIDE, HAH?
THE BLACK CLIFFS? AY? LIKE BEFORE?
THE LAST INHUMAN.
...
AH-GOOD, OLD ONE. I KNOW IT COSTS YOU TO SPEAK.
COME BOARD, COME BOARD...

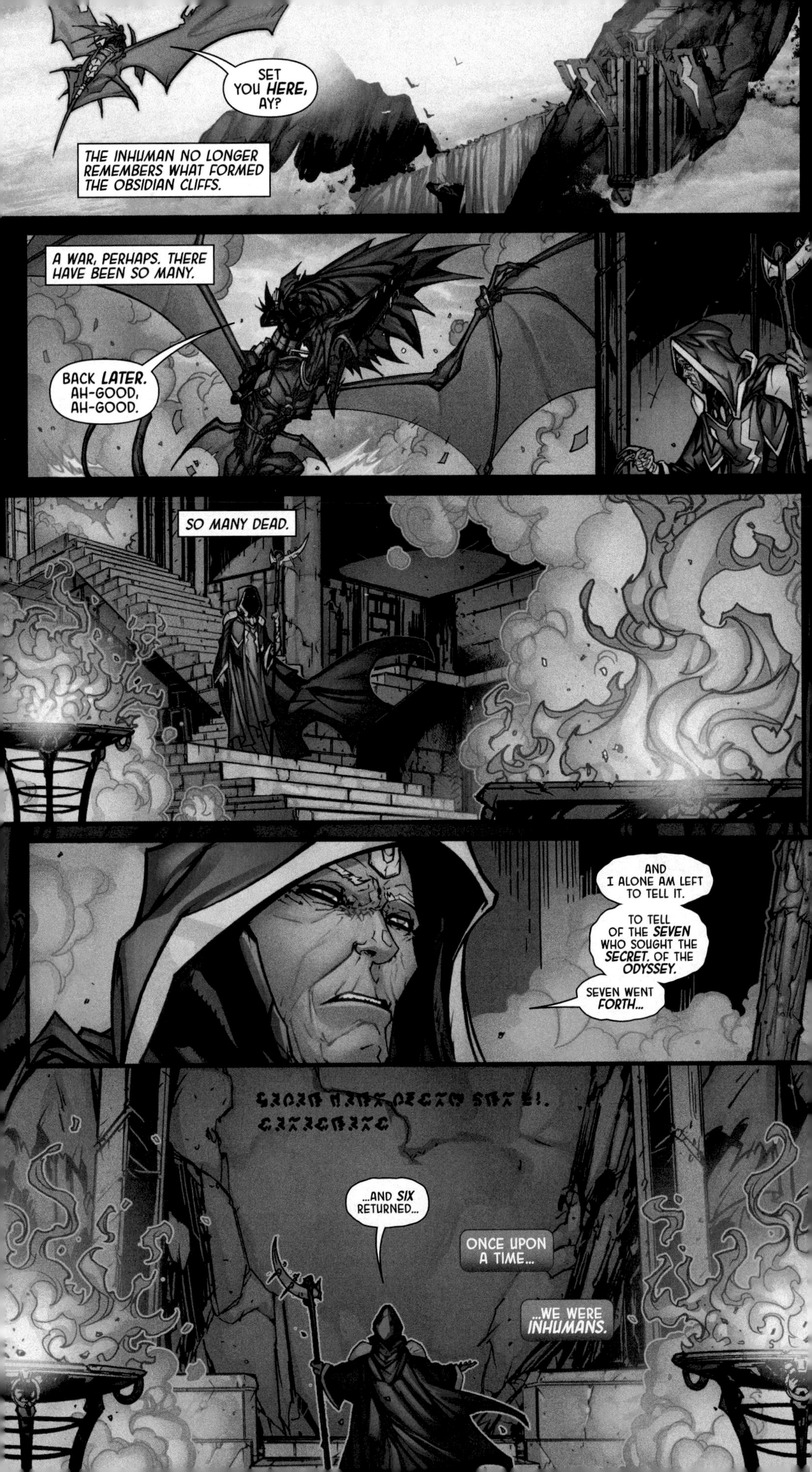
SET YOU HERE, AY?
THE INHUMAN NO LONGER REMEMBERS WHAT FORMED THE OBSIDIAN CLIFFS.
A WAR, PERHAPS. THERE HAVE BEEN SO MANY.
BACK LATER. AH-GOOD, AH-GOOD.
SO MANY DEAD.
AND I ALONE AM LEFT TO TELL IT.
TO TELL OF THE SEVEN WHO SOUGHT THE SECRET. OF THE ODYSSEY.
SEVEN WENT FORTH...
...AND SIX RETURNED...
ONCE UPON A TIME...
...WE WERE INHUMANS.

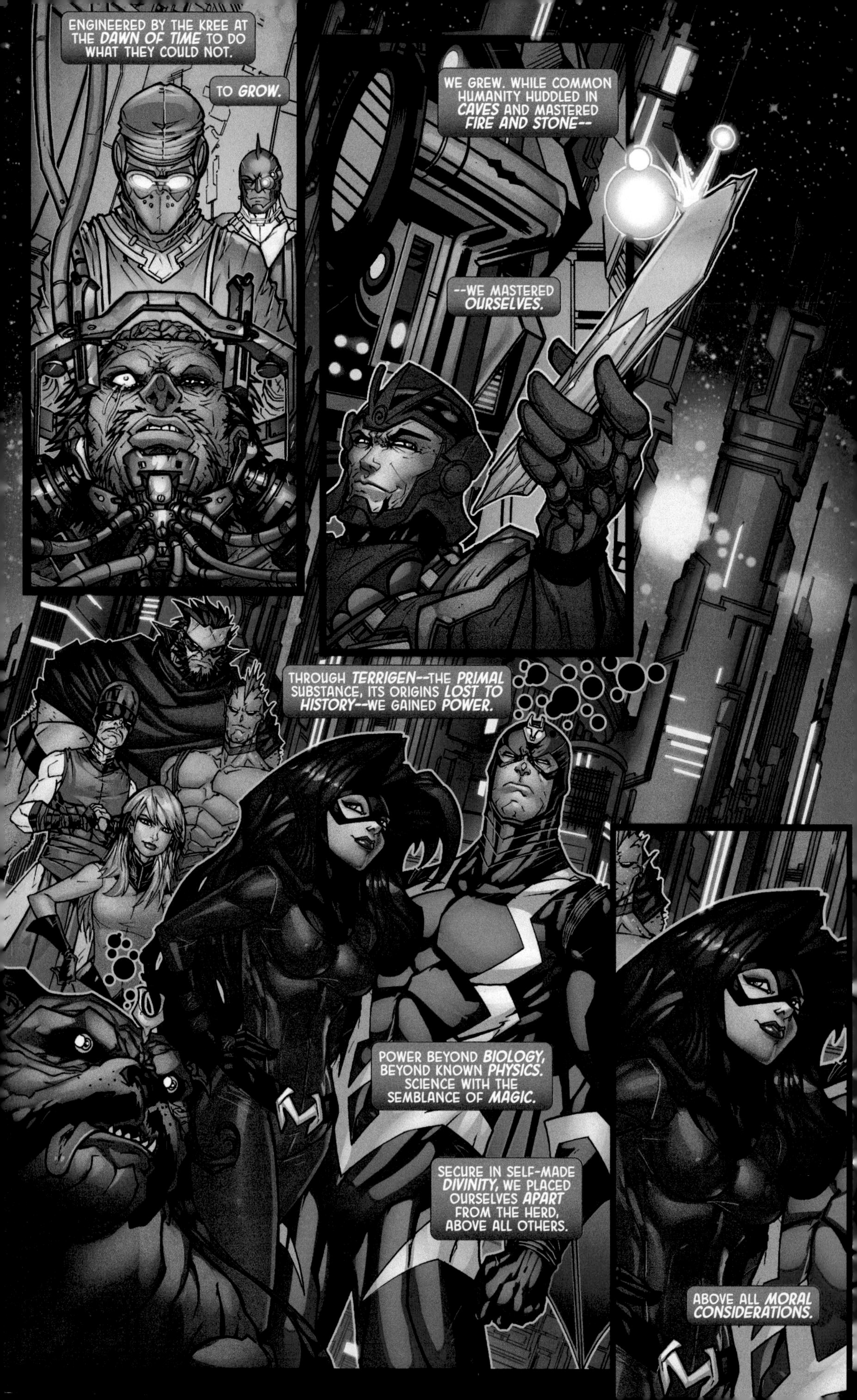
ENGINEERED BY THE KREE AT THE DAWN OF TIME TO DO WHAT THEY COULD NOT.
TO GROW.
WE GREW. WHILE COMMON HUMANITY HUDDLED IN CAVES AND MASTERED FIRE AND STONE--
--WE MASTERED OURSELVES.
THROUGH TERRIGEN--THE PRIMAL SUBSTANCE, ITS ORIGINS LOST TO HISTORY--WE GAINED POWER.
POWER BEYOND BIOLOGY, BEYOND KNOWN PHYSICS. SCIENCE WITH THE SEMBLANCE OF MAGIC.
SECURE IN SELF-MADE DIVINITY, WE PLACED OURSELVES APART FROM THE HERD, ABOVE ALL OTHERS.
ABOVE ALL MORAL CONSIDERATIONS.

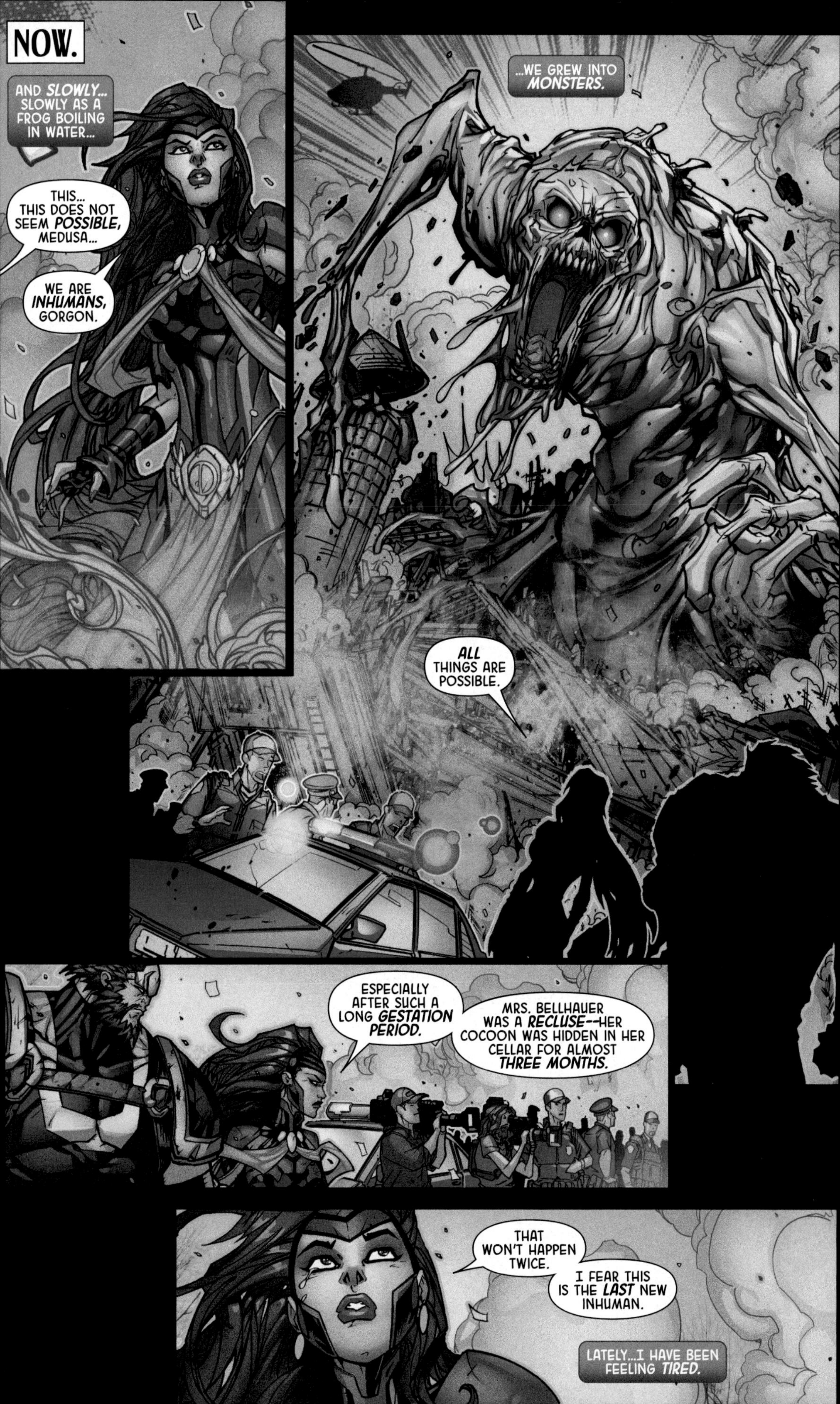
NOW.
AND SLOWLY... SLOWLY AS A FROG BOILING IN WATER...
THIS... THIS DOES NOT SEEM POSSIBLE, MEDUSA...
WE ARE INHUMANS, GORGON.
...WE GREW INTO MONSTERS.
ALL THINGS ARE POSSIBLE.
ESPECIALLY AFTER SUCH A LONG GESTATION PERIOD.
MRS. BELLHAUER WAS A RECLUSE--HER COCOON WAS HIDDEN IN HER CELLAR FOR ALMOST THREE MONTHS.
THAT WON'T HAPPEN TWICE.
I FEAR THIS IS THE LAST NEW INHUMAN.
LATELY...I HAVE BEEN FEELING TIRED.

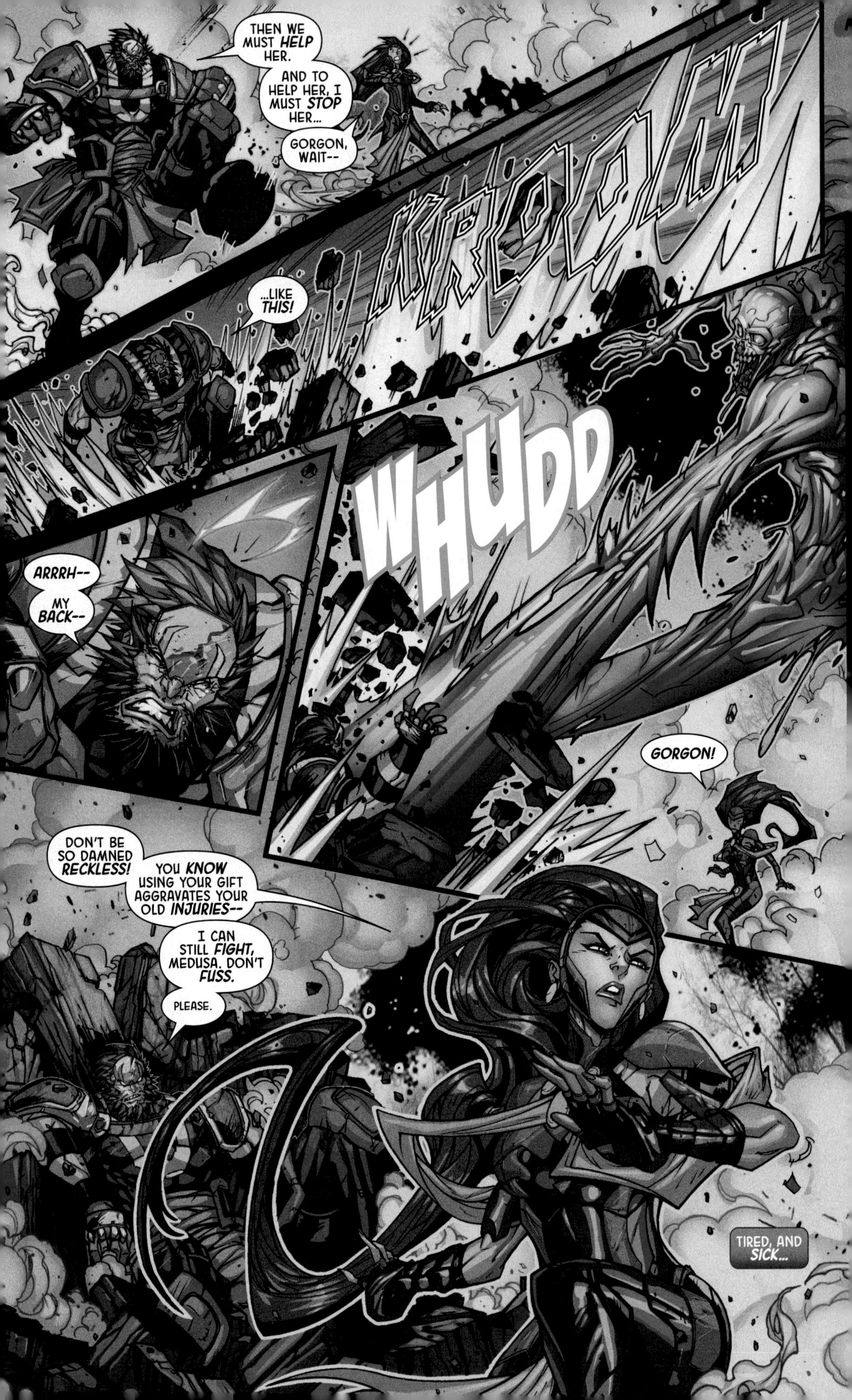
THEN WE MUST HELP HER.
AND TO HELP HER, I MUST STOP HER...
GORGON, WAIT--
KROOOM
...LIKE THIS!
WHUDD
ARRRH--
MY BACK--
GORGON!
DON'T BE SO DAMNED RECKLESS!
YOU KNOW USING YOUR GIFT AGGRAVATES YOUR OLD INJURIES--
I CAN STILL FIGHT, MEDUSA. DON'T FUSS.
PLEASE.
TIRED, AND SICK...

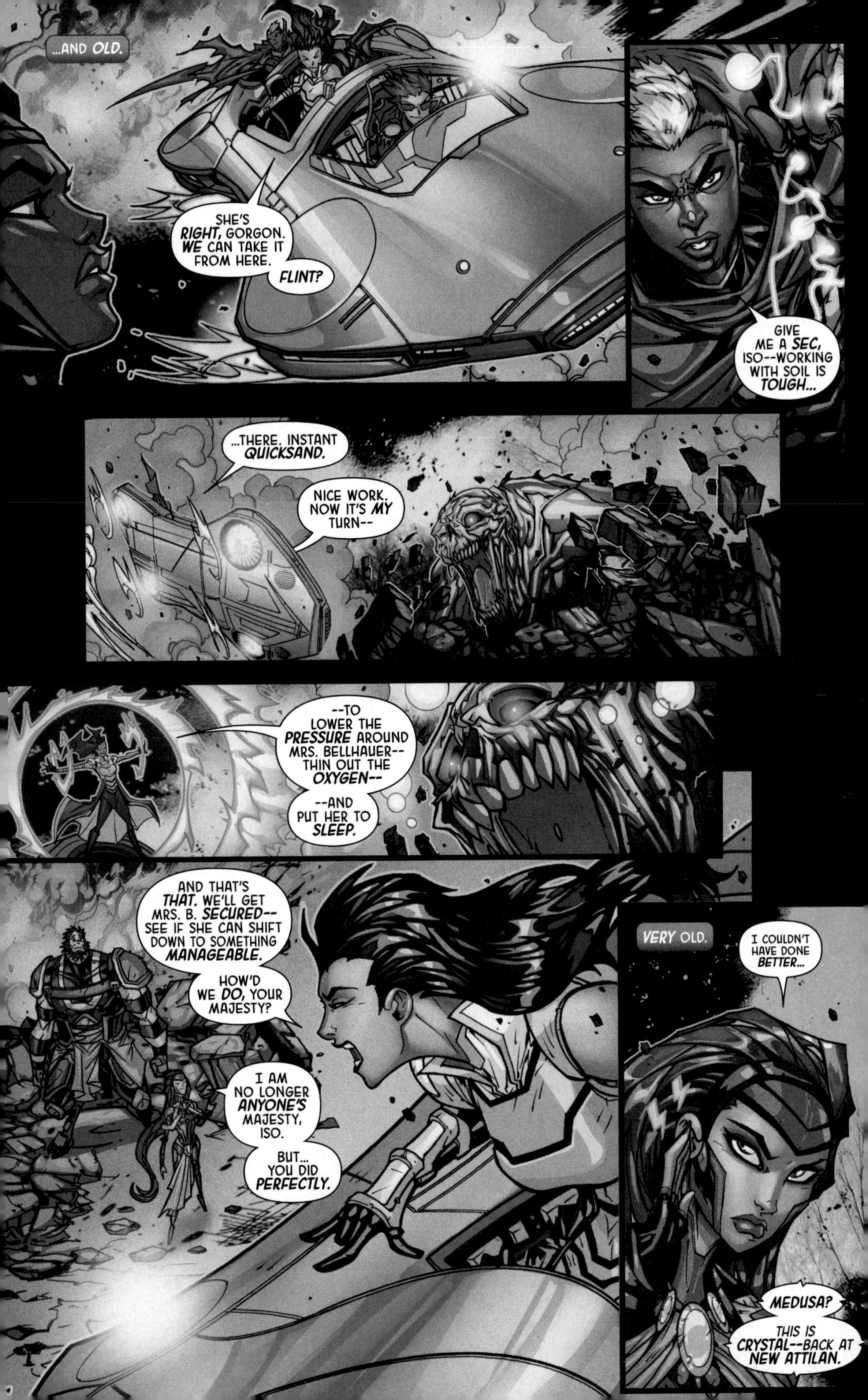
...AND OLD.
SHE'S RIGHT, GORGON. WE CAN TAKE IT FROM HERE.
FLINT?
GIVE ME A SEC, ISO--WORKING WITH SOIL IS TOUGH...
...THERE. INSTANT QUICKSAND.
NICE WORK. NOW IT'S MY TURN--
--TO LOWER THE PRESSURE AROUND MRS. BELLHAUER--THIN OUT THE OXYGEN--
--AND PUT HER TO SLEEP.
AND THAT'S THAT. WE'LL GET MRS. B. SECURED--SEE IF SHE CAN SHIFT DOWN TO SOMETHING MANAGEABLE.
HOW'D WE DO, YOUR MAJESTY?
I AM NO LONGER ANYONE'S MAJESTY, ISO.
BUT... YOU DID PERFECTLY.
VERY OLD.
I COULDN'T HAVE DONE BETTER...
MEDUSA?
THIS IS CRYSTAL--BACK AT NEW ATTILAN.

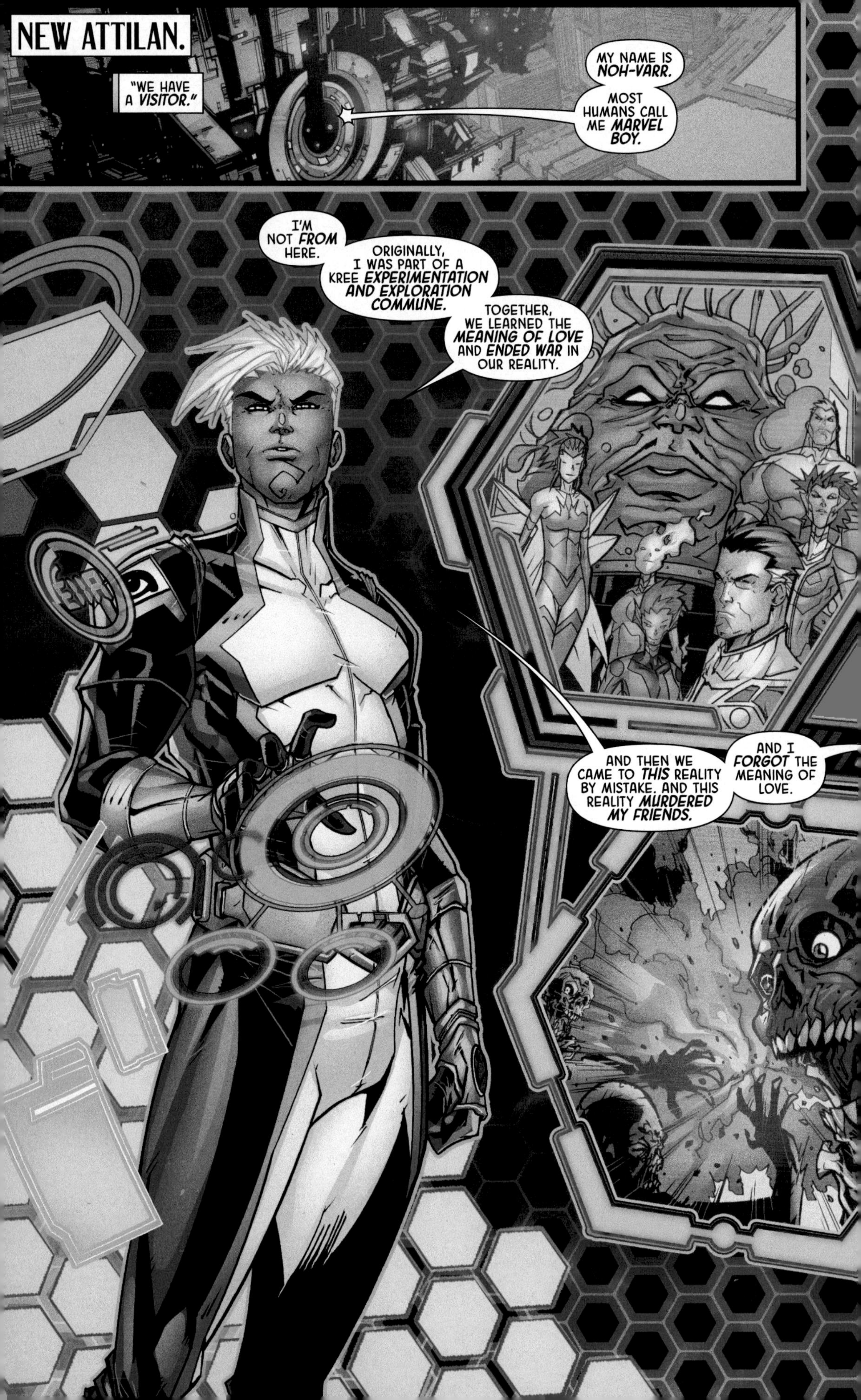
NEW ATTILAN.
"WE HAVE A VISITOR."
MY NAME IS NOH-VARR.
MOST HUMANS CALL ME MARVEL BOY.
I'M NOT FROM HERE.
ORIGINALLY, I WAS PART OF A KREE EXPERIMENTATION AND EXPLORATION COMMUNE.
TOGETHER, WE LEARNED THE MEANING OF LOVE AND ENDED WAR IN OUR REALITY.
AND THEN WE CAME TO THIS REALITY BY MISTAKE. AND THIS REALITY MURDERED MY FRIENDS.
AND I FORGOT THE MEANING OF LOVE.

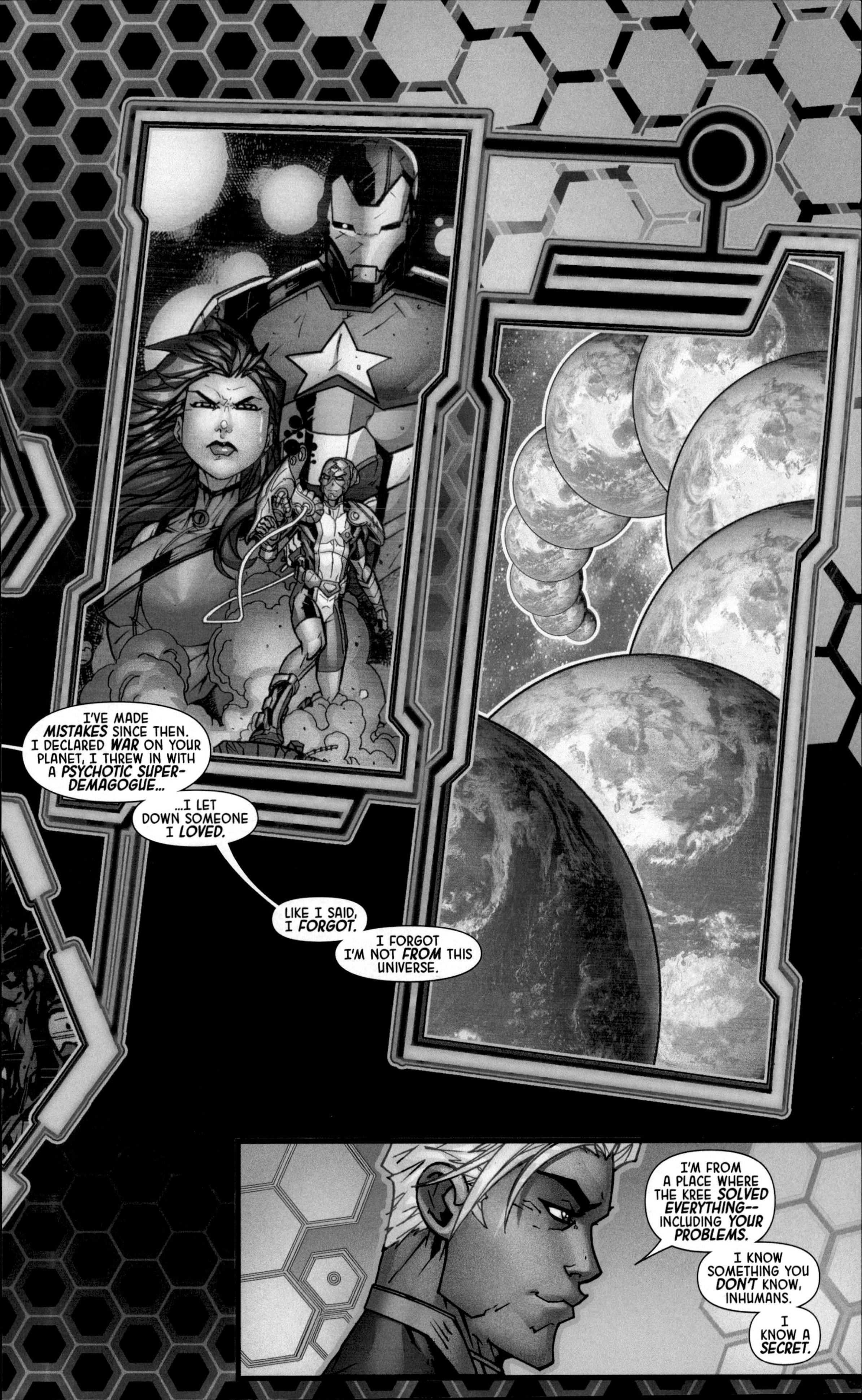

I'VE MADE MISTAKES SINCE THEN. I DECLARED WAR ON YOUR PLANET, I THREW IN WITH A PSYCHOTIC SUPER-DEMAGOGUE...
...I LET DOWN SOMEONE I LOVED.
LIKE I SAID, I FORGOT.
I FORGOT I'M NOT FROM THIS UNIVERSE.
I'M FROM A PLACE WHERE THE KREE SOLVED EVERYTHING-- INCLUDING YOUR PROBLEMS.
I KNOW SOMETHING YOU DON'T KNOW, INHUMANS.
I KNOW A SECRET.

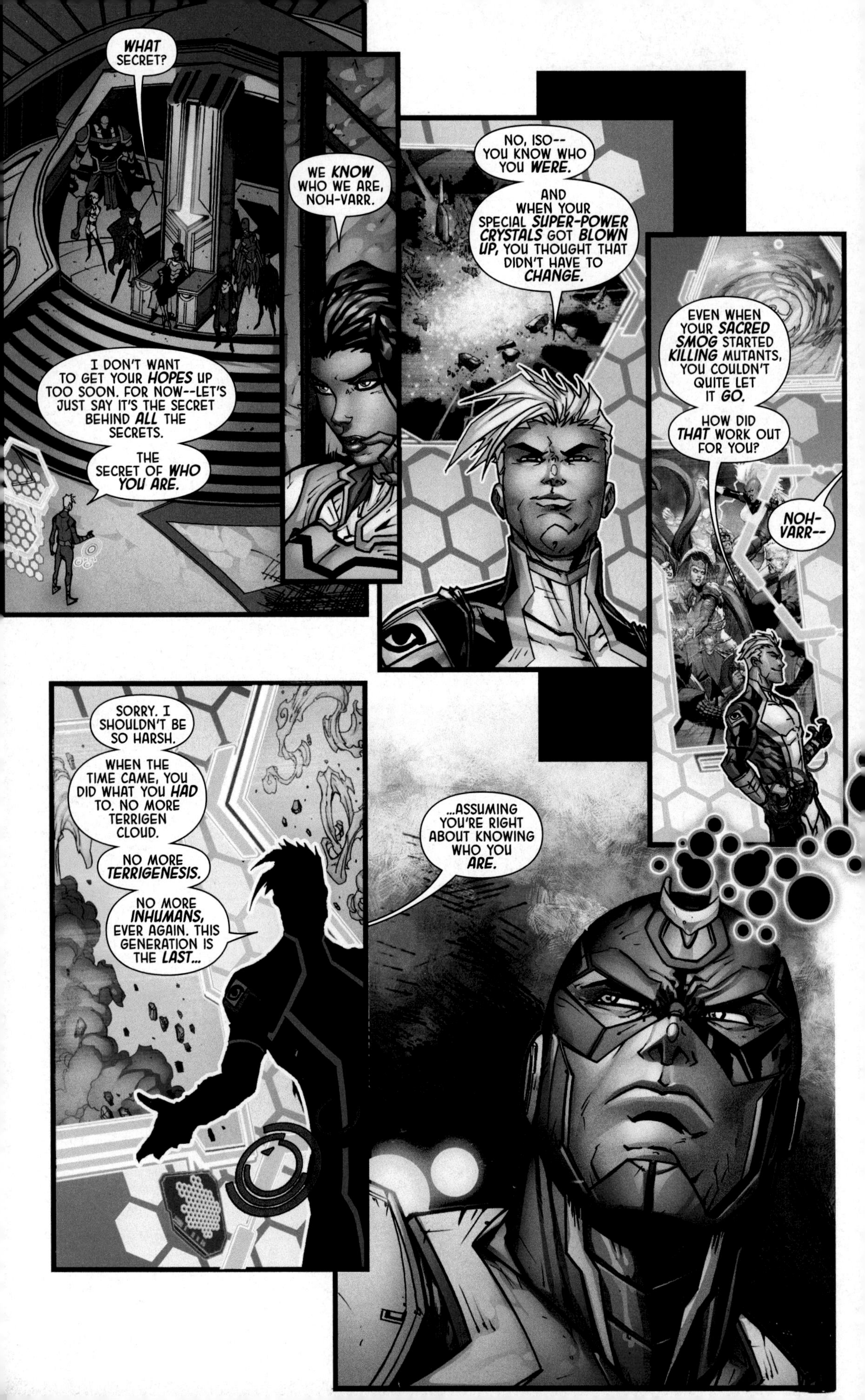
WHAT SECRET?
I DON'T WANT TO GET YOUR HOPES UP TOO SOON. FOR NOW--LET'S JUST SAY IT'S THE SECRET BEHIND ALL THE SECRETS.
THE SECRET OF WHO YOU ARE.
WE KNOW WHO WE ARE, NOH-VARR.
NO, ISO-- YOU KNOW WHO YOU WERE.
AND WHEN YOUR SPECIAL SUPER-POWER CRYSTALS GOT BLOWN UP, YOU THOUGHT THAT DIDN'T HAVE TO CHANGE.
EVEN WHEN YOUR SACRED SMOG STARTED KILLING MUTANTS, YOU COULDN'T QUITE LET IT GO.
HOW DID THAT WORK OUT FOR YOU?
NOH-VARR--
SORRY. I SHOULDN'T BE SO HARSH.
WHEN THE TIME CAME, YOU DID WHAT YOU HAD TO. NO MORE TERRIGEN CLOUD.
NO MORE TERRIGENESIS.
NO MORE INHUMANS, EVER AGAIN. THIS GENERATION IS THE LAST...
...ASSUMING YOU'RE RIGHT ABOUT KNOWING WHO YOU ARE.

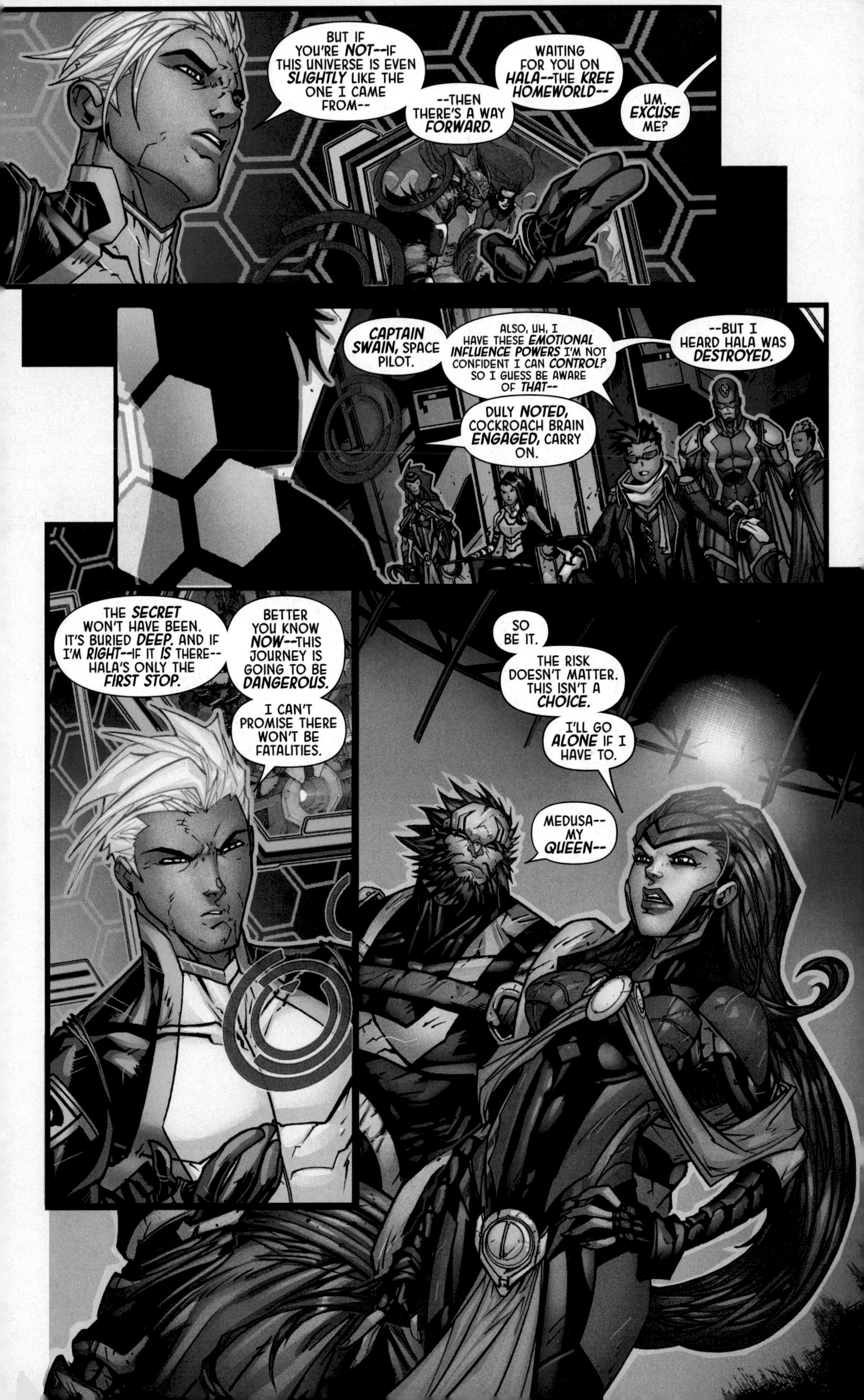
BUT IF YOU'RE NOT--IF THIS UNIVERSE IS EVEN SLIGHTLY LIKE THE ONE I CAME FROM--
--THEN THERE'S A WAY FORWARD.
WAITING FOR YOU ON HALA--THE KREE HOMEWORLD--
UM. EXCUSE ME?
CAPTAIN SWAIN, SPACE PILOT.
ALSO, UH, I HAVE THESE EMOTIONAL INFLUENCE POWERS I'M NOT CONFIDENT I CAN CONTROL? SO I GUESS BE AWARE OF THAT--
DULY NOTED, COCKROACH BRAIN ENGAGED, CARRY ON.
--BUT I HEARD HALA WAS DESTROYED.
THE SECRET WON'T HAVE BEEN. IT'S BURIED DEEP. AND IF I'M RIGHT--IF IT IS THERE--HALA'S ONLY THE FIRST STOP.
BETTER YOU KNOW NOW--THIS JOURNEY IS GOING TO BE DANGEROUS.
I CAN'T PROMISE THERE WON'T BE FATALITIES.
SO BE IT.
THE RISK DOESN'T MATTER. THIS ISN'T A CHOICE.
I'LL GO ALONE IF I HAVE TO.
MEDUSA--MY QUEEN--

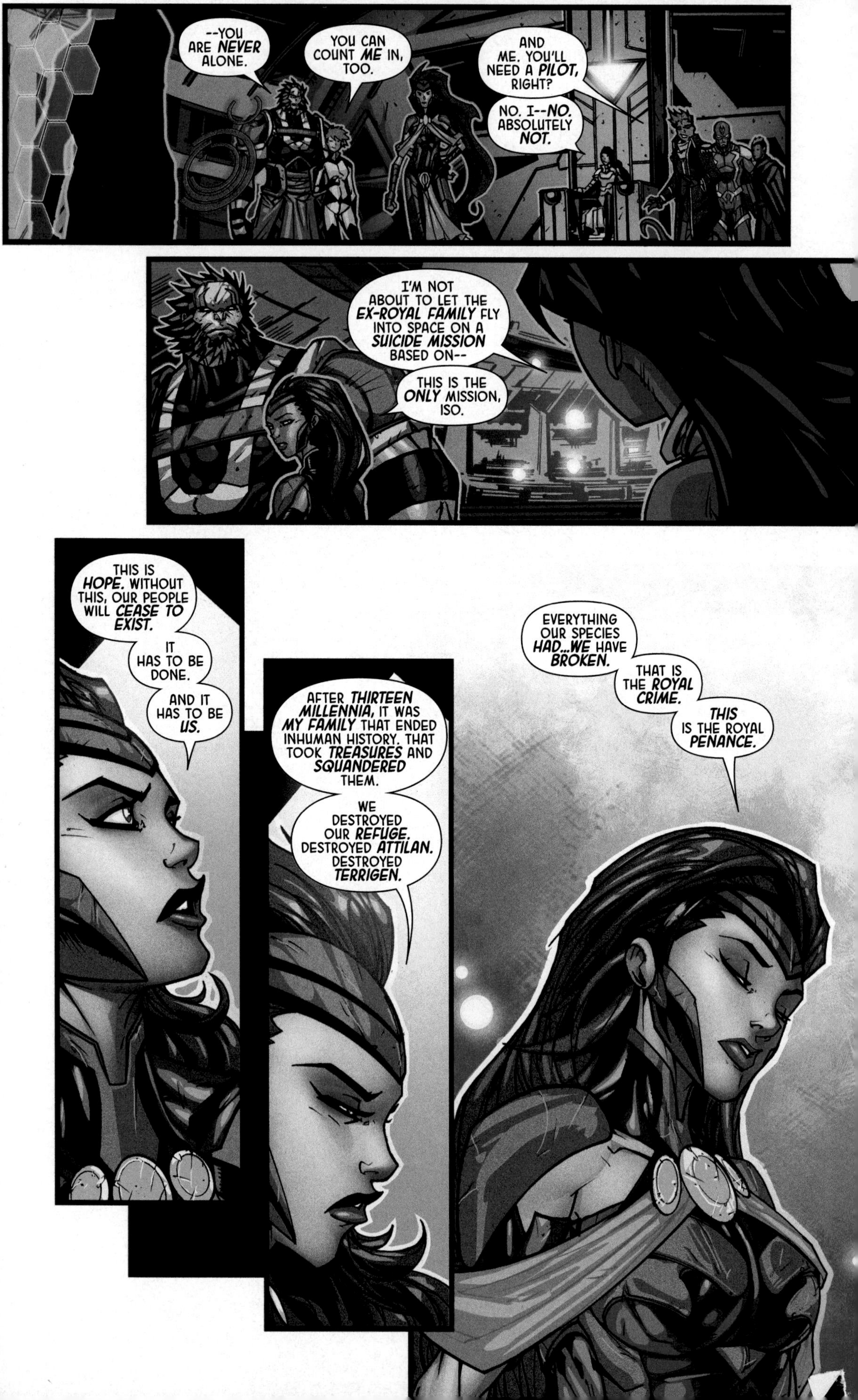
--YOU ARE NEVER ALONE.
YOU CAN COUNT ME IN, TOO.
AND ME. YOU'LL NEED A PILOT, RIGHT?
NO. I--NO. ABSOLUTELY NOT.
I'M NOT ABOUT TO LET THE EX-ROYAL FAMILY FLY INTO SPACE ON A SUICIDE MISSION BASED ON--
THIS IS THE ONLY MISSION, ISO.
THIS IS HOPE. WITHOUT THIS, OUR PEOPLE WILL CEASE TO EXIST.
IT HAS TO BE DONE.
AND IT HAS TO BE US.
AFTER THIRTEEN MILLENNIA, IT WAS MY FAMILY THAT ENDED INHUMAN HISTORY. THAT TOOK TREASURES AND SQUANDERED THEM.
WE DESTROYED OUR REFUGE. DESTROYED ATTILAN. DESTROYED TERRIGEN.
EVERYTHING OUR SPECIES HAD...WE HAVE BROKEN.
THAT IS THE ROYAL CRIME.
THIS IS THE ROYAL PENANCE.

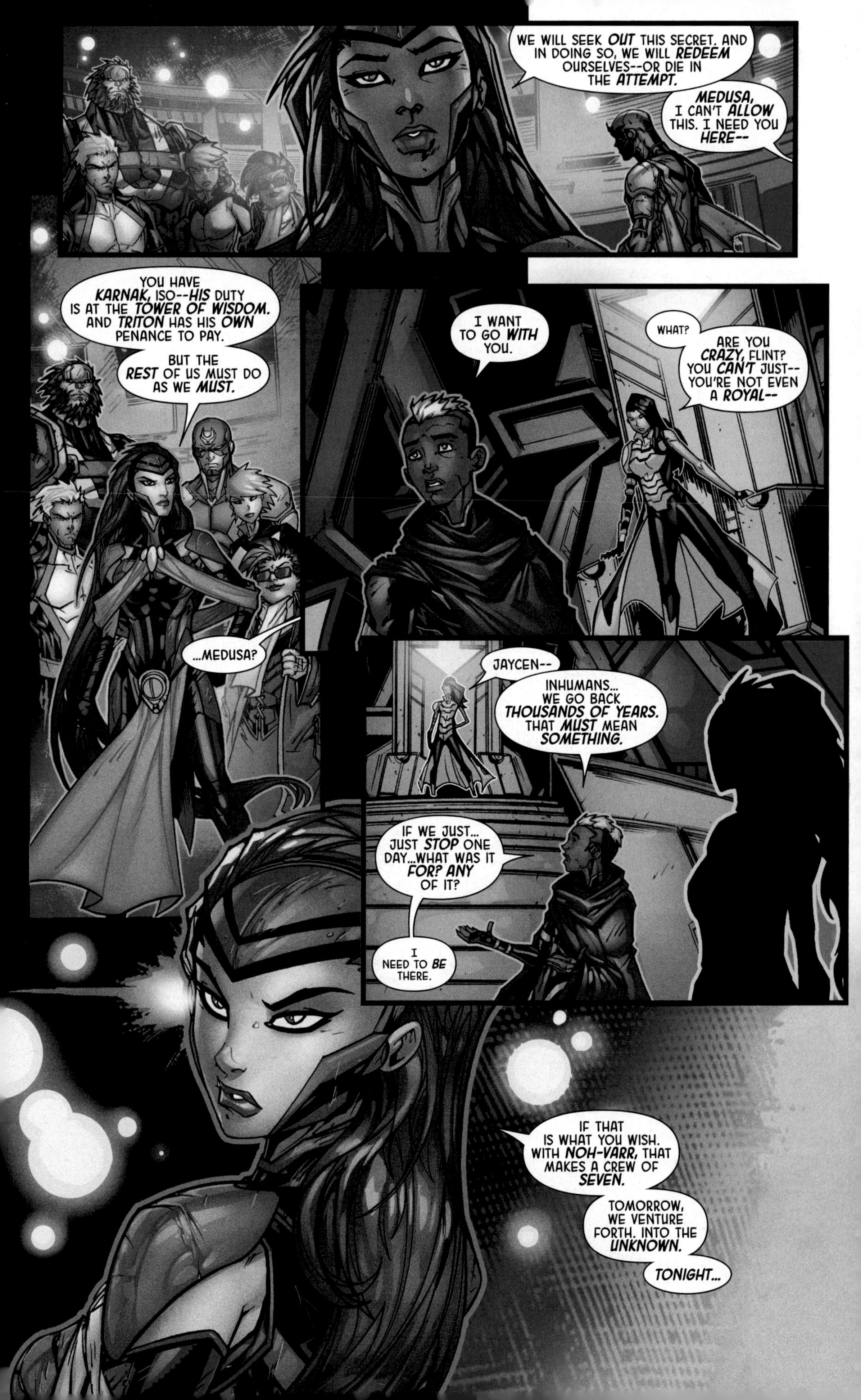

WE WILL SEEK OUT THIS SECRET. AND IN DOING SO, WE WILL REDEEM OURSELVES--OR DIE IN THE ATTEMPT.
MEDUSA, I CAN'T ALLOW THIS. I NEED YOU HERE--
YOU HAVE KARNAK, ISO--HIS DUTY IS AT THE TOWER OF WISDOM. AND TRITON HAS HIS OWN PENANCE TO PAY.
BUT THE REST OF US MUST DO AS WE MUST.
...MEDUSA?
I WANT TO GO WITH YOU.
WHAT?
ARE YOU CRAZY, FLINT? YOU CAN'T JUST-- YOU'RE NOT EVEN A ROYAL--
JAYCEN--
INHUMANS... WE GO BACK THOUSANDS OF YEARS. THAT MUST MEAN SOMETHING.
IF WE JUST... JUST STOP ONE DAY...WHAT WAS IT FOR? ANY OF IT?
I NEED TO BE THERE.
IF THAT IS WHAT YOU WISH. WITH NOH-VARR, THAT MAKES A CREW OF SEVEN.
TOMORROW, WE VENTURE FORTH. INTO THE UNKNOWN.
TONIGHT...

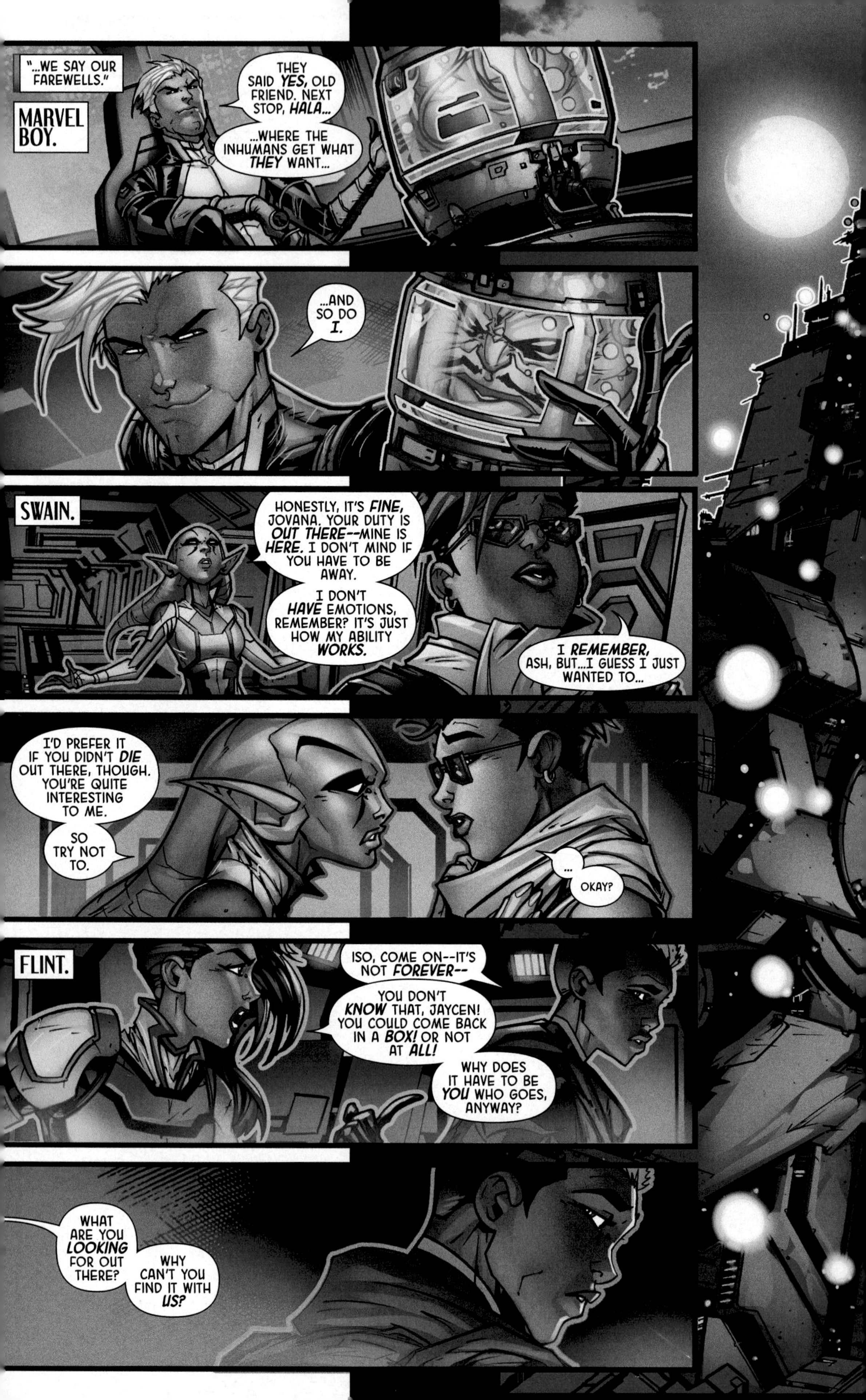
"...WE SAY OUR FAREWELLS."
MARVEL BOY.
THEY SAID YES, OLD FRIEND. NEXT STOP, HALA...
...WHERE THE INHUMANS GET WHAT THEY WANT...
...AND SO DO I.
SWAIN.
HONESTLY, IT'S FINE, JOVANA. YOUR DUTY IS OUT THERE--MINE IS HERE. I DON'T MIND IF YOU HAVE TO BE AWAY.
I DON'T HAVE EMOTIONS, REMEMBER? IT'S JUST HOW MY ABILITY WORKS.
I REMEMBER, ASH, BUT...I GUESS I JUST WANTED TO...
I'D PREFER IT IF YOU DIDN'T DIE OUT THERE, THOUGH. YOU'RE QUITE INTERESTING TO ME.
SO TRY NOT TO.
...
OKAY?
FLINT.
ISO, COME ON--IT'S NOT FOREVER--
YOU DON'T KNOW THAT, JAYCEN! YOU COULD COME BACK IN A BOX! OR NOT AT ALL!
WHY DOES IT HAVE TO BE YOU WHO GOES, ANYWAY?
WHAT ARE YOU LOOKING FOR OUT THERE?
WHY CAN'T YOU FIND IT WITH US?

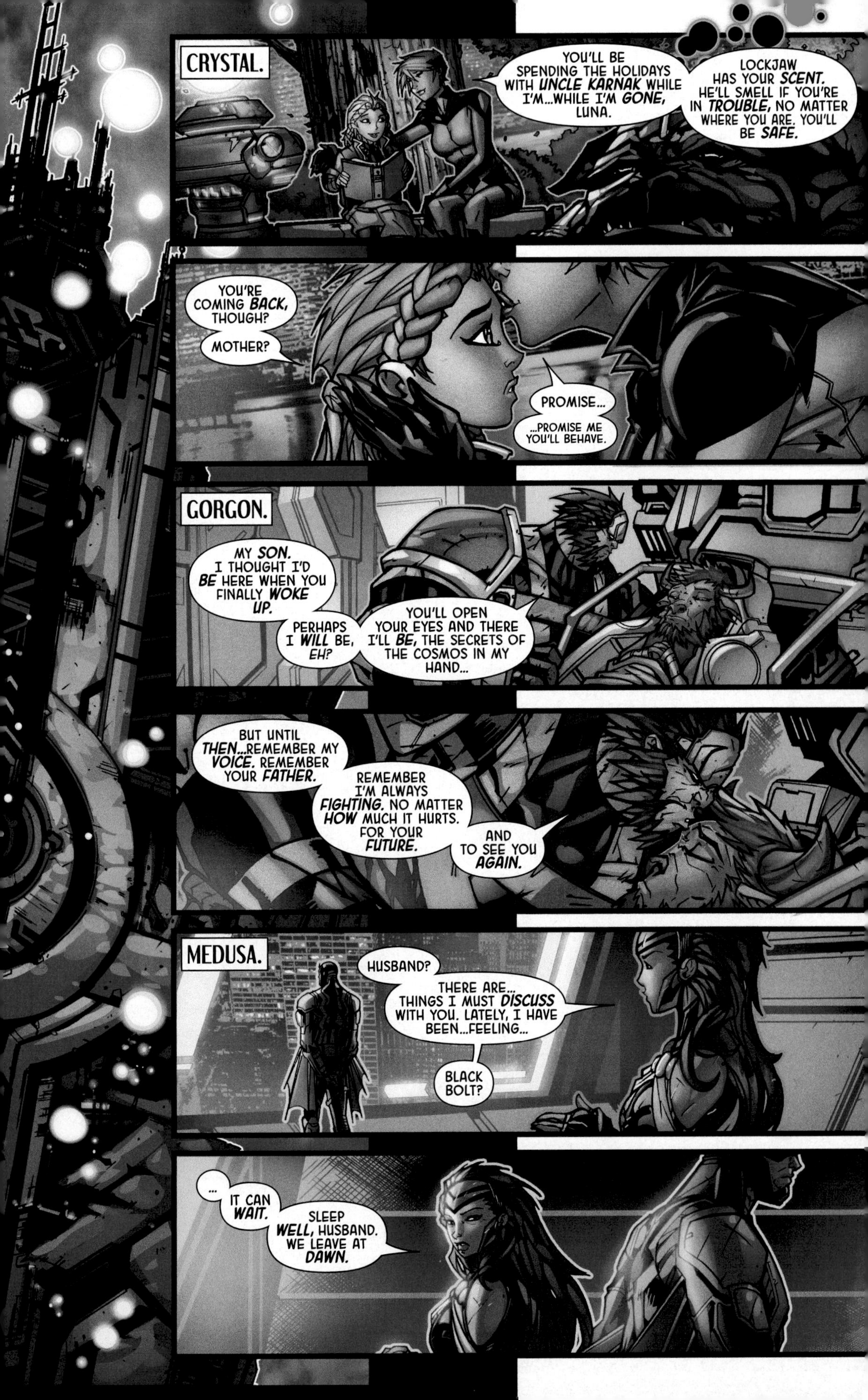
CRYSTAL.
YOU'LL BE SPENDING THE HOLIDAYS WITH UNCLE KARNAK WHILE I'M...WHILE I'M GONE, LUNA.
LOCKJAW HAS YOUR SCENT. HE'LL SMELL IF YOU'RE IN TROUBLE, NO MATTER WHERE YOU ARE. YOU'LL BE SAFE.
YOU'RE COMING BACK, THOUGH?
MOTHER?
PROMISE...
...PROMISE ME YOU'LL BEHAVE.
GORGON.
MY SON. I THOUGHT I'D BE HERE WHEN YOU FINALLY WOKE UP.
PERHAPS I WILL BE, EH?
YOU'LL OPEN YOUR EYES AND THERE I'LL BE, THE SECRETS OF THE COSMOS IN MY HAND...
BUT UNTIL THEN...REMEMBER MY VOICE. REMEMBER YOUR FATHER.
REMEMBER I'M ALWAYS FIGHTING. NO MATTER HOW MUCH IT HURTS. FOR YOUR FUTURE.
AND TO SEE YOU AGAIN.
MEDUSA.
HUSBAND?
THERE ARE... THINGS I MUST DISCUSS WITH YOU. LATELY, I HAVE BEEN...FEELING...
BLACK BOLT?
...
IT CAN WAIT.
SLEEP WELL, HUSBAND. WE LEAVE AT DAWN.

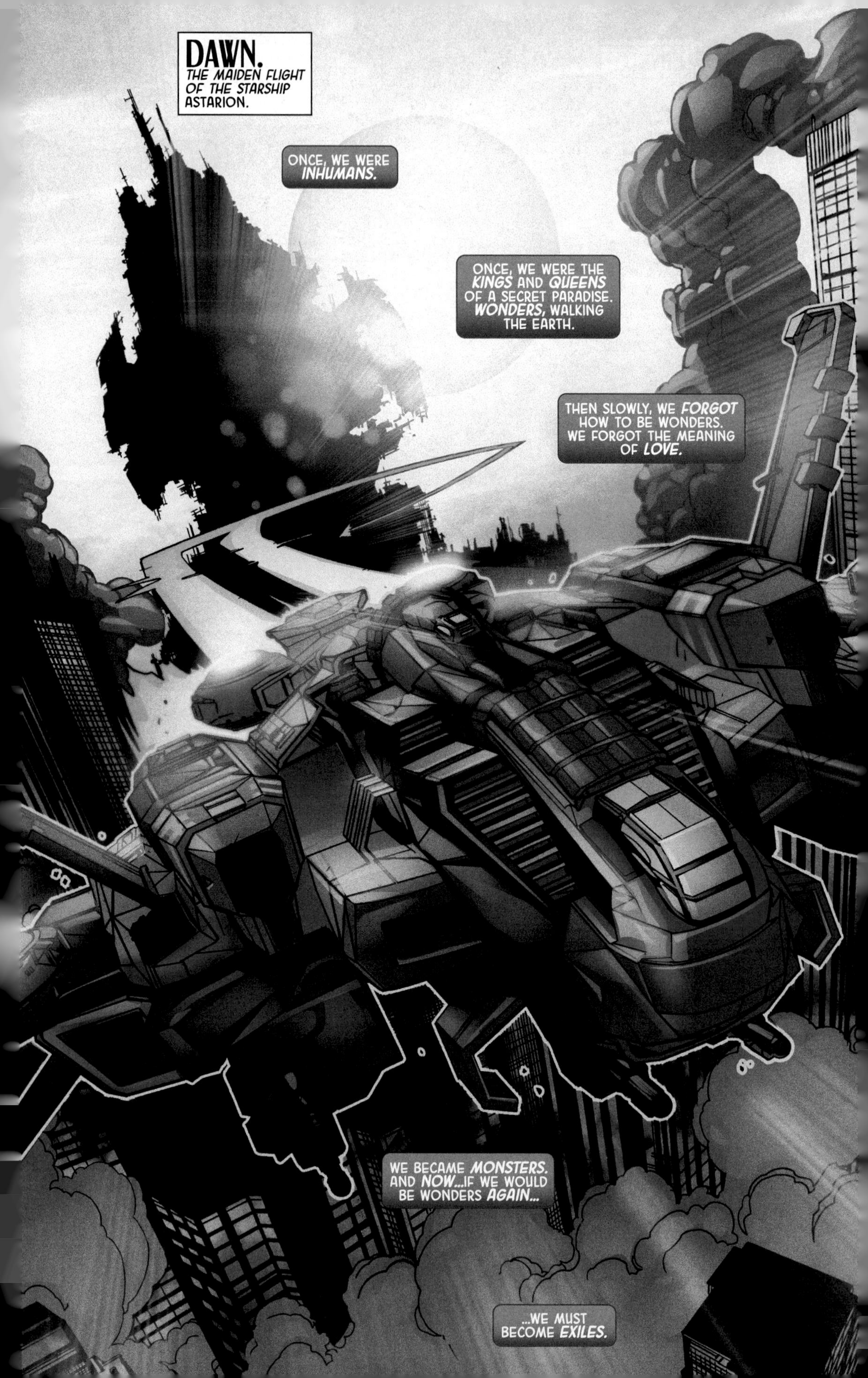
DAWN. THE MAIDEN FLIGHT OF THE STARSHIP ASTARION.
ONCE, WE WERE INHUMANS.
ONCE, WE WERE THE KINGS AND QUEENS OF A SECRET PARADISE. WONDERS, WALKING THE EARTH.
THEN SLOWLY, WE FORGOT HOW TO BE WONDERS. WE FORGOT THE MEANING OF LOVE.
WE BECAME MONSTERS. AND NOW...IF WE WOULD BE WONDERS AGAIN...
...WE MUST BECOME EXILES.

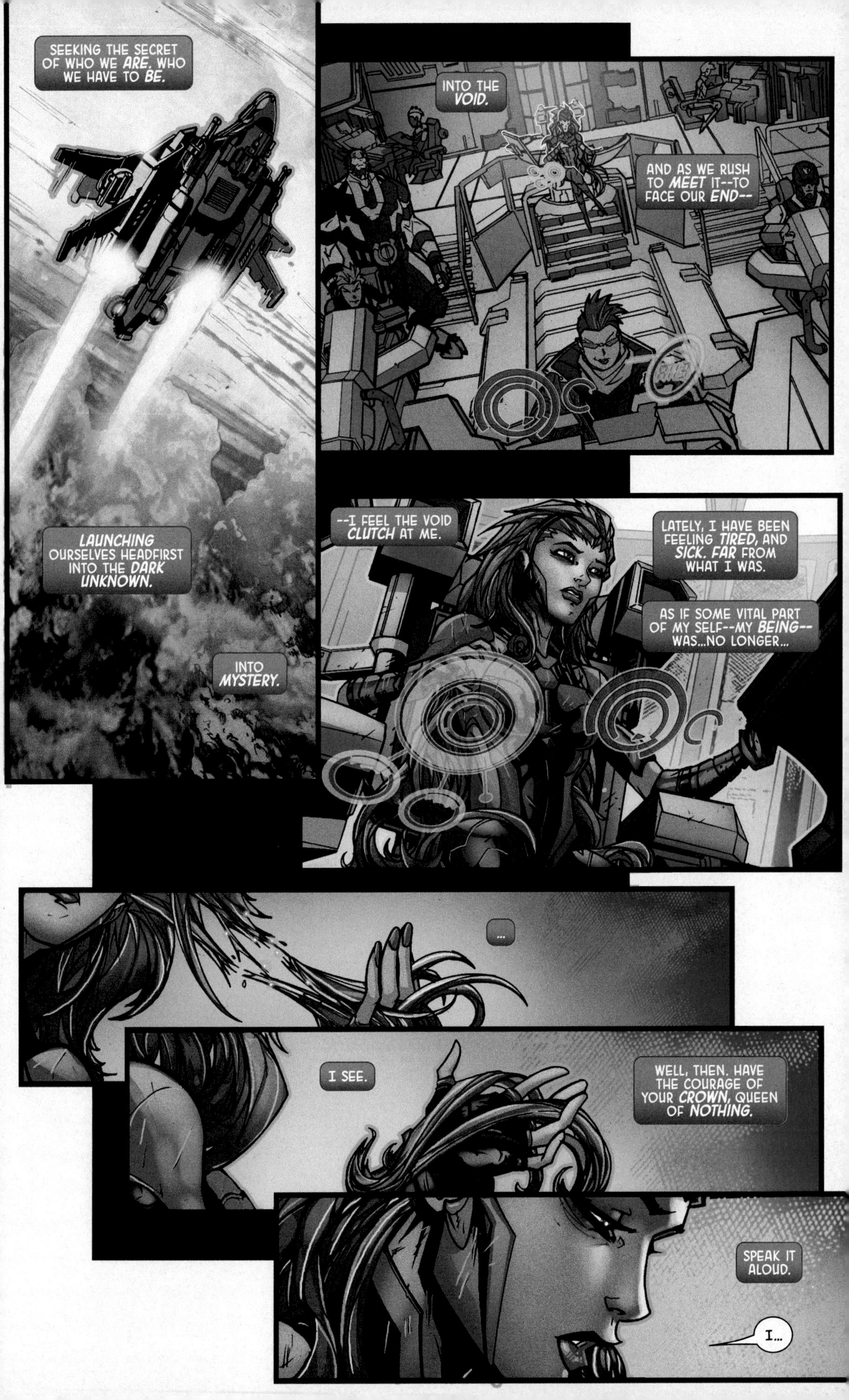
SEEKING THE SECRET OF WHO WE ARE. WHO WE HAVE TO BE.
LAUNCHING OURSELVES HEADFIRST INTO THE DARK UNKNOWN.
INTO MYSTERY.
INTO THE VOID.
AND AS WE RUSH TO MEET IT--TO FACE OUR END--
--I FEEL THE VOID CLUTCH AT ME.
LATELY, I HAVE BEEN FEELING TIRED, AND SICK. FAR FROM WHAT I WAS.
AS IF SOME VITAL PART OF MY SELF--MY BEING--WAS...NO LONGER...
...
I SEE.
WELL, THEN. HAVE THE COURAGE OF YOUR CROWN, QUEEN OF NOTHING.
SPEAK IT ALOUD.
I...

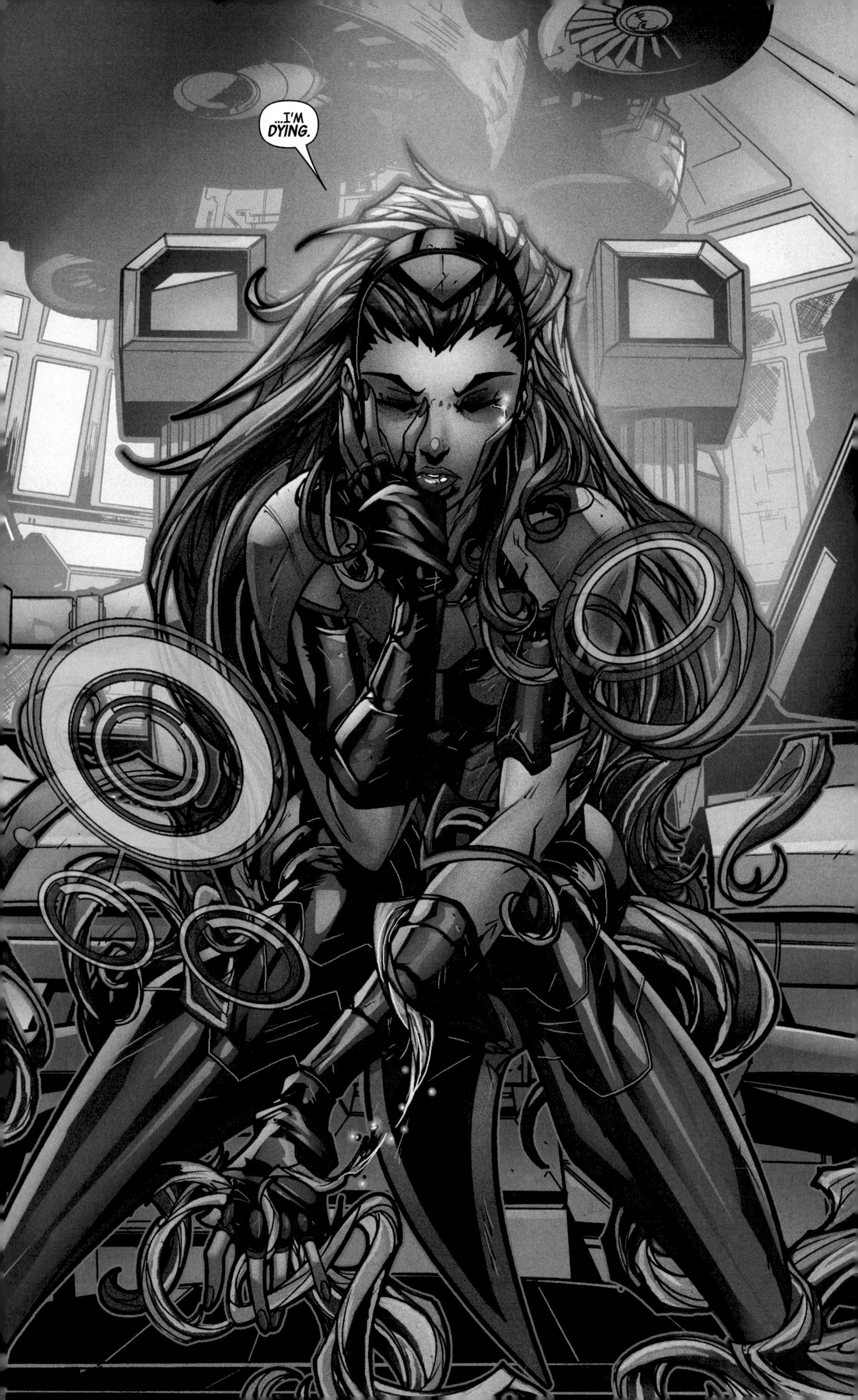
...I'M DYING.

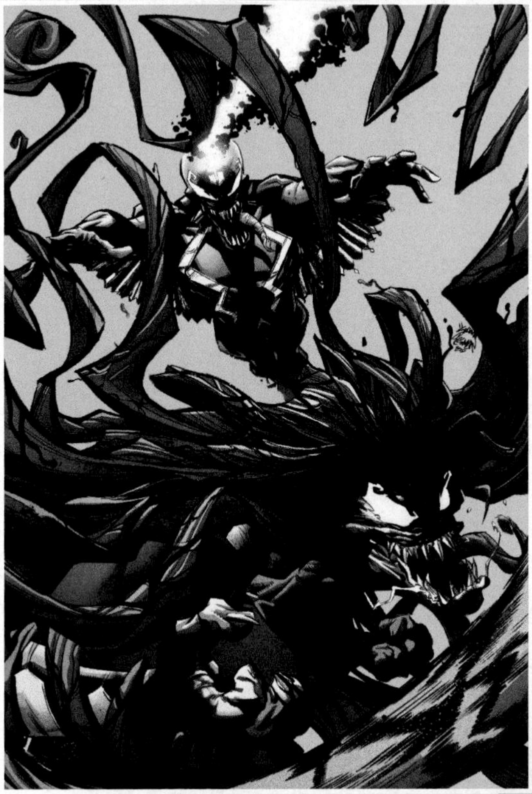

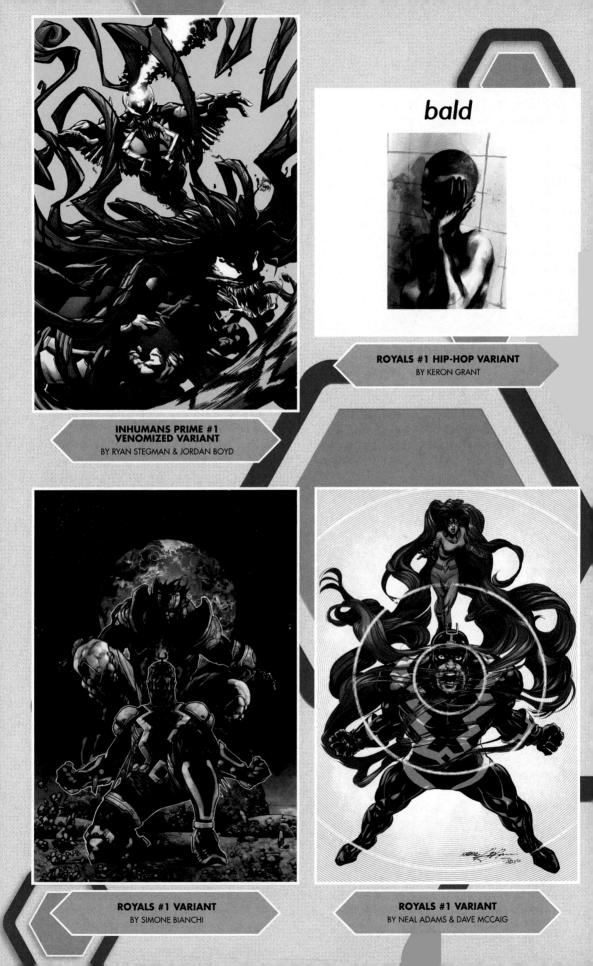

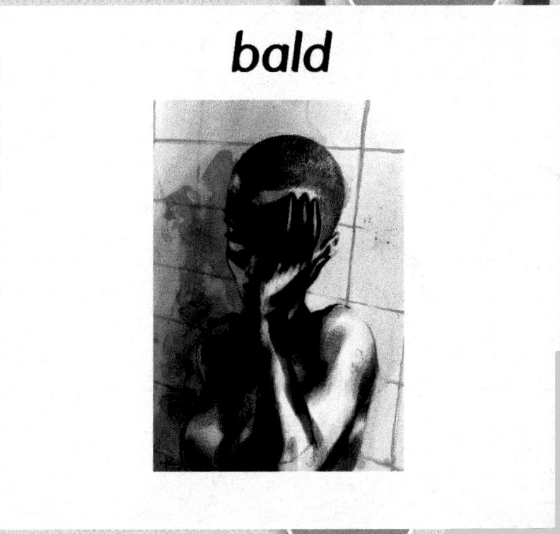
bald

**ROYALS #1 HIP-HOP VARIANT**
BY KERON GRANT

**INHUMANS PRIME #1 VENOMIZED VARIANT**
BY RYAN STEGMAN & JORDAN BOYD

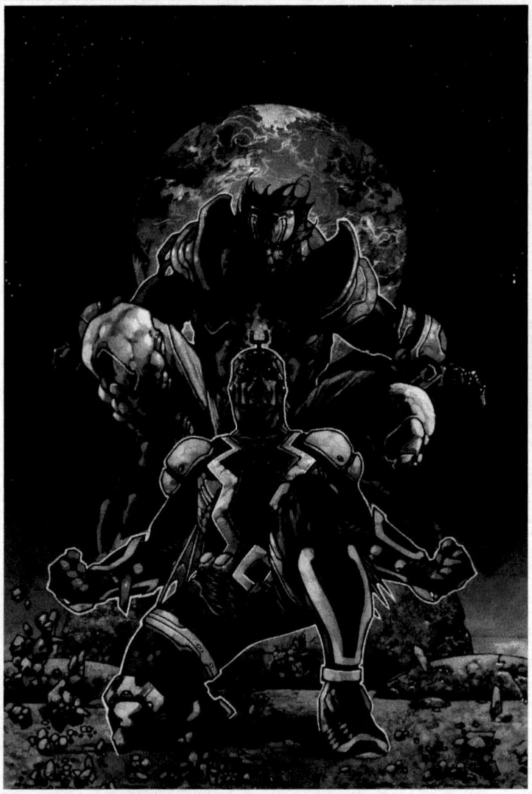

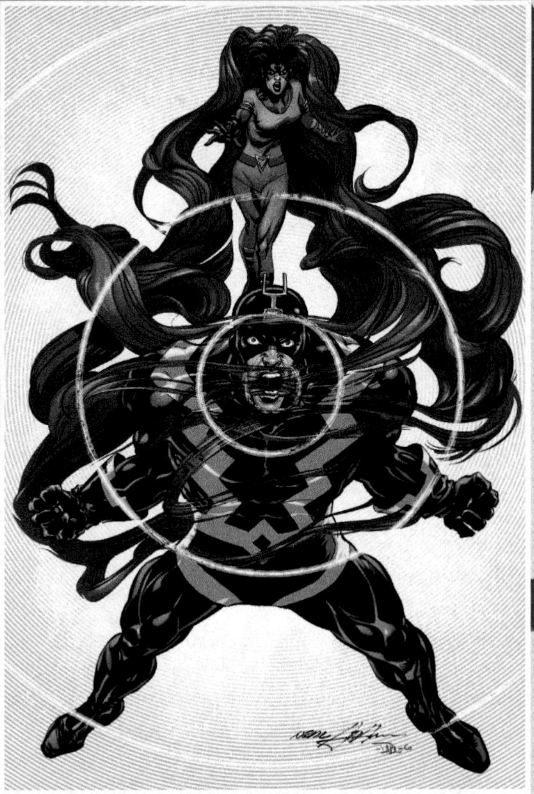

**ROYALS #1 VARIANT**
BY SIMONE BIANCHI

**ROYALS #1 VARIANT**
BY NEAL ADAMS & DAVE MCCAIG

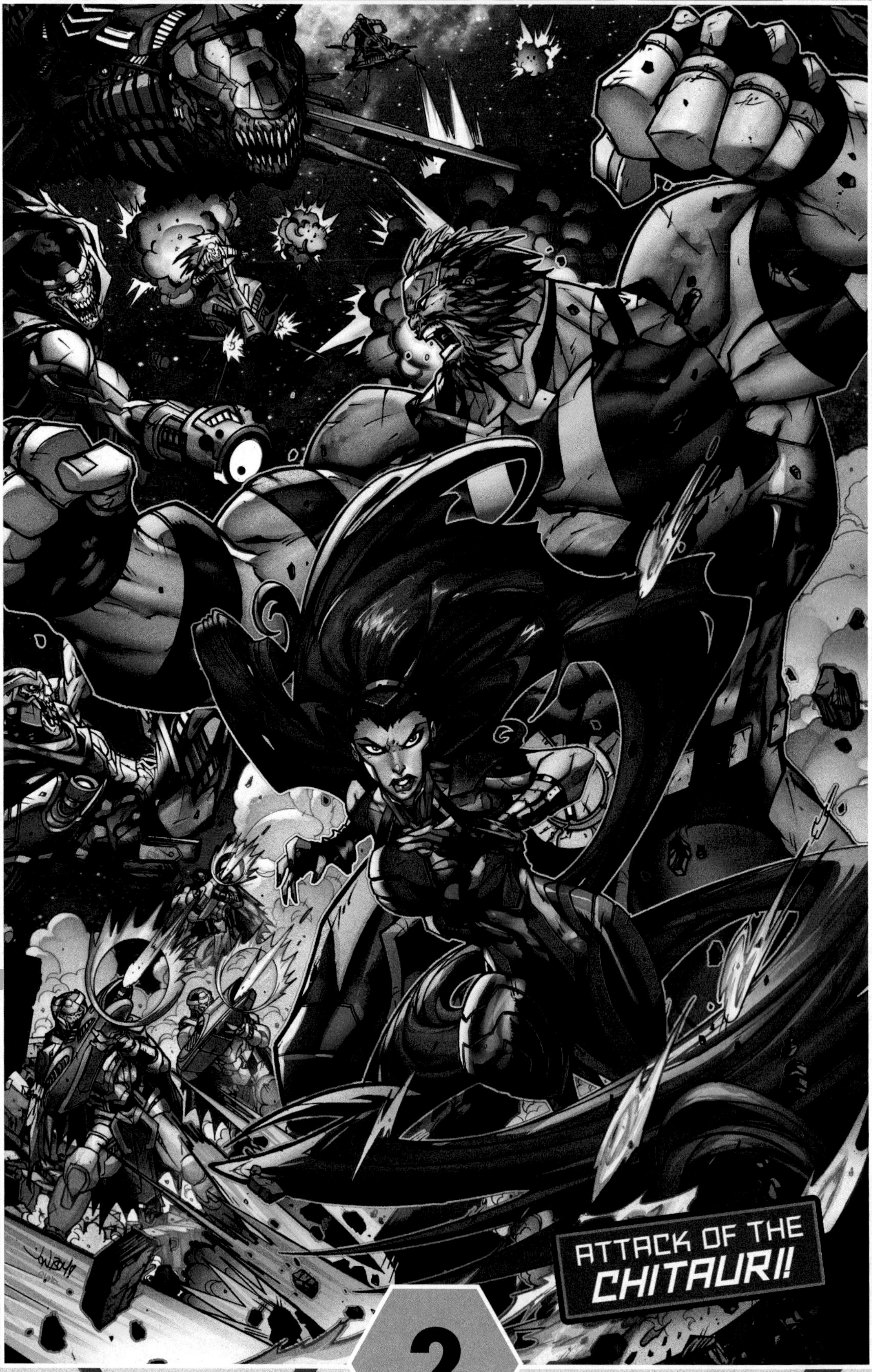
ATTACK OF THE
CHITAURI!!

2

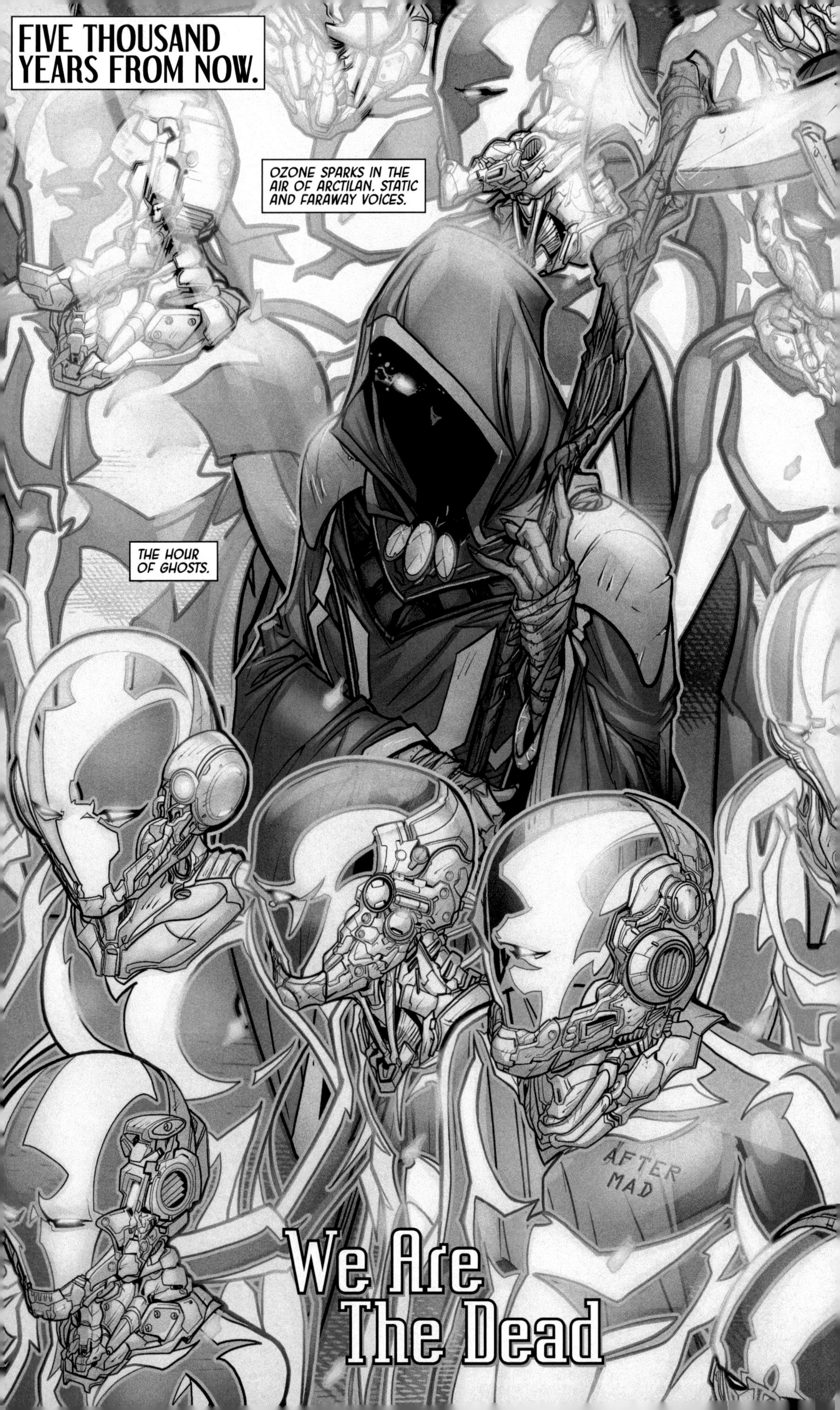
FIVE THOUSAND YEARS FROM NOW.
OZONE SPARKS IN THE AIR OF ARCTILAN. STATIC AND FARAWAY VOICES.
THE HOUR OF GHOSTS.
AFTER MAD
We Are The Dead

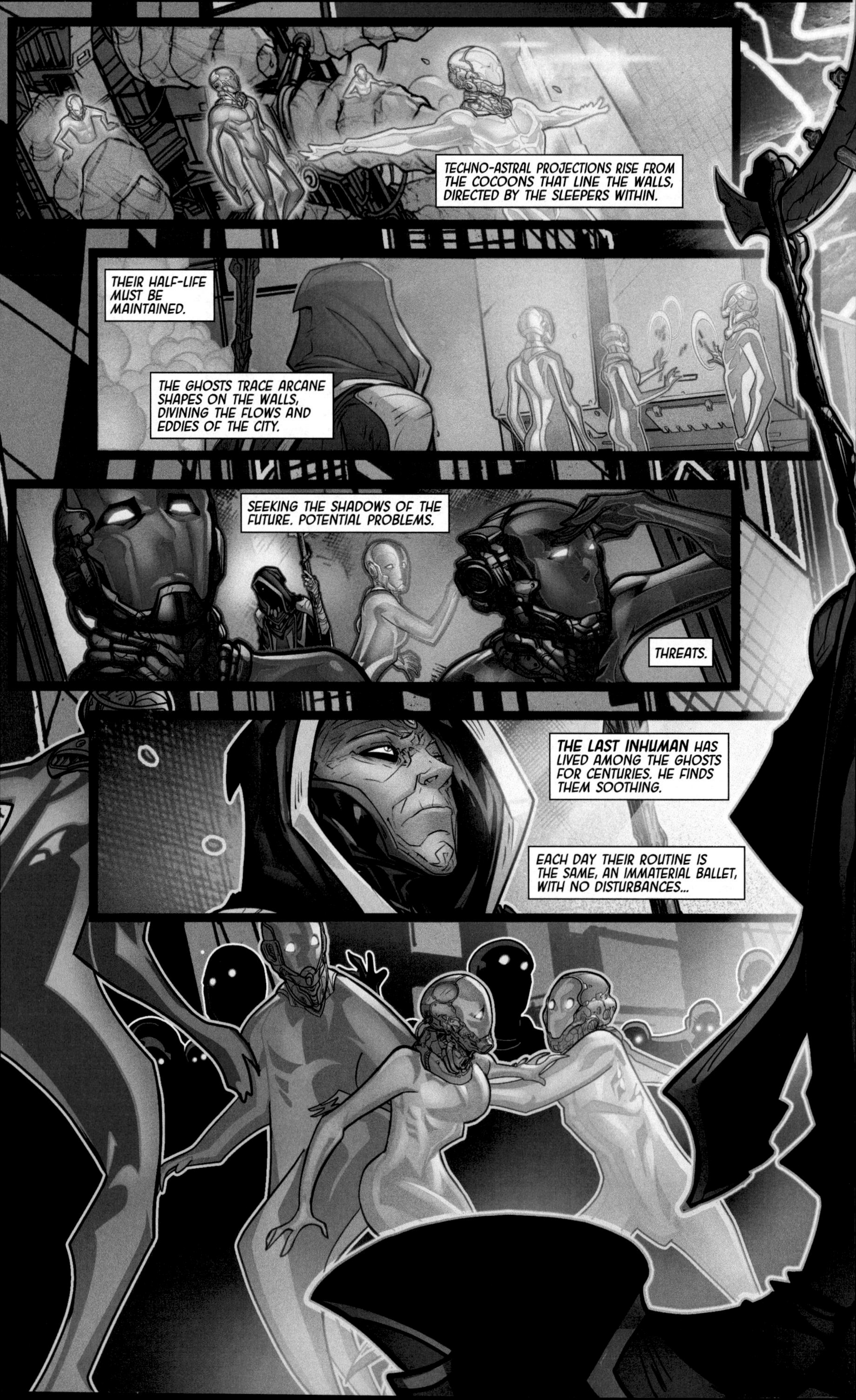
TECHNO-ASTRAL PROJECTIONS RISE FROM THE COCOONS THAT LINE THE WALLS, DIRECTED BY THE SLEEPERS WITHIN.
THEIR HALF-LIFE MUST BE MAINTAINED.
THE GHOSTS TRACE ARCANE SHAPES ON THE WALLS, DIVINING THE FLOWS AND EDDIES OF THE CITY.
SEEKING THE SHADOWS OF THE FUTURE. POTENTIAL PROBLEMS.
THREATS.
THE LAST INHUMAN HAS LIVED AMONG THE GHOSTS FOR CENTURIES. HE FINDS THEM SOOTHING.
EACH DAY THEIR ROUTINE IS THE SAME, AN IMMATERIAL BALLET, WITH NO DISTURBANCES...

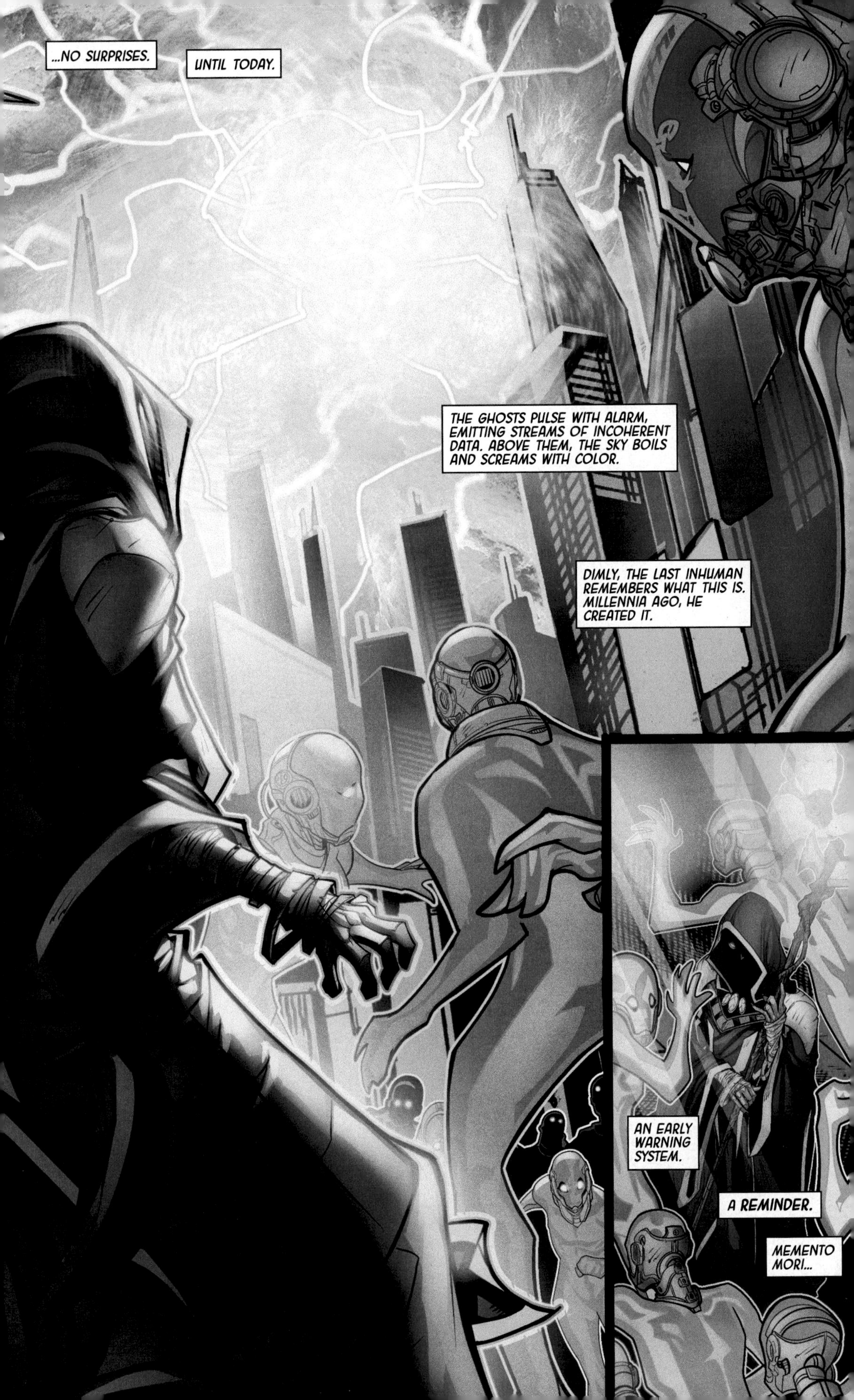
...NO SURPRISES.
UNTIL TODAY.
THE GHOSTS PULSE WITH ALARM, EMITTING STREAMS OF INCOHERENT DATA. ABOVE THEM, THE SKY BOILS AND SCREAMS WITH COLOR.
DIMLY, THE LAST INHUMAN REMEMBERS WHAT THIS IS. MILLENNIA AGO, HE CREATED IT.
AN EARLY WARNING SYSTEM.
A REMINDER.
MEMENTO MORI...

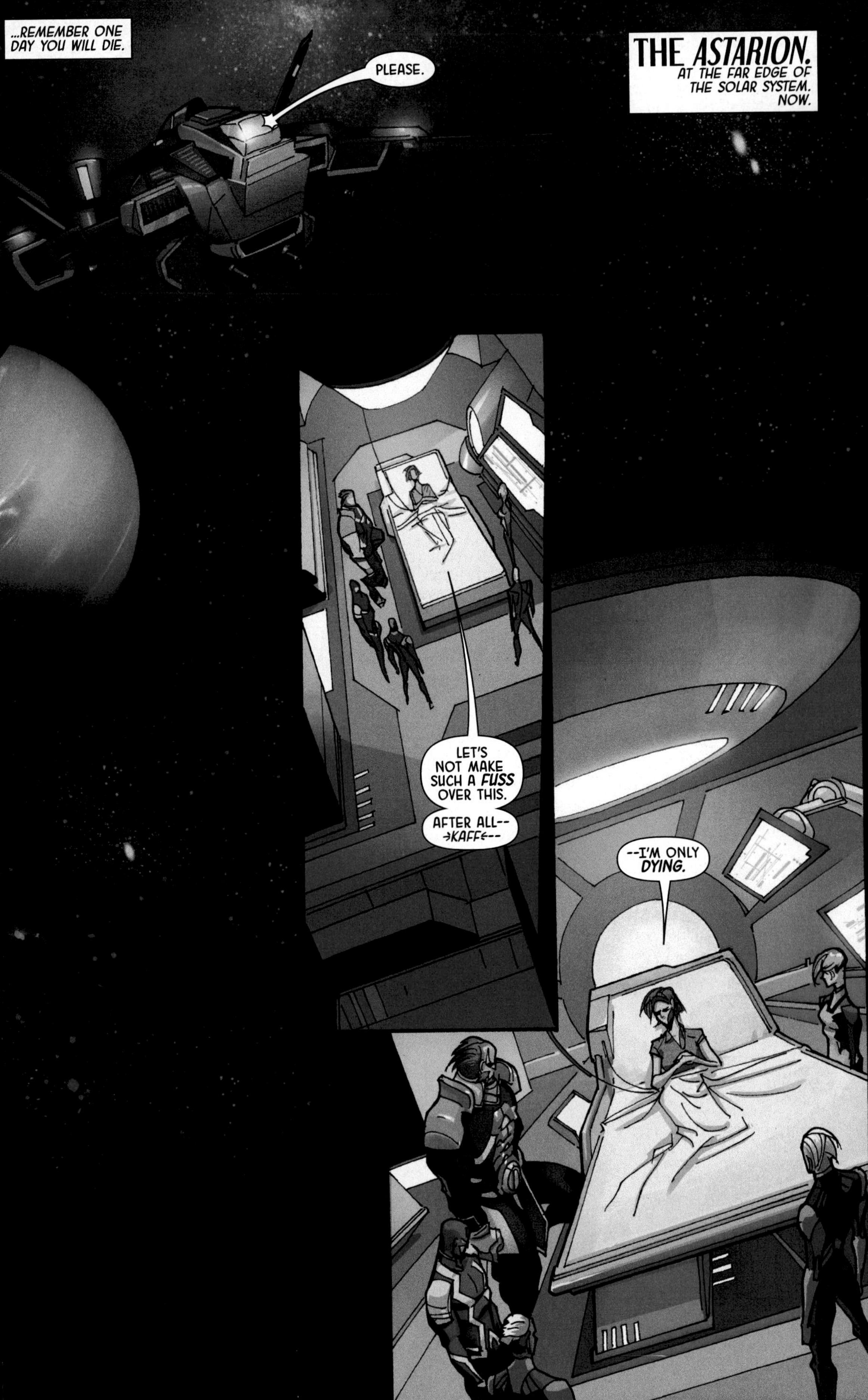
...REMEMBER ONE DAY YOU WILL DIE.
PLEASE.
THE ASTARION.
AT THE FAR EDGE OF THE SOLAR SYSTEM. NOW.
LET'S NOT MAKE SUCH A FUSS OVER THIS.
AFTER ALL-- →KAFF←--
--I'M ONLY DYING.

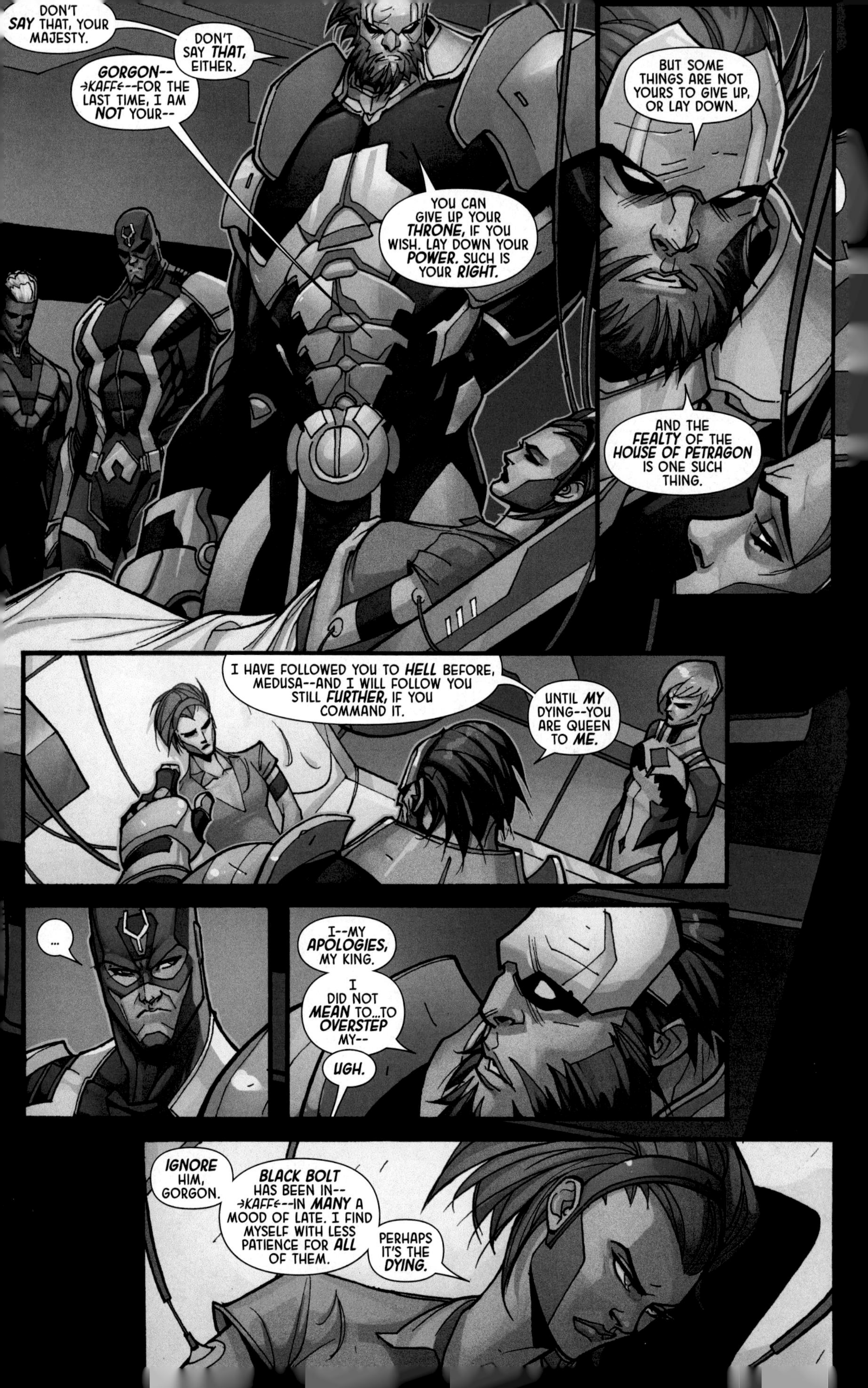
DON'T SAY THAT, YOUR MAJESTY.
DON'T SAY THAT, EITHER.
GORGON-- →KAFF←--FOR THE LAST TIME, I AM NOT YOUR--
YOU CAN GIVE UP YOUR THRONE, IF YOU WISH. LAY DOWN YOUR POWER. SUCH IS YOUR RIGHT.
BUT SOME THINGS ARE NOT YOURS TO GIVE UP, OR LAY DOWN.
AND THE FEALTY OF THE HOUSE OF PETRAGON IS ONE SUCH THING.
I HAVE FOLLOWED YOU TO HELL BEFORE, MEDUSA--AND I WILL FOLLOW YOU STILL FURTHER, IF YOU COMMAND IT.
UNTIL MY DYING--YOU ARE QUEEN TO ME.
...
I--MY APOLOGIES, MY KING.
I DID NOT MEAN TO...TO OVERSTEP MY--
UGH.
IGNORE HIM, GORGON.
BLACK BOLT HAS BEEN IN-- →KAFF←--IN MANY A MOOD OF LATE. I FIND MYSELF WITH LESS PATIENCE FOR ALL OF THEM.
PERHAPS IT'S THE DYING.

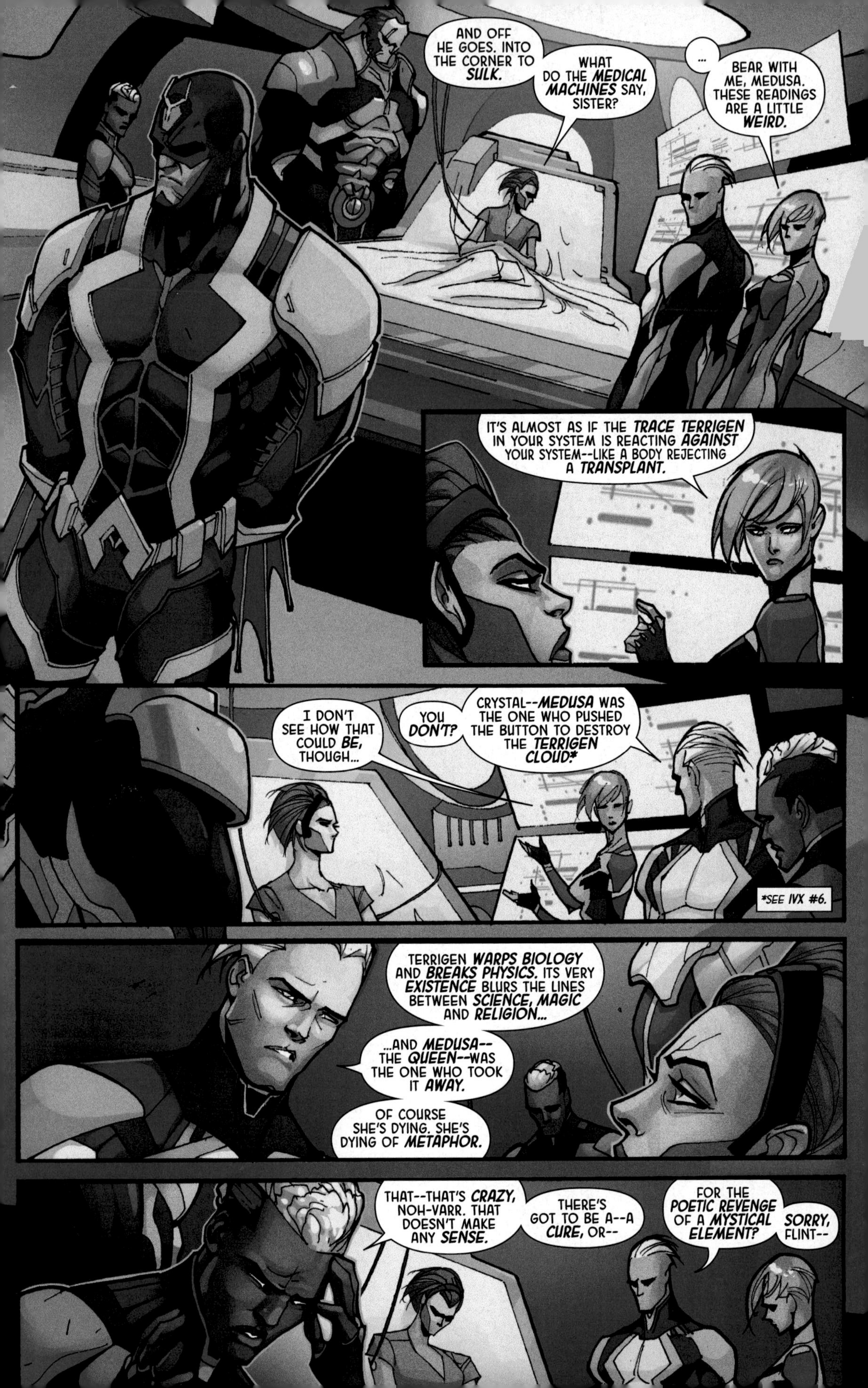
AND OFF HE GOES. INTO THE CORNER TO SULK.
WHAT DO THE MEDICAL MACHINES SAY, SISTER?
...
BEAR WITH ME, MEDUSA. THESE READINGS ARE A LITTLE WEIRD.
IT'S ALMOST AS IF THE TRACE TERRIGEN IN YOUR SYSTEM IS REACTING AGAINST YOUR SYSTEM--LIKE A BODY REJECTING A TRANSPLANT.
I DON'T SEE HOW THAT COULD BE, THOUGH...
YOU DON'T?
CRYSTAL--MEDUSA WAS THE ONE WHO PUSHED THE BUTTON TO DESTROY THE TERRIGEN CLOUD!*
*SEE IVX #6.
TERRIGEN WARPS BIOLOGY AND BREAKS PHYSICS. ITS VERY EXISTENCE BLURS THE LINES BETWEEN SCIENCE, MAGIC AND RELIGION...
...AND MEDUSA--THE QUEEN--WAS THE ONE WHO TOOK IT AWAY.
OF COURSE SHE'S DYING. SHE'S DYING OF METAPHOR.
THAT--THAT'S CRAZY, NOH-VARR. THAT DOESN'T MAKE ANY SENSE.
THERE'S GOT TO BE A--A CURE, OR--
FOR THE POETIC REVENGE OF A MYSTICAL ELEMENT?
SORRY, FLINT--

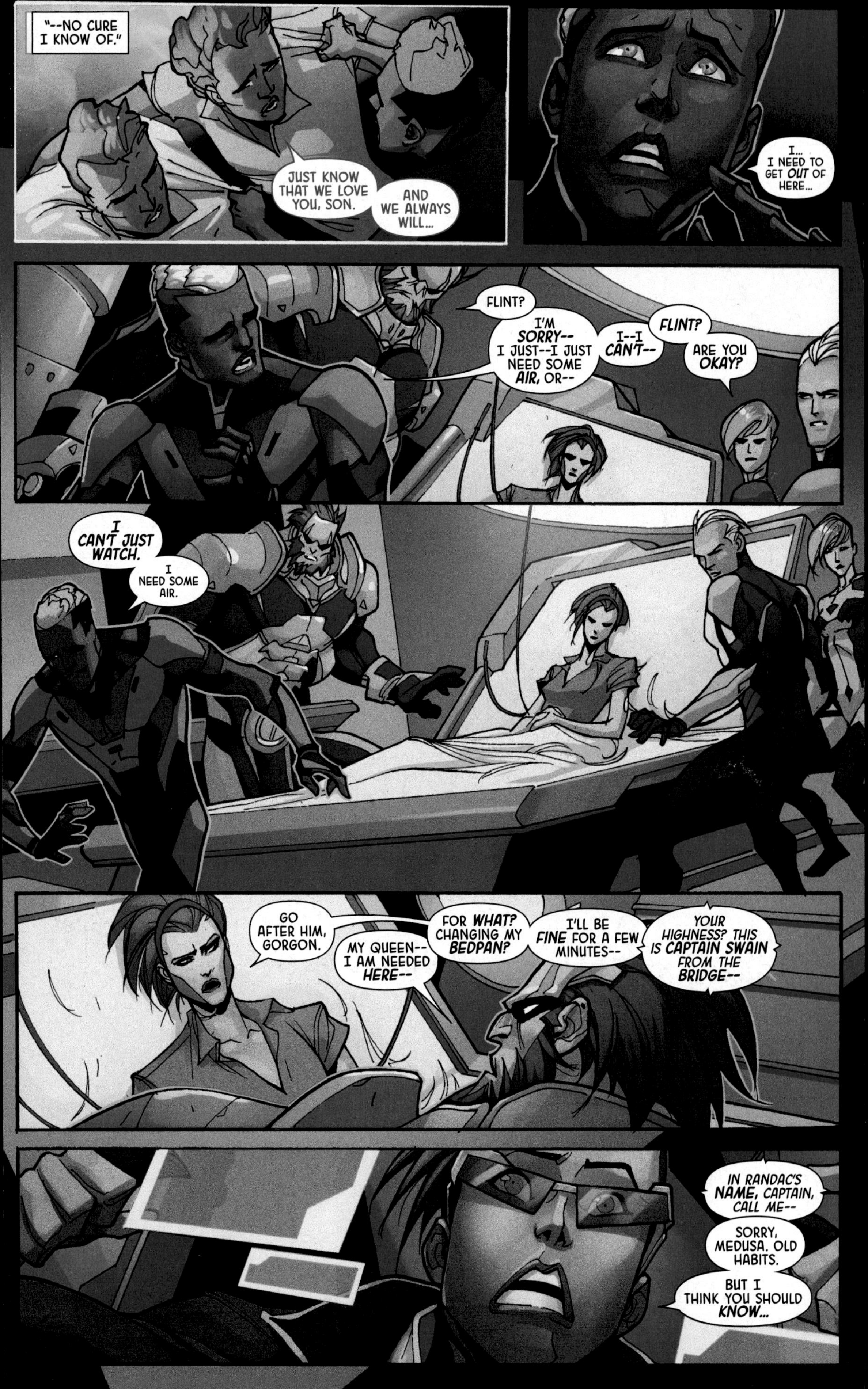
"--NO CURE I KNOW OF."
JUST KNOW THAT WE LOVE YOU, SON.
AND WE ALWAYS WILL...
I... I NEED TO GET OUT OF HERE...
FLINT?
I'M SORRY-- I JUST--I JUST NEED SOME AIR, OR--
I--I CAN'T--
FLINT?
ARE YOU OKAY?
I CAN'T JUST WATCH.
I NEED SOME AIR.
GO AFTER HIM, GORGON.
MY QUEEN-- I AM NEEDED HERE--
FOR WHAT? CHANGING MY BEDPAN?
I'LL BE FINE FOR A FEW MINUTES--
YOUR HIGHNESS? THIS IS CAPTAIN SWAIN FROM THE BRIDGE--
IN RANDAC'S NAME, CAPTAIN, CALL ME--
SORRY, MEDUSA. OLD HABITS.
BUT I THINK YOU SHOULD KNOW...

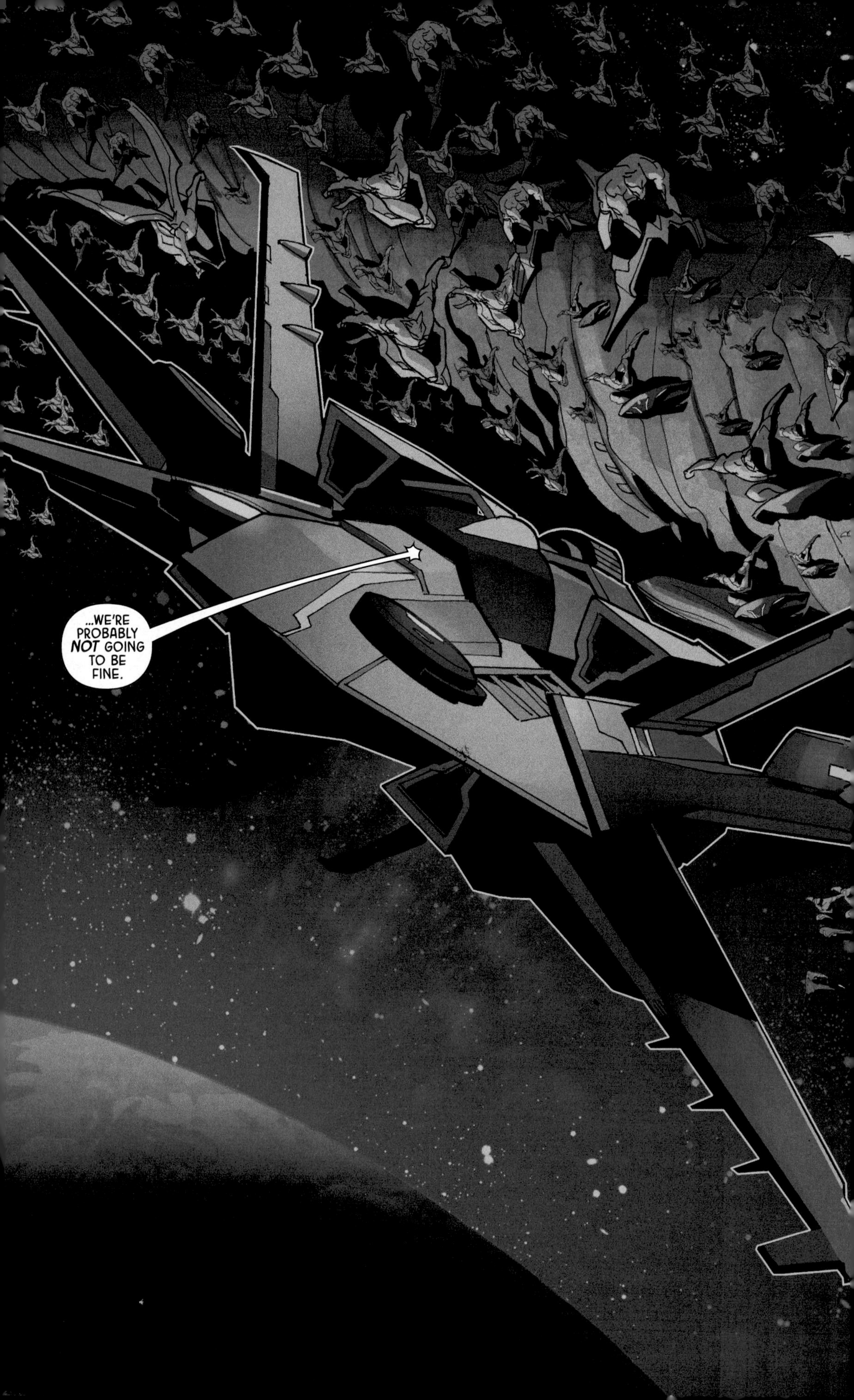
...WE'RE PROBABLY NOT GOING TO BE FINE.

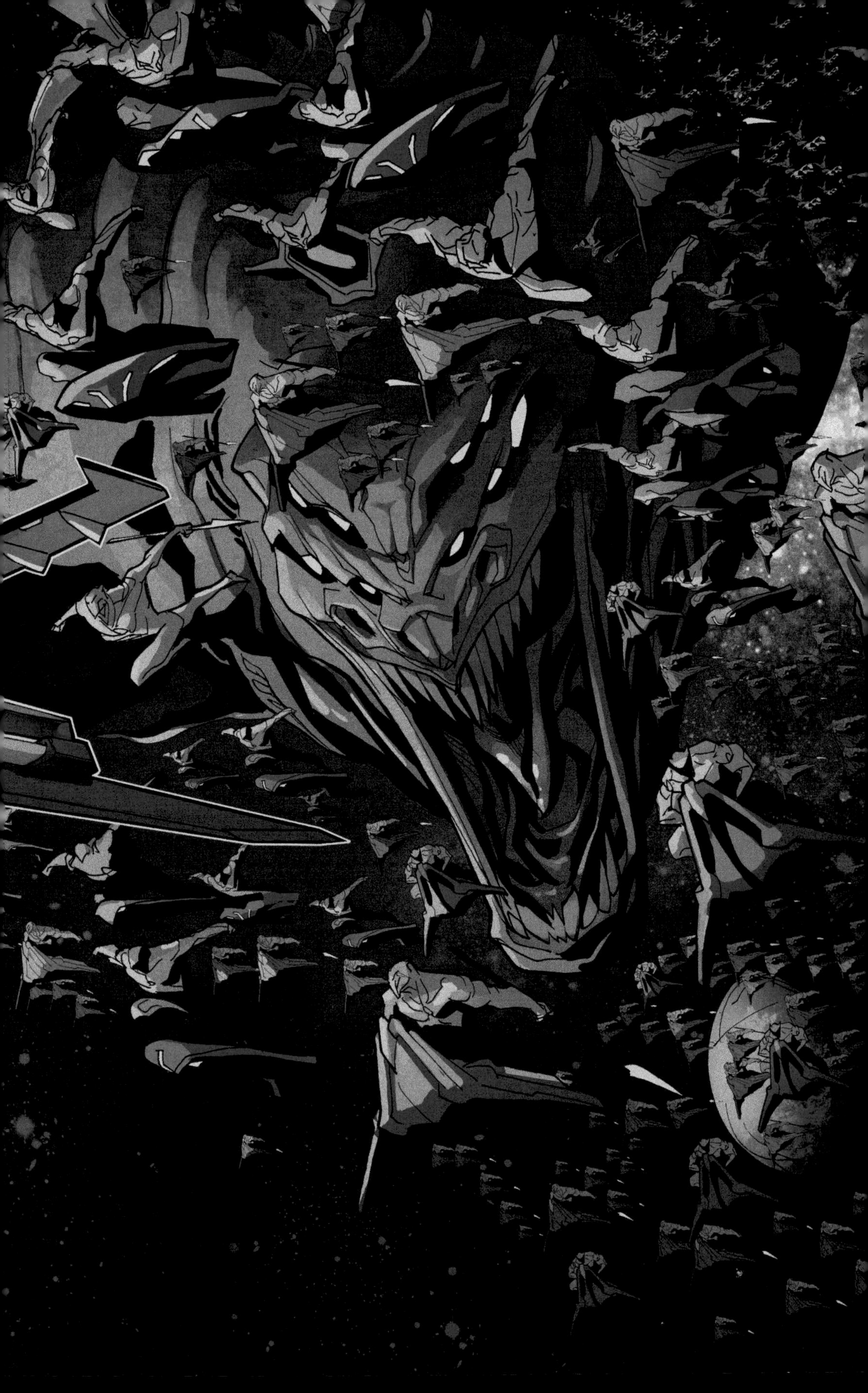

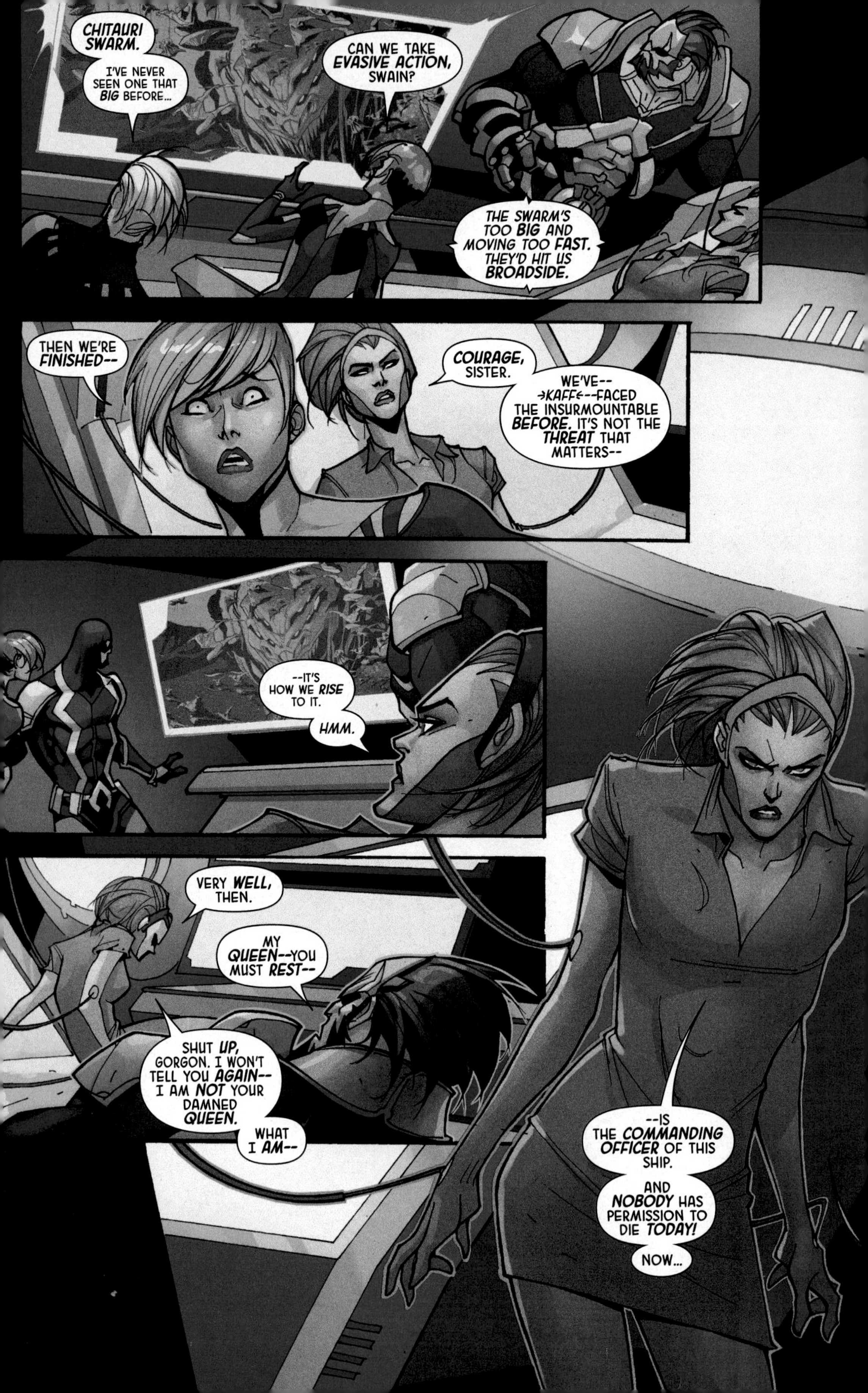

CHITAURI SWARM.
I'VE NEVER SEEN ONE THAT BIG BEFORE...
CAN WE TAKE EVASIVE ACTION, SWAIN?
THE SWARM'S TOO BIG AND MOVING TOO FAST. THEY'D HIT US BROADSIDE.
THEN WE'RE FINISHED--
COURAGE, SISTER.
WE'VE-- →KAFF← --FACED THE INSURMOUNTABLE BEFORE. IT'S NOT THE THREAT THAT MATTERS--
--IT'S HOW WE RISE TO IT.
HMM.
VERY WELL, THEN.
MY QUEEN--YOU MUST REST--
SHUT UP, GORGON. I WON'T TELL YOU AGAIN-- I AM NOT YOUR DAMNED QUEEN.
WHAT I AM--
--IS THE COMMANDING OFFICER OF THIS SHIP.
AND NOBODY HAS PERMISSION TO DIE TODAY!
NOW...

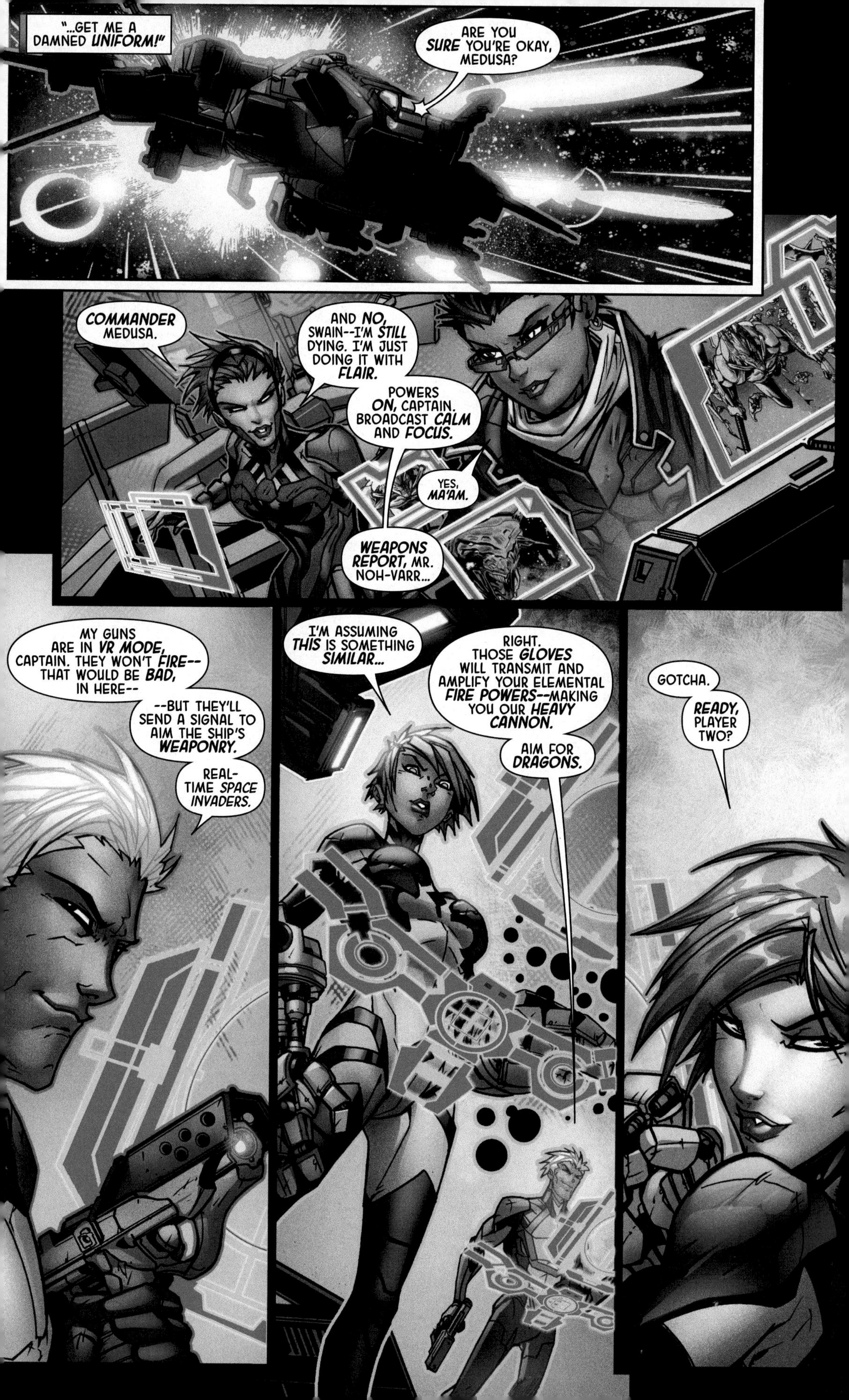
"...GET ME A DAMNED UNIFORM!"
ARE YOU SURE YOU'RE OKAY, MEDUSA?
COMMANDER MEDUSA.
AND NO, SWAIN--I'M STILL DYING. I'M JUST DOING IT WITH FLAIR.
POWERS ON, CAPTAIN. BROADCAST CALM AND FOCUS.
YES, MA'AM.
WEAPONS REPORT, MR. NOH-VARR...
MY GUNS ARE IN VR MODE, CAPTAIN. THEY WON'T FIRE--THAT WOULD BE BAD, IN HERE--
--BUT THEY'LL SEND A SIGNAL TO AIM THE SHIP'S WEAPONRY.
REAL-TIME SPACE INVADERS.
I'M ASSUMING THIS IS SOMETHING SIMILAR...
RIGHT. THOSE GLOVES WILL TRANSMIT AND AMPLIFY YOUR ELEMENTAL FIRE POWERS--MAKING YOU OUR HEAVY CANNON.
AIM FOR DRAGONS.
GOTCHA.
READY, PLAYER TWO?

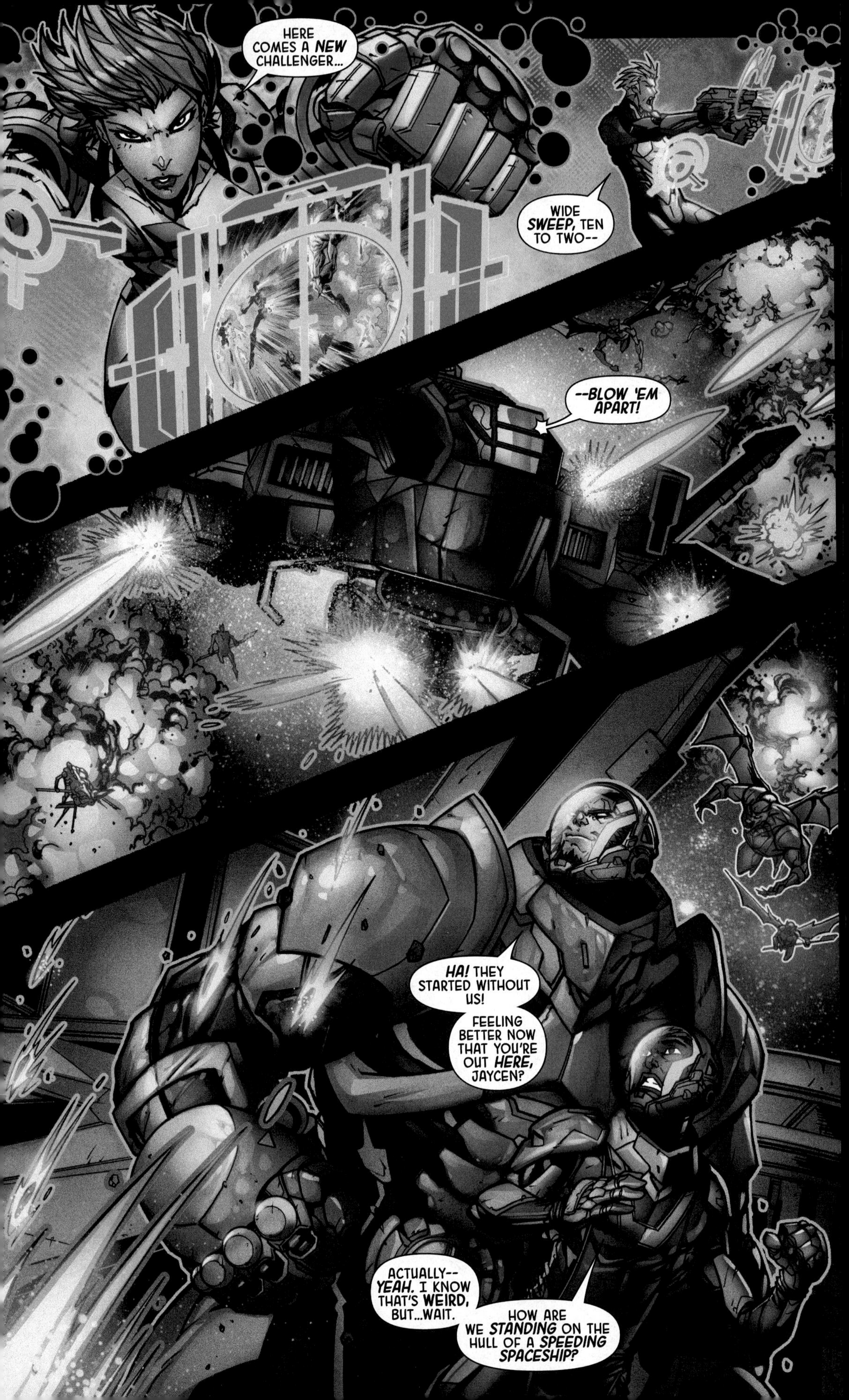

HERE COMES A NEW CHALLENGER...
WIDE SWEEP, TEN TO TWO--
--BLOW 'EM APART!
HA! THEY STARTED WITHOUT US!
FEELING BETTER NOW THAT YOU'RE OUT HERE, JAYCEN?
ACTUALLY-- YEAH. I KNOW THAT'S WEIRD, BUT...WAIT.
HOW ARE WE STANDING ON THE HULL OF A SPEEDING SPACESHIP?

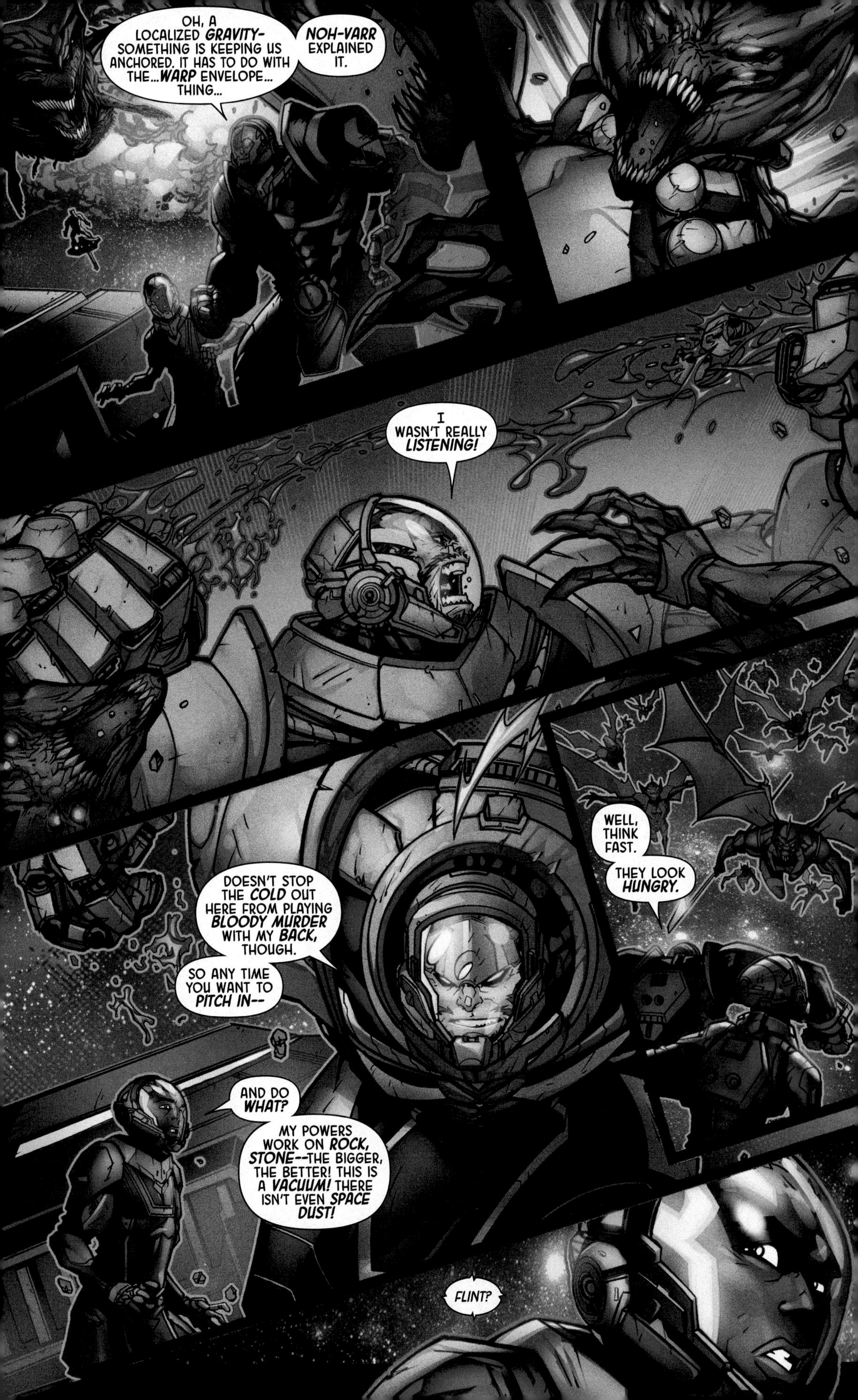
OH, A LOCALIZED GRAVITY-SOMETHING IS KEEPING US ANCHORED. IT HAS TO DO WITH THE...WARP ENVELOPE... THING...
NOH-VARR EXPLAINED IT.
I WASN'T REALLY LISTENING!
DOESN'T STOP THE COLD OUT HERE FROM PLAYING BLOODY MURDER WITH MY BACK, THOUGH.
SO ANY TIME YOU WANT TO PITCH IN--
WELL, THINK FAST.
THEY LOOK HUNGRY.
AND DO WHAT?
MY POWERS WORK ON ROCK, STONE--THE BIGGER, THE BETTER! THIS IS A VACUUM! THERE ISN'T EVEN SPACE DUST!
FLINT?

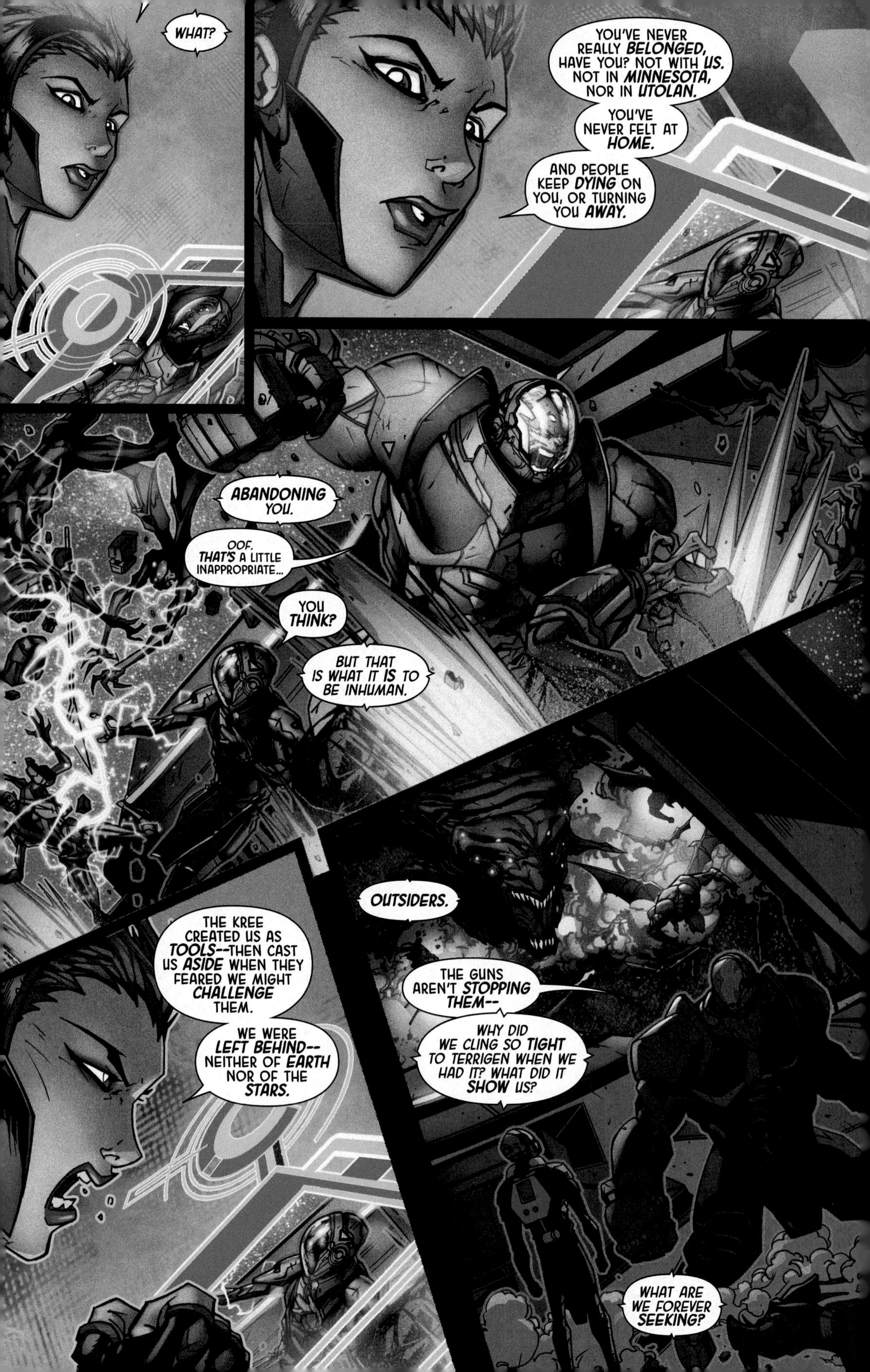
WHAT?
YOU'VE NEVER REALLY BELONGED, HAVE YOU? NOT WITH US. NOT IN MINNESOTA, NOR IN UTOLAN.
YOU'VE NEVER FELT AT HOME.
AND PEOPLE KEEP DYING ON YOU, OR TURNING YOU AWAY.
ABANDONING YOU.
OOF. THAT'S A LITTLE INAPPROPRIATE...
YOU THINK?
BUT THAT IS WHAT IT IS TO BE INHUMAN.
OUTSIDERS.
THE KREE CREATED US AS TOOLS--THEN CAST US ASIDE WHEN THEY FEARED WE MIGHT CHALLENGE THEM.
WE WERE LEFT BEHIND--NEITHER OF EARTH NOR OF THE STARS.
THE GUNS AREN'T STOPPING THEM--
WHY DID WE CLING SO TIGHT TO TERRIGEN WHEN WE HAD IT? WHAT DID IT SHOW US?
WHAT ARE WE FOREVER SEEKING?

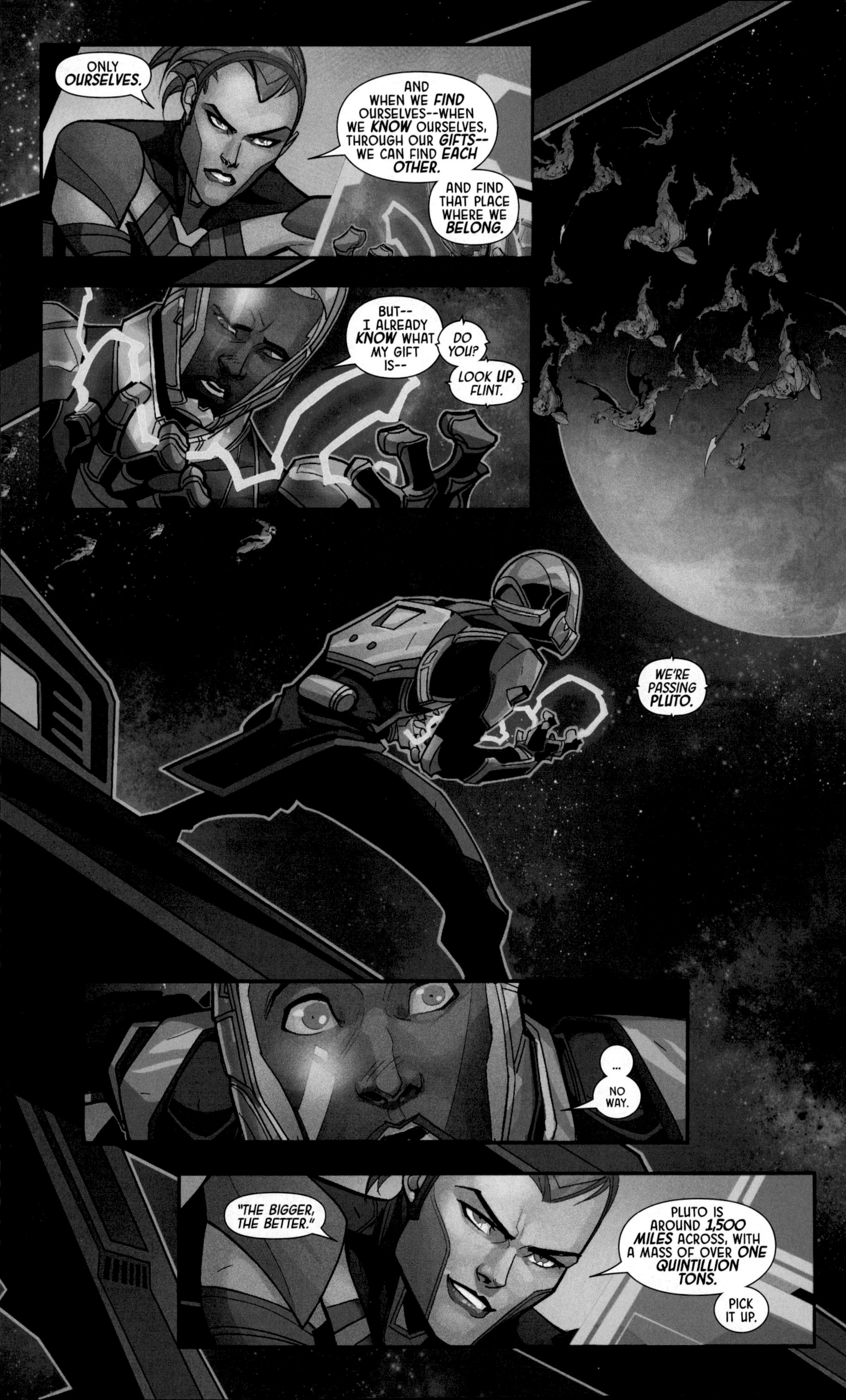
ONLY OURSELVES.
AND WHEN WE FIND OURSELVES--WHEN WE KNOW OURSELVES, THROUGH OUR GIFTS-- WE CAN FIND EACH OTHER.
AND FIND THAT PLACE WHERE WE BELONG.
BUT-- I ALREADY KNOW WHAT MY GIFT IS--
DO YOU?
LOOK UP, FLINT.
WE'RE PASSING PLUTO.
...
NO WAY.
"THE BIGGER, THE BETTER."
PLUTO IS AROUND 1,500 MILES ACROSS, WITH A MASS OF OVER ONE QUINTILLION TONS.
PICK IT UP.

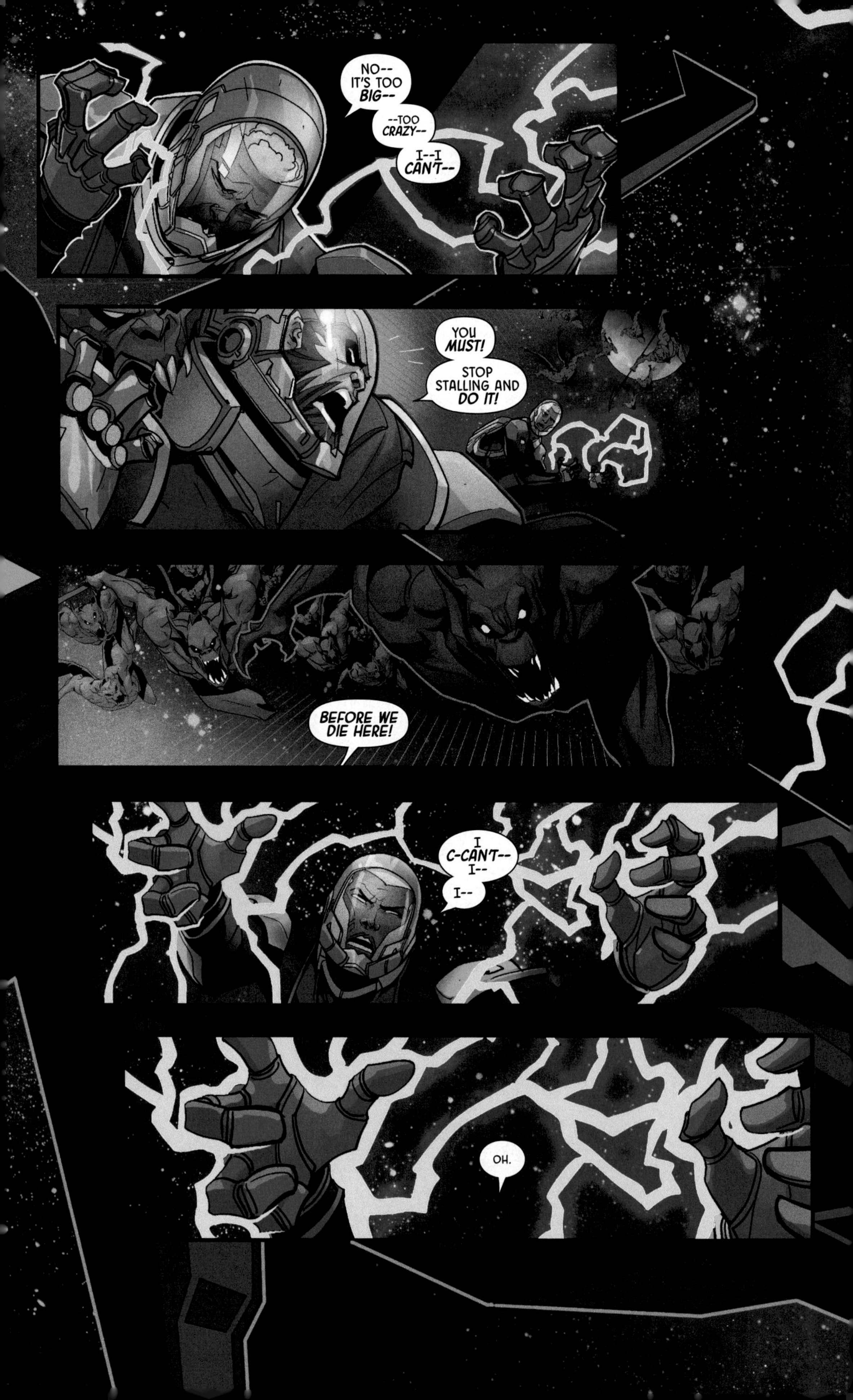
NO-- IT'S TOO BIG--
--TOO CRAZY--
I--I CAN'T--
YOU MUST!
STOP STALLING AND DO IT!
BEFORE WE DIE HERE!
I C-CAN'T-- I--
I--
OH.

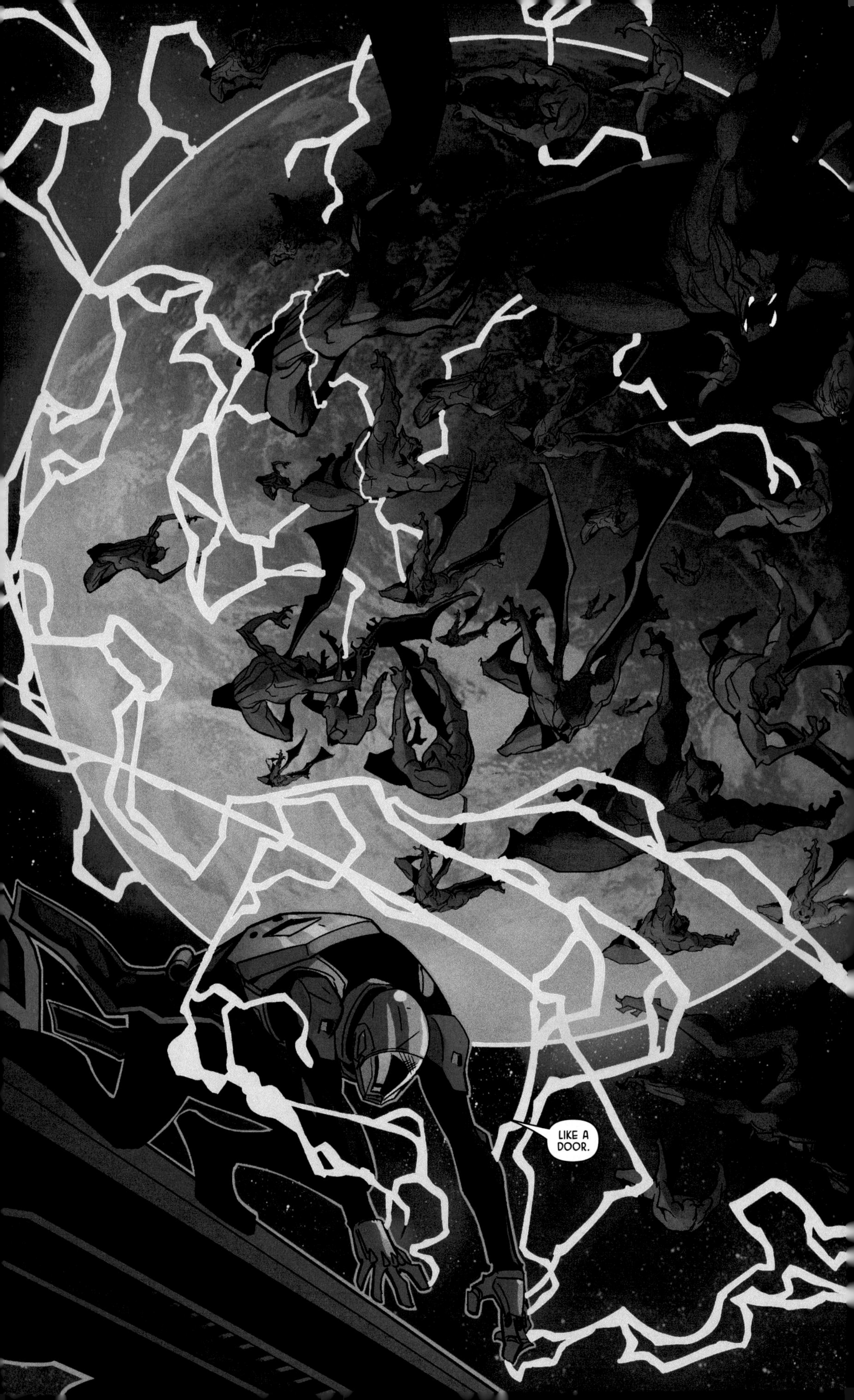
LIKE A DOOR.

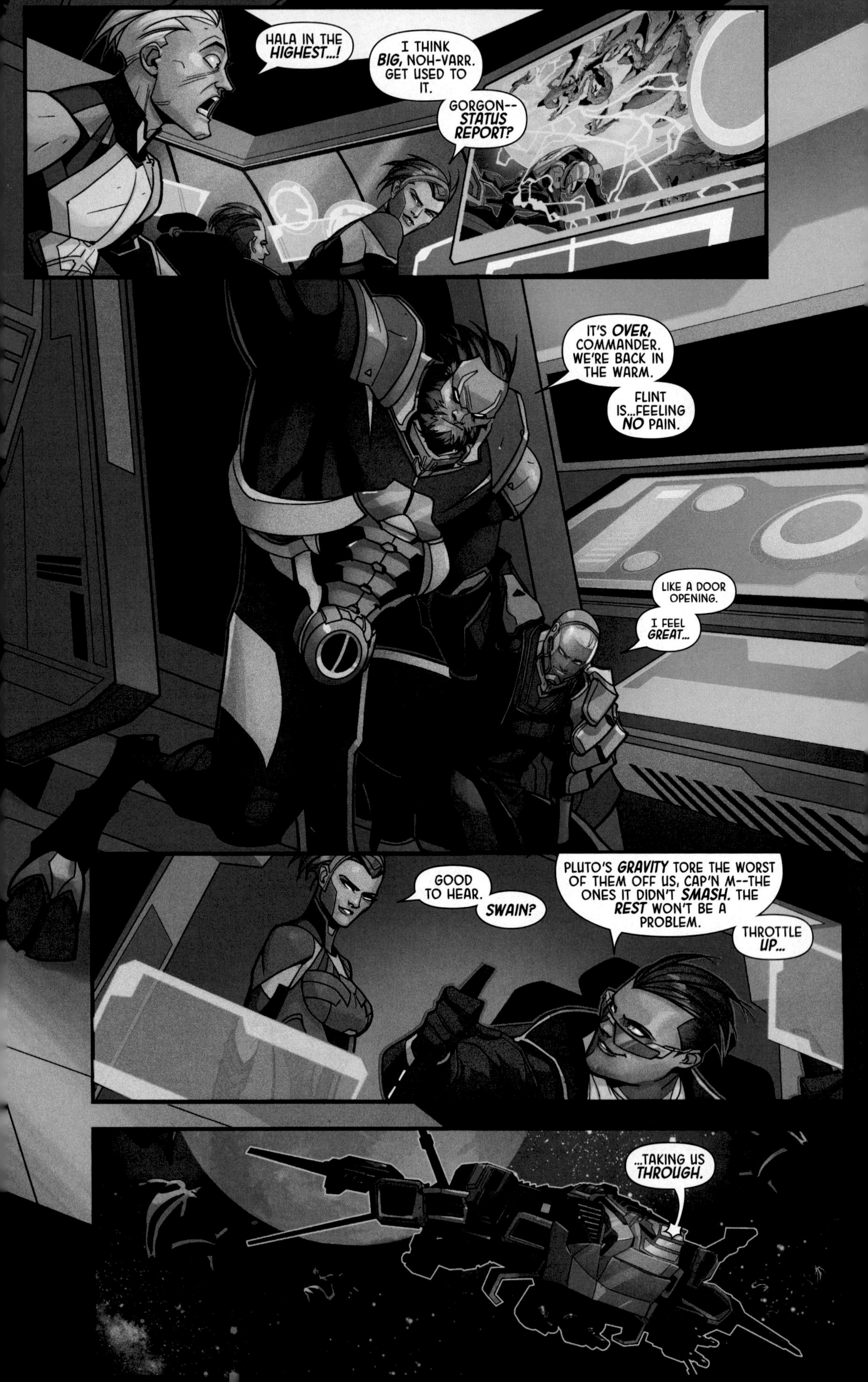

HALA IN THE HIGHEST...!
I THINK BIG, NOH-VARR. GET USED TO IT.
GORGON-- STATUS REPORT?
IT'S OVER, COMMANDER. WE'RE BACK IN THE WARM.
FLINT IS...FEELING NO PAIN.
LIKE A DOOR OPENING.
I FEEL GREAT...
GOOD TO HEAR. SWAIN?
PLUTO'S GRAVITY TORE THE WORST OF THEM OFF US, CAP'N M--THE ONES IT DIDN'T SMASH. THE REST WON'T BE A PROBLEM.
THROTTLE UP...
...TAKING US THROUGH.

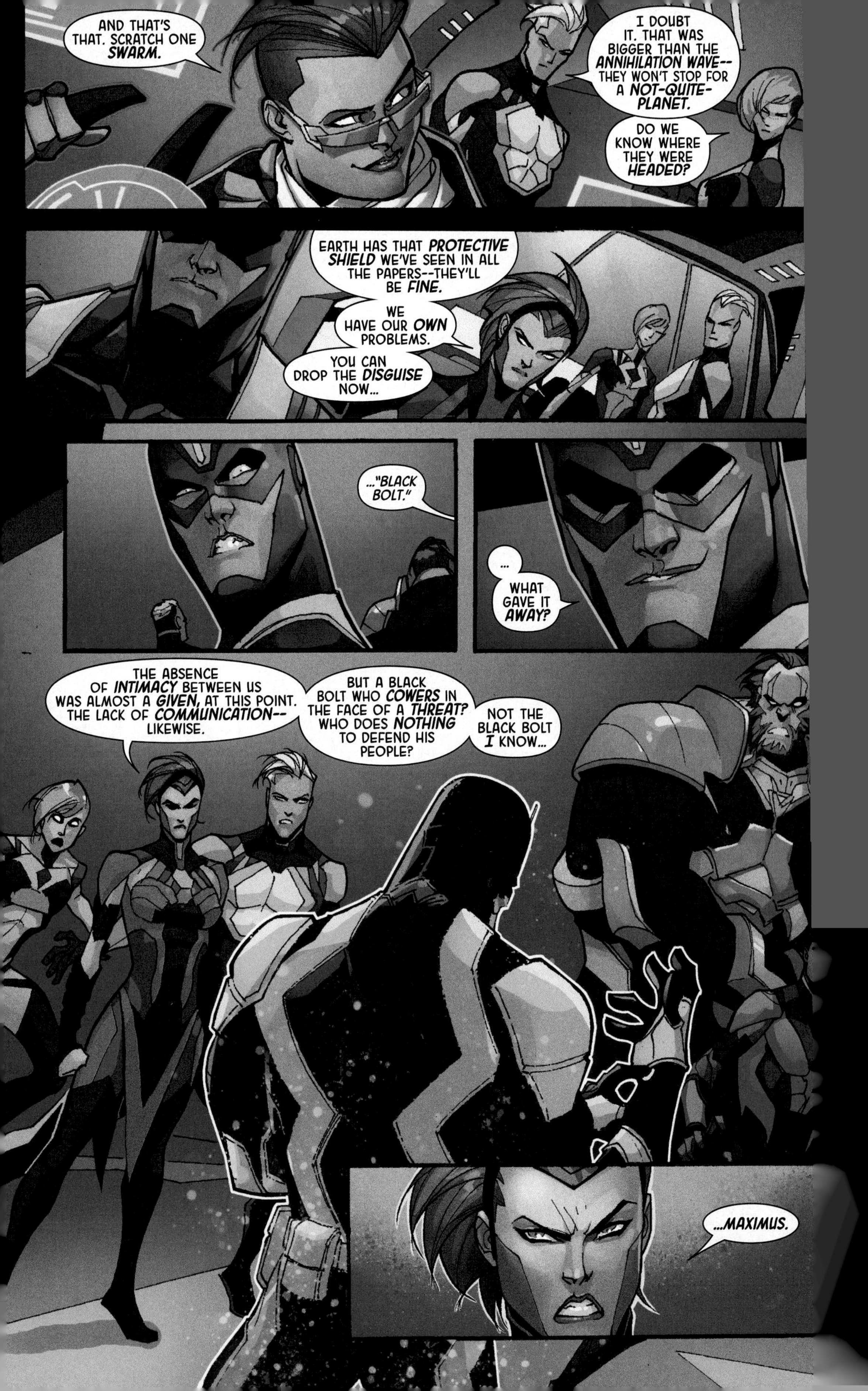
AND THAT'S THAT. SCRATCH ONE *SWARM.*
I DOUBT IT. THAT WAS BIGGER THAN THE *ANNIHILATION WAVE--* THEY WON'T STOP FOR A *NOT-QUITE-PLANET.*
DO WE KNOW WHERE THEY WERE *HEADED?*
EARTH HAS THAT *PROTECTIVE SHIELD* WE'VE SEEN IN ALL THE PAPERS--THEY'LL BE *FINE.*
WE HAVE OUR *OWN* PROBLEMS.
YOU CAN DROP THE *DISGUISE* NOW...
..."*BLACK BOLT.*"
... WHAT GAVE IT *AWAY?*
THE ABSENCE OF *INTIMACY* BETWEEN US WAS ALMOST A *GIVEN,* AT THIS POINT. THE LACK OF *COMMUNICATION--* LIKEWISE.
BUT A BLACK BOLT WHO *COWERS* IN THE FACE OF A *THREAT?* WHO DOES *NOTHING* TO DEFEND HIS PEOPLE?
NOT THE BLACK BOLT *I* KNOW...
*...MAXIMUS.*

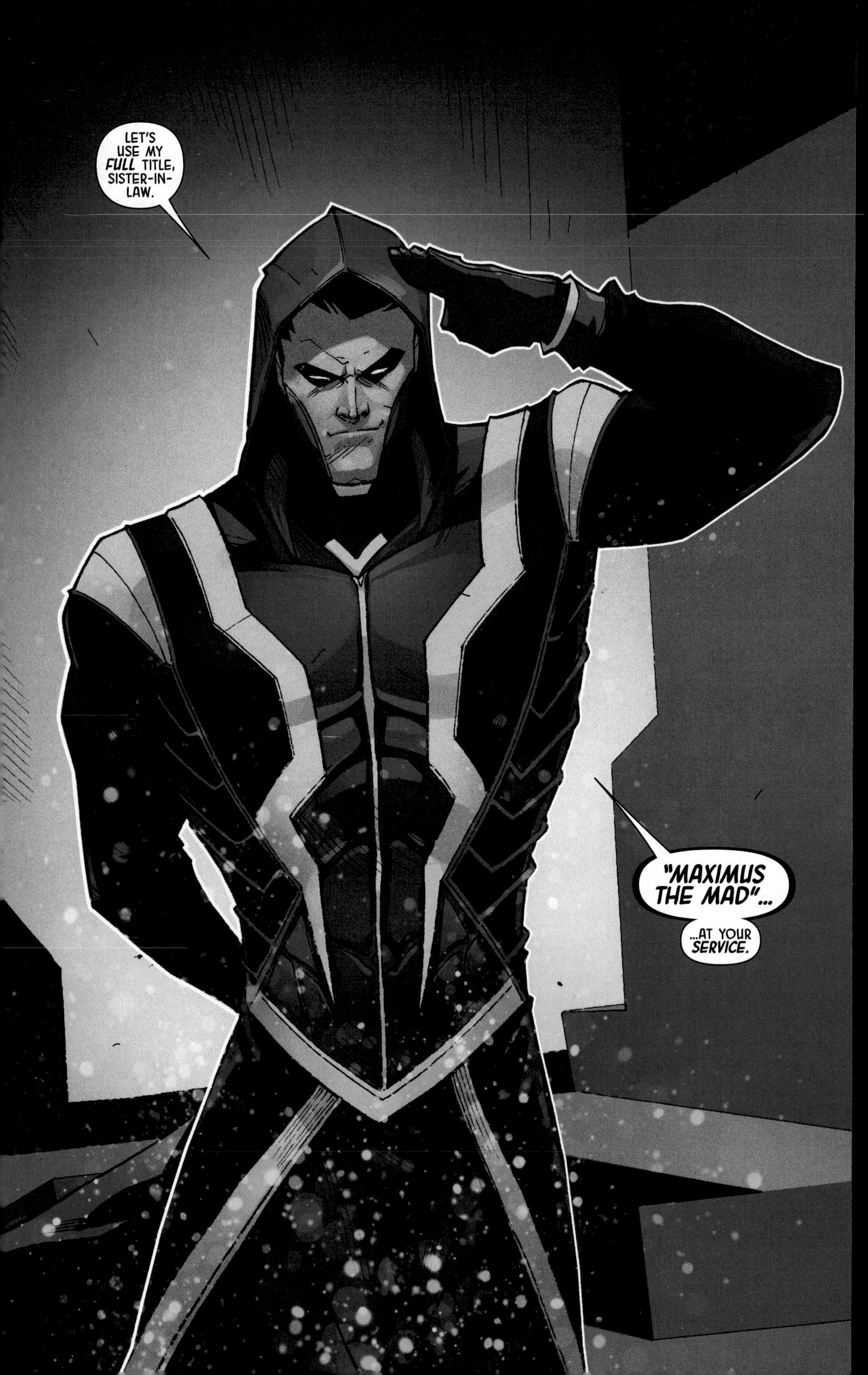
LET'S USE MY *FULL* TITLE, SISTER-IN-LAW.
"MAXIMUS THE MAD"...
...AT YOUR *SERVICE*.

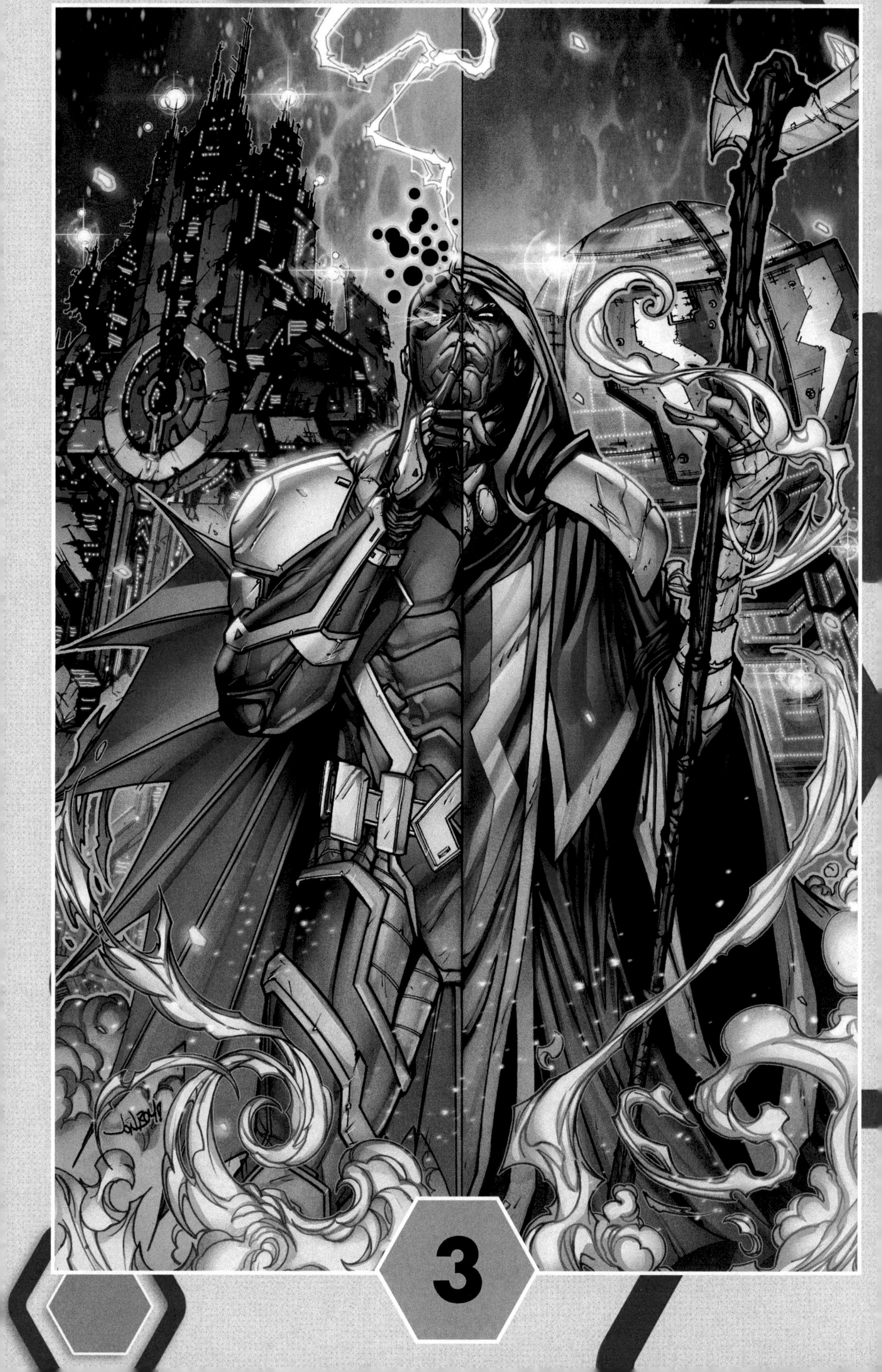

3

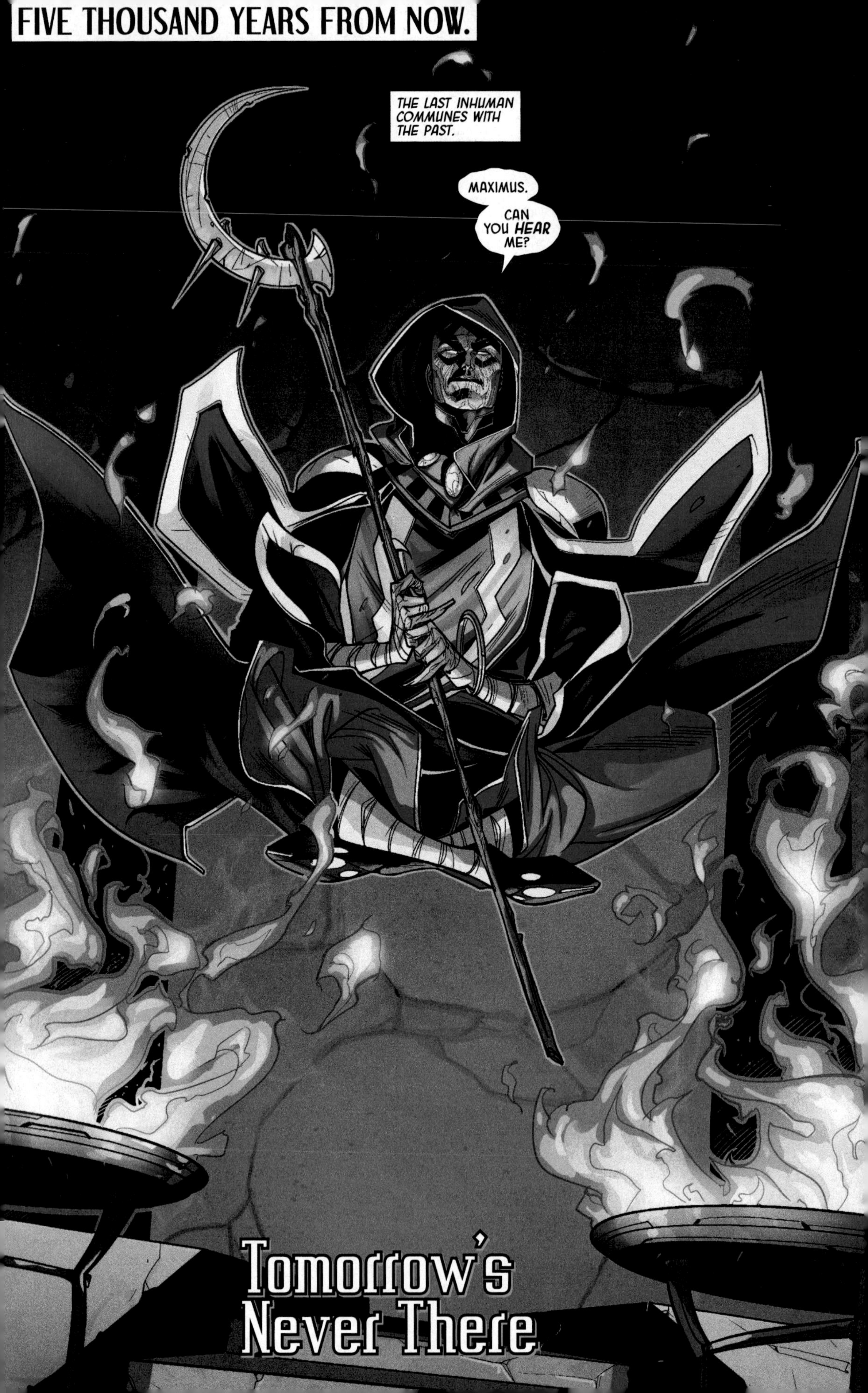
FIVE THOUSAND YEARS FROM NOW.
THE LAST INHUMAN COMMUNES WITH THE PAST.
MAXIMUS.
CAN YOU HEAR ME?
Tomorrow's Never There

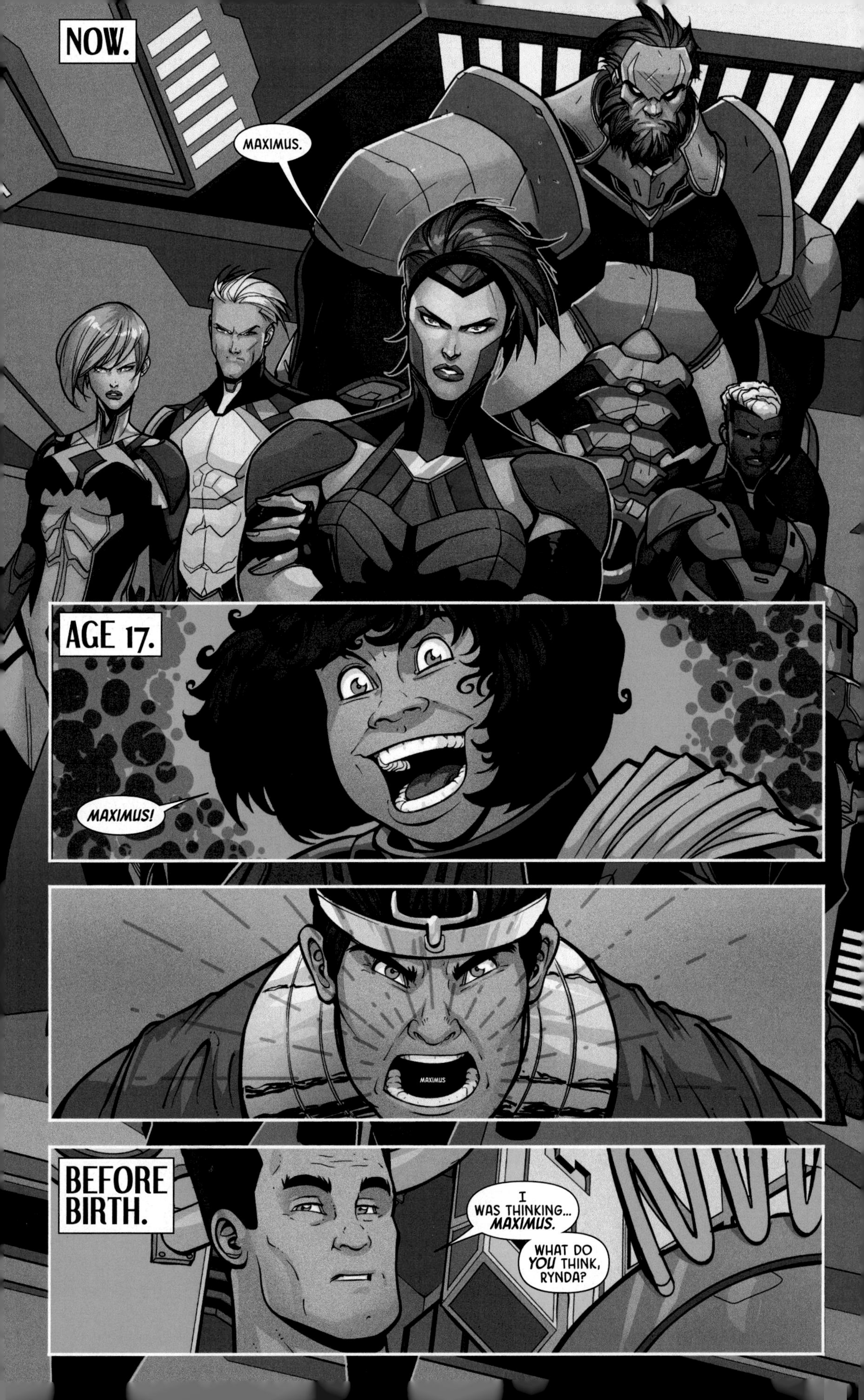
NOW.
MAXIMUS.
AGE 17.
MAXIMUS!
MAXIMUS
BEFORE BIRTH.
I WAS THINKING... MAXIMUS.
WHAT DO YOU THINK, RYNDA?

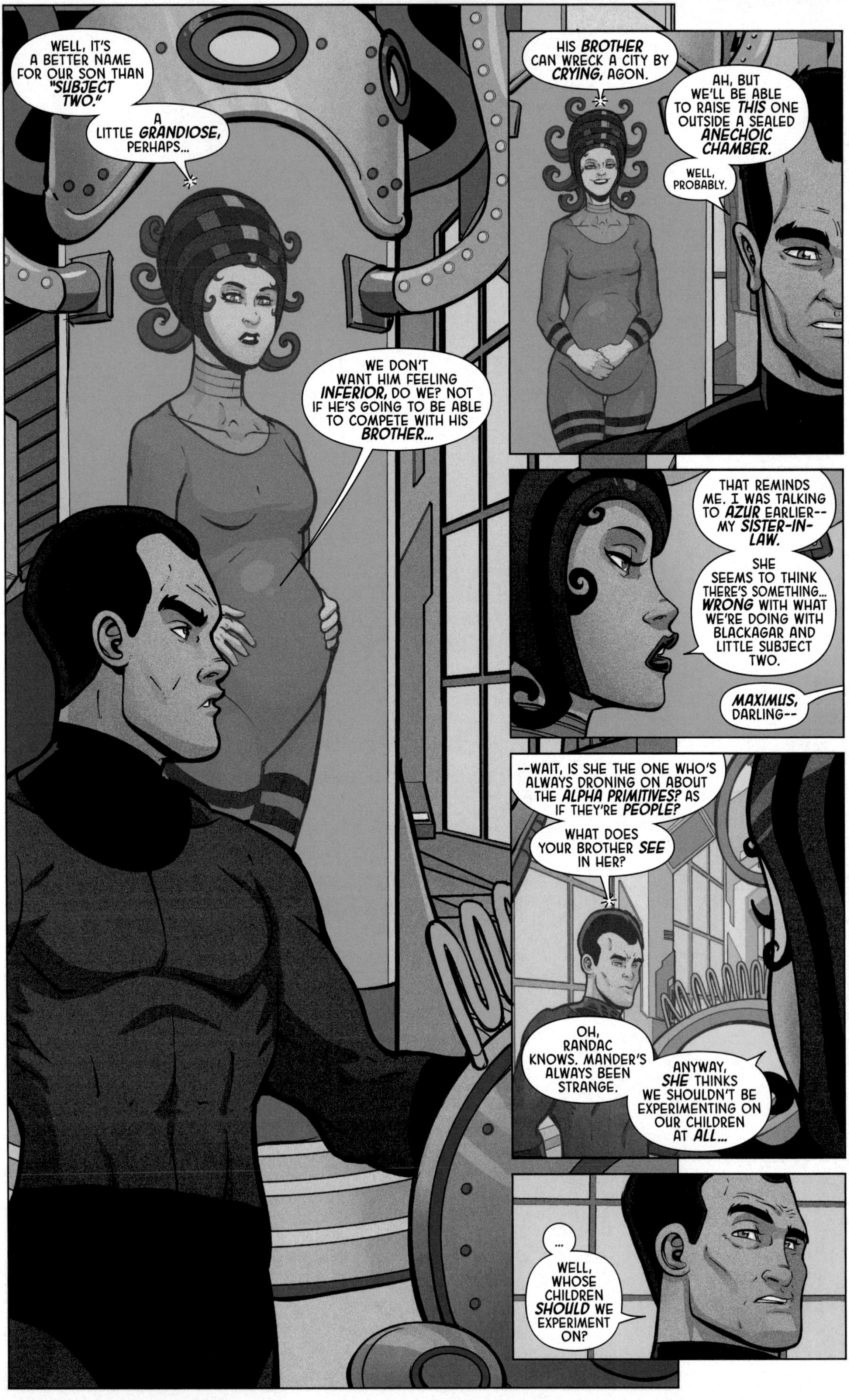
WELL, IT'S A BETTER NAME FOR OUR SON THAN "SUBJECT TWO."
A LITTLE GRANDIOSE, PERHAPS...
WE DON'T WANT HIM FEELING INFERIOR, DO WE? NOT IF HE'S GOING TO BE ABLE TO COMPETE WITH HIS BROTHER...
HIS BROTHER CAN WRECK A CITY BY CRYING, AGON.
AH, BUT WE'LL BE ABLE TO RAISE THIS ONE OUTSIDE A SEALED ANECHOIC CHAMBER.
WELL, PROBABLY.
THAT REMINDS ME. I WAS TALKING TO AZUR EARLIER-- MY SISTER-IN-LAW.
SHE SEEMS TO THINK THERE'S SOMETHING... WRONG WITH WHAT WE'RE DOING WITH BLACKAGAR AND LITTLE SUBJECT TWO.
MAXIMUS, DARLING--
--WAIT, IS SHE THE ONE WHO'S ALWAYS DRONING ON ABOUT THE ALPHA PRIMITIVES? AS IF THEY'RE PEOPLE?
WHAT DOES YOUR BROTHER SEE IN HER?
OH, RANDAC KNOWS. MANDER'S ALWAYS BEEN STRANGE.
ANYWAY, SHE THINKS WE SHOULDN'T BE EXPERIMENTING ON OUR CHILDREN AT ALL...
...
WELL, WHOSE CHILDREN SHOULD WE EXPERIMENT ON?

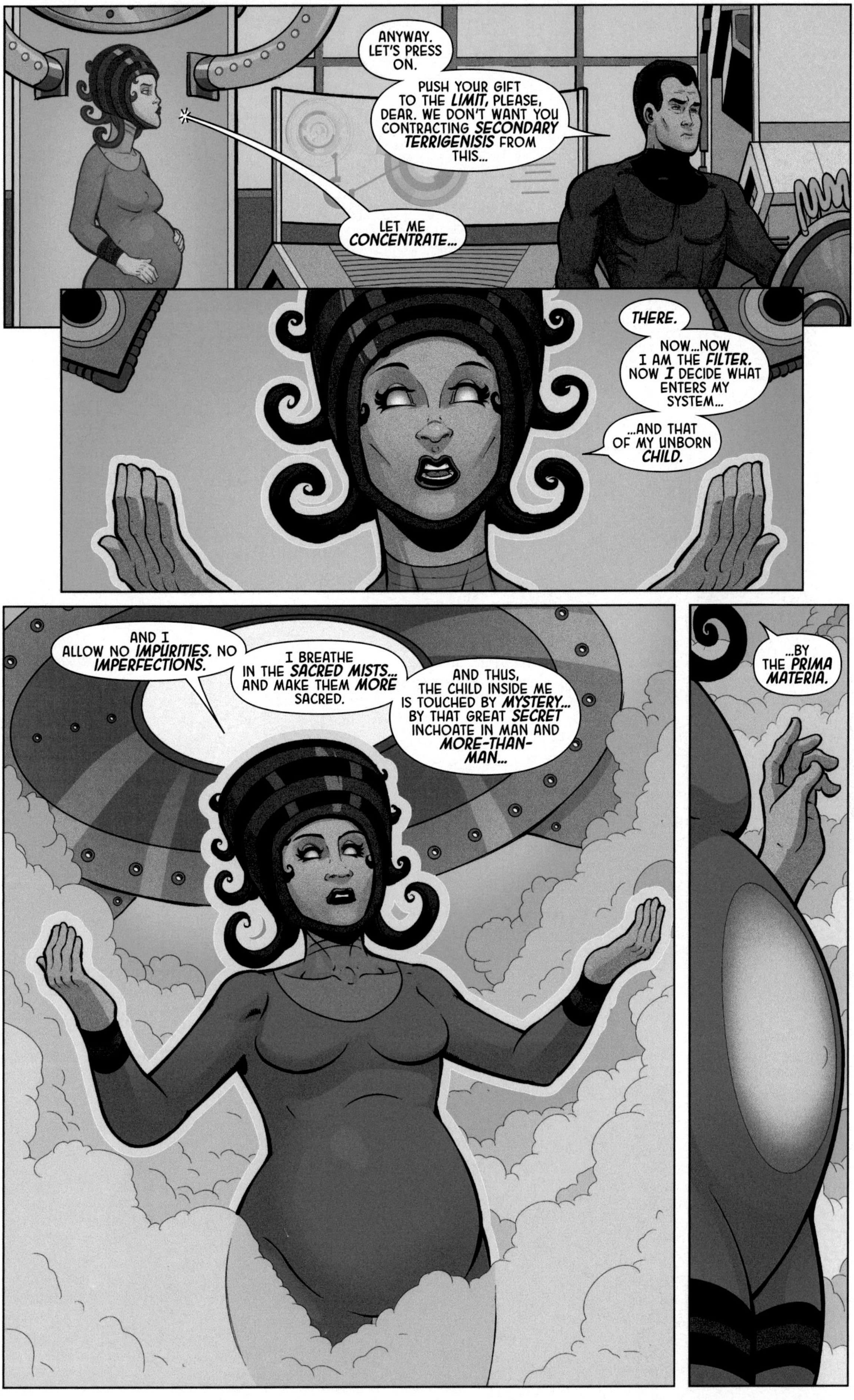
ANYWAY. LET'S PRESS ON.
PUSH YOUR GIFT TO THE LIMIT, PLEASE, DEAR. WE DON'T WANT YOU CONTRACTING SECONDARY TERRIGENISIS FROM THIS...
LET ME CONCENTRATE...
THERE.
NOW...NOW I AM THE FILTER. NOW I DECIDE WHAT ENTERS MY SYSTEM...
...AND THAT OF MY UNBORN CHILD.
AND I ALLOW NO IMPURITIES. NO IMPERFECTIONS.
I BREATHE IN THE SACRED MISTS... AND MAKE THEM MORE SACRED.
AND THUS, THE CHILD INSIDE ME IS TOUCHED BY MYSTERY... BY THAT GREAT SECRET INCHOATE IN MAN AND MORE-THAN-MAN...
...BY THE PRIMA MATERIA.

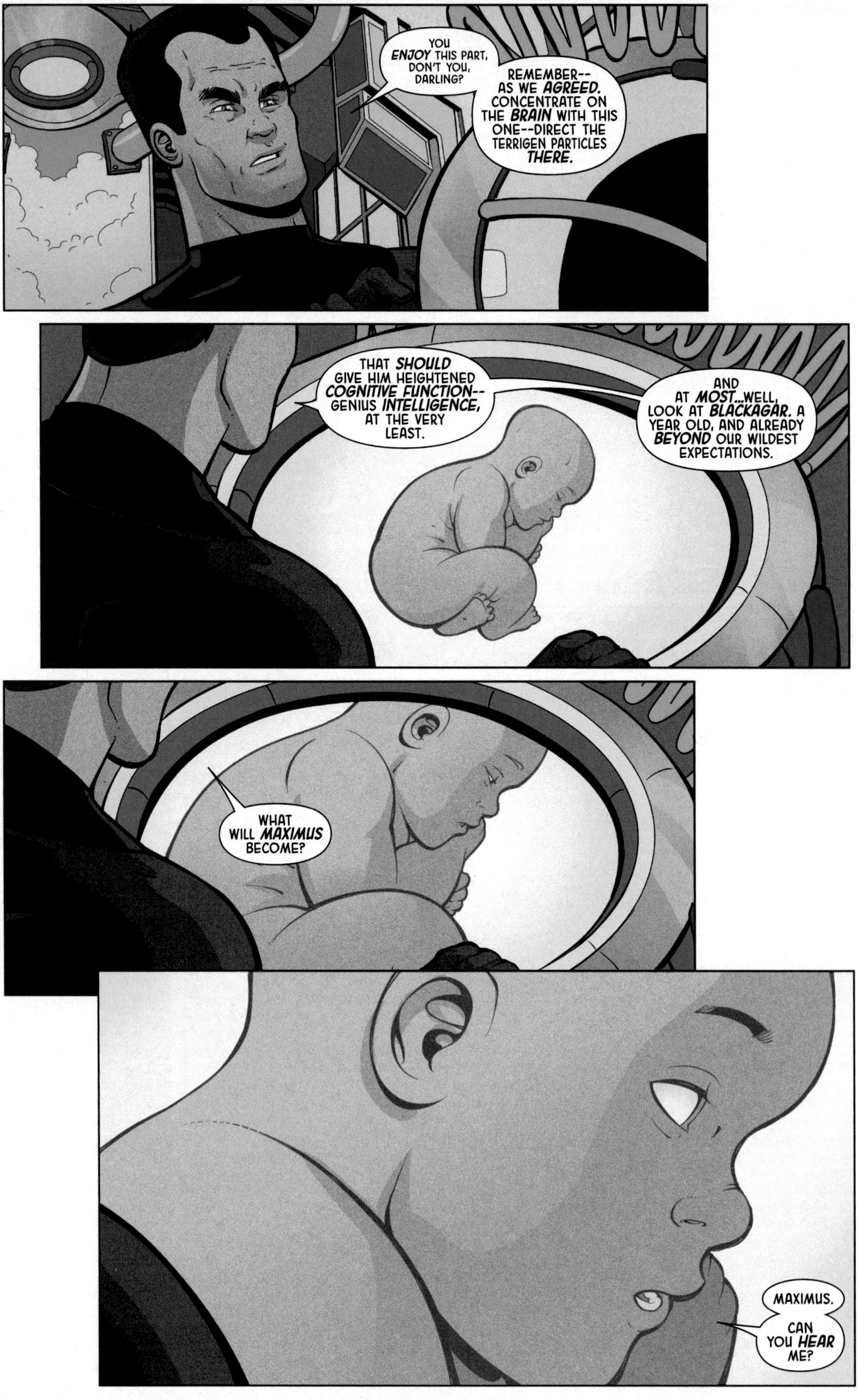
YOU ENJOY THIS PART, DON'T YOU, DARLING?
REMEMBER-- AS WE AGREED. CONCENTRATE ON THE BRAIN WITH THIS ONE--DIRECT THE TERRIGEN PARTICLES THERE.
THAT SHOULD GIVE HIM HEIGHTENED COGNITIVE FUNCTION-- GENIUS INTELLIGENCE, AT THE VERY LEAST.
AND AT MOST...WELL, LOOK AT BLACKAGAR. A YEAR OLD, AND ALREADY BEYOND OUR WILDEST EXPECTATIONS.
WHAT WILL MAXIMUS BECOME?
MAXIMUS.
CAN YOU HEAR ME?

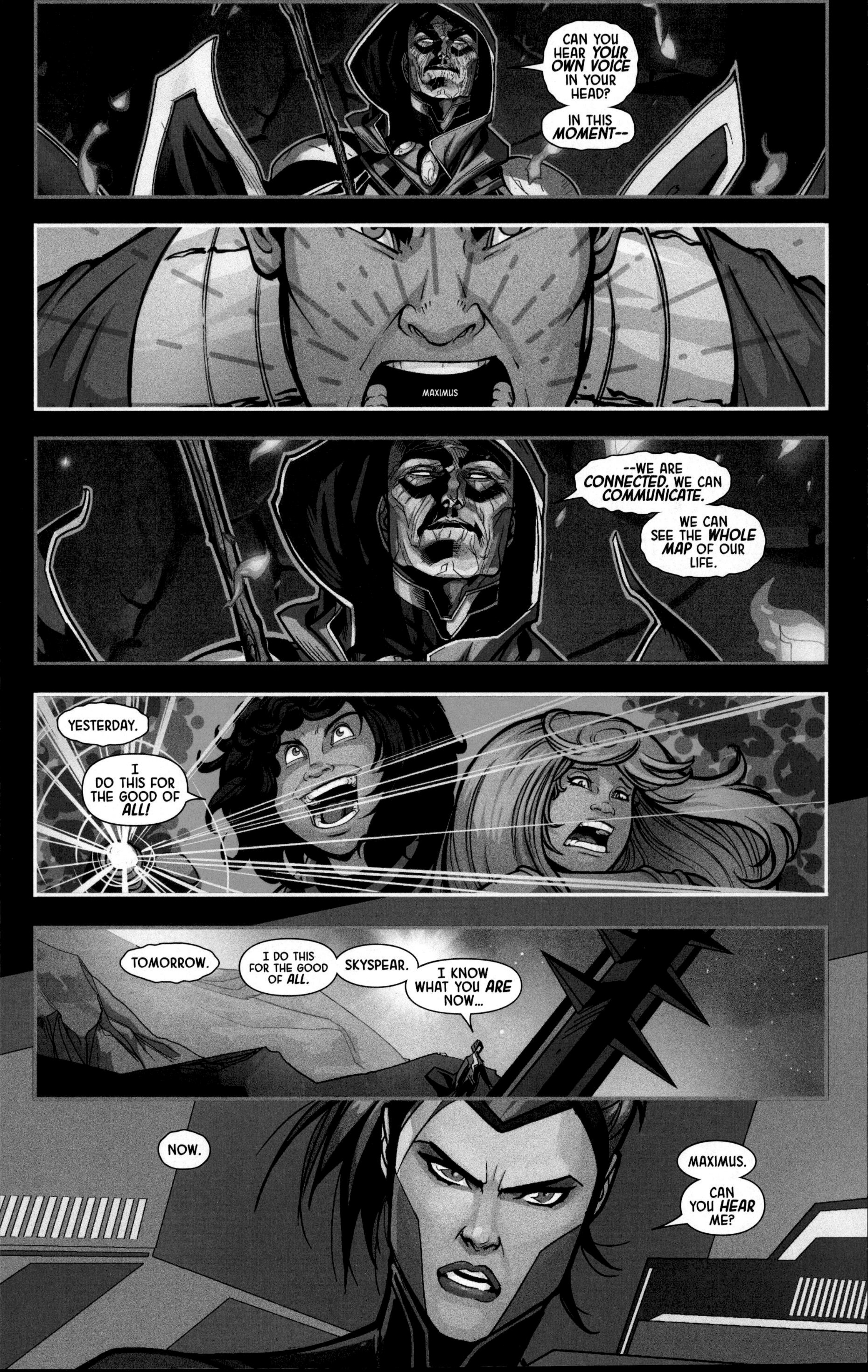
CAN YOU HEAR YOUR OWN VOICE IN YOUR HEAD?
IN THIS MOMENT--
MAXIMUS
--WE ARE CONNECTED. WE CAN COMMUNICATE.
WE CAN SEE THE WHOLE MAP OF OUR LIFE.
YESTERDAY.
I DO THIS FOR THE GOOD OF ALL!
TOMORROW.
I DO THIS FOR THE GOOD OF ALL.
SKYSPEAR.
I KNOW WHAT YOU ARE NOW...
NOW.
MAXIMUS.
CAN YOU HEAR ME?

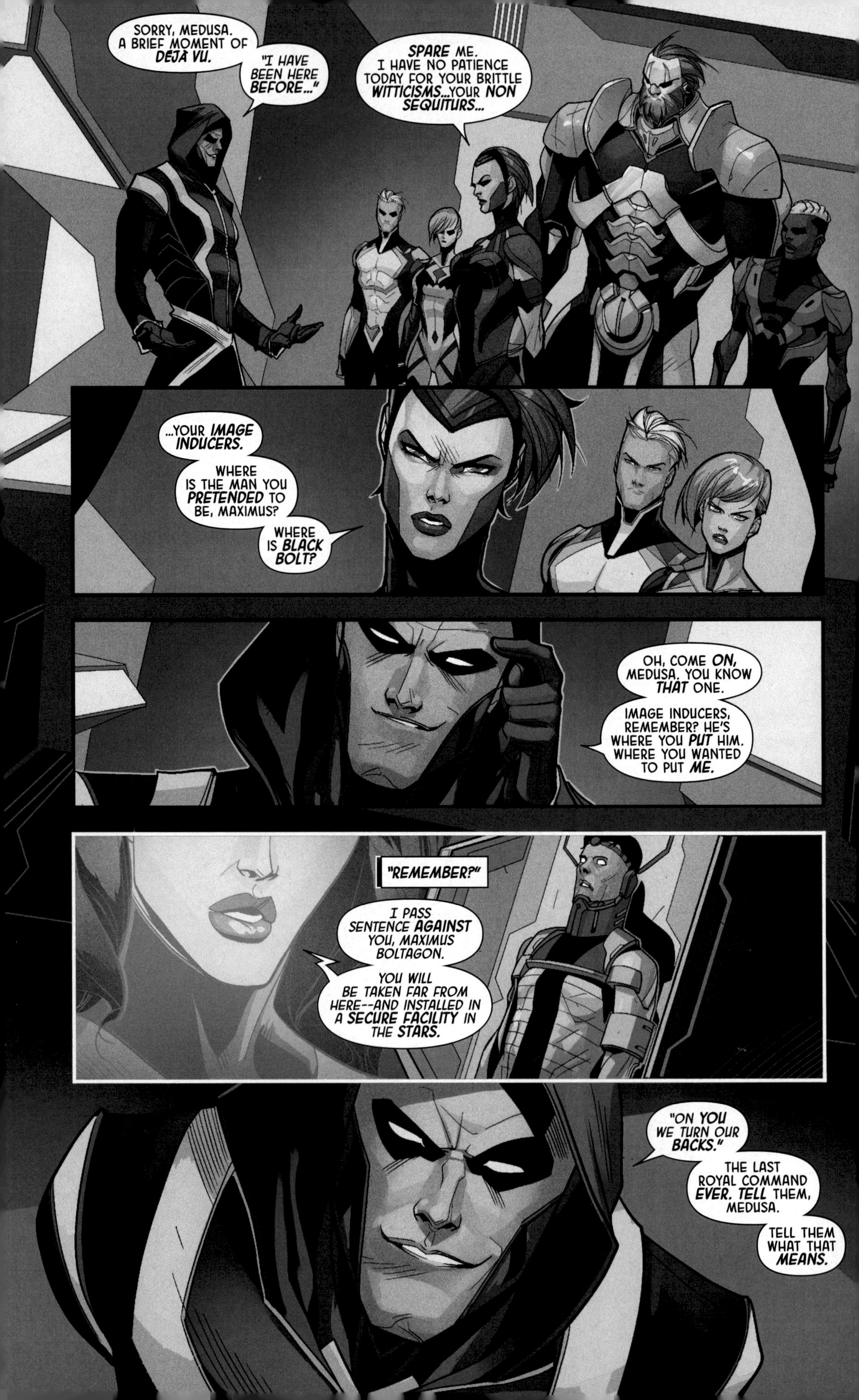
SORRY, MEDUSA. A BRIEF MOMENT OF DÉJÀ VU.
"I HAVE BEEN HERE BEFORE..."
SPARE ME. I HAVE NO PATIENCE TODAY FOR YOUR BRITTLE WITTICISMS...YOUR NON SEQUITURS...
...YOUR IMAGE INDUCERS.
WHERE IS THE MAN YOU PRETENDED TO BE, MAXIMUS?
WHERE IS BLACK BOLT?
OH, COME ON, MEDUSA. YOU KNOW THAT ONE.
IMAGE INDUCERS, REMEMBER? HE'S WHERE YOU PUT HIM. WHERE YOU WANTED TO PUT ME.
"REMEMBER?"
I PASS SENTENCE AGAINST YOU, MAXIMUS BOLTAGON.
YOU WILL BE TAKEN FAR FROM HERE--AND INSTALLED IN A SECURE FACILITY IN THE STARS.
"ON YOU WE TURN OUR BACKS."
THE LAST ROYAL COMMAND EVER. TELL THEM, MEDUSA.
TELL THEM WHAT THAT MEANS.

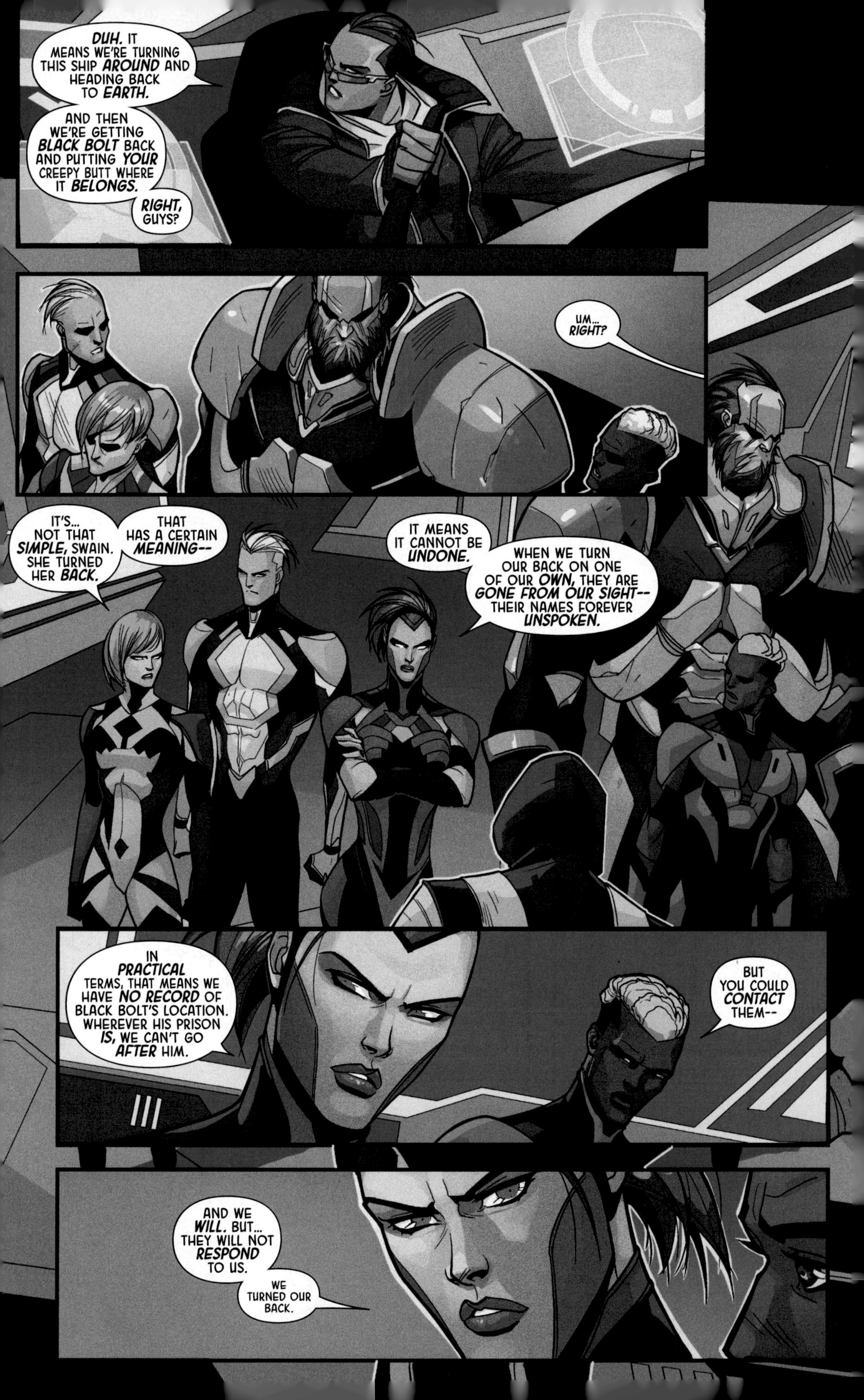
DUH. IT MEANS WE'RE TURNING THIS SHIP AROUND AND HEADING BACK TO EARTH.
AND THEN WE'RE GETTING BLACK BOLT BACK AND PUTTING YOUR CREEPY BUTT WHERE IT BELONGS.
RIGHT, GUYS?
UM... RIGHT?
IT'S... NOT THAT SIMPLE, SWAIN. SHE TURNED HER BACK.
THAT HAS A CERTAIN MEANING--
IT MEANS IT CANNOT BE UNDONE.
WHEN WE TURN OUR BACK ON ONE OF OUR OWN, THEY ARE GONE FROM OUR SIGHT-- THEIR NAMES FOREVER UNSPOKEN.
IN PRACTICAL TERMS, THAT MEANS WE HAVE NO RECORD OF BLACK BOLT'S LOCATION. WHEREVER HIS PRISON IS, WE CAN'T GO AFTER HIM.
BUT YOU COULD CONTACT THEM--
AND WE WILL. BUT... THEY WILL NOT RESPOND TO US.
WE TURNED OUR BACK.

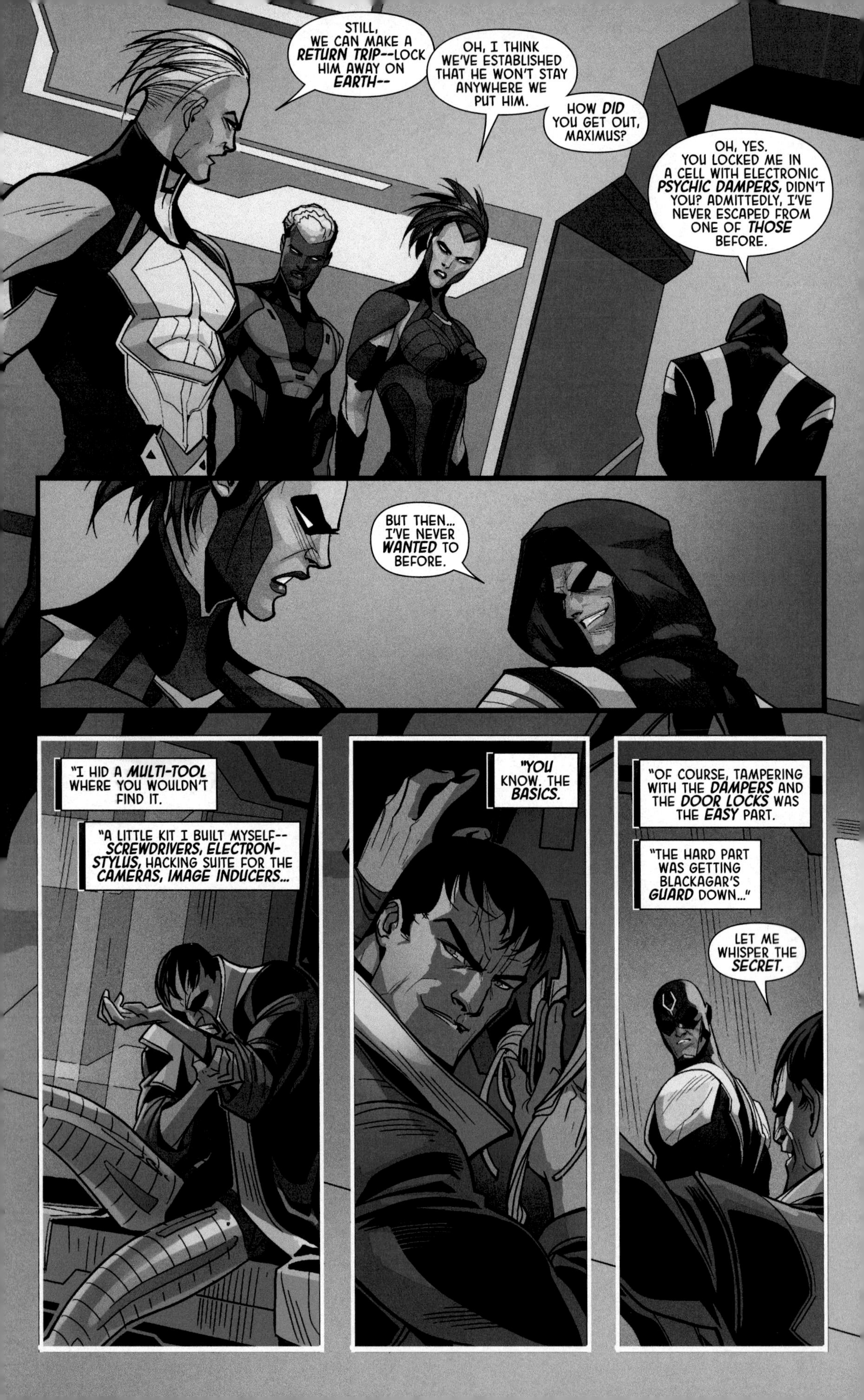
STILL, WE CAN MAKE A RETURN TRIP--LOCK HIM AWAY ON EARTH--
OH, I THINK WE'VE ESTABLISHED THAT HE WON'T STAY ANYWHERE WE PUT HIM.
HOW DID YOU GET OUT, MAXIMUS?
OH, YES. YOU LOCKED ME IN A CELL WITH ELECTRONIC PSYCHIC DAMPERS, DIDN'T YOU? ADMITTEDLY, I'VE NEVER ESCAPED FROM ONE OF THOSE BEFORE.
BUT THEN... I'VE NEVER WANTED TO BEFORE.
"I HID A MULTI-TOOL WHERE YOU WOULDN'T FIND IT.
"A LITTLE KIT I BUILT MYSELF--SCREWDRIVERS, ELECTRON-STYLUS, HACKING SUITE FOR THE CAMERAS, IMAGE INDUCERS...
"YOU KNOW. THE BASICS.
"OF COURSE, TAMPERING WITH THE DAMPERS AND THE DOOR LOCKS WAS THE EASY PART.
"THE HARD PART WAS GETTING BLACKAGAR'S GUARD DOWN..."
LET ME WHISPER THE SECRET.

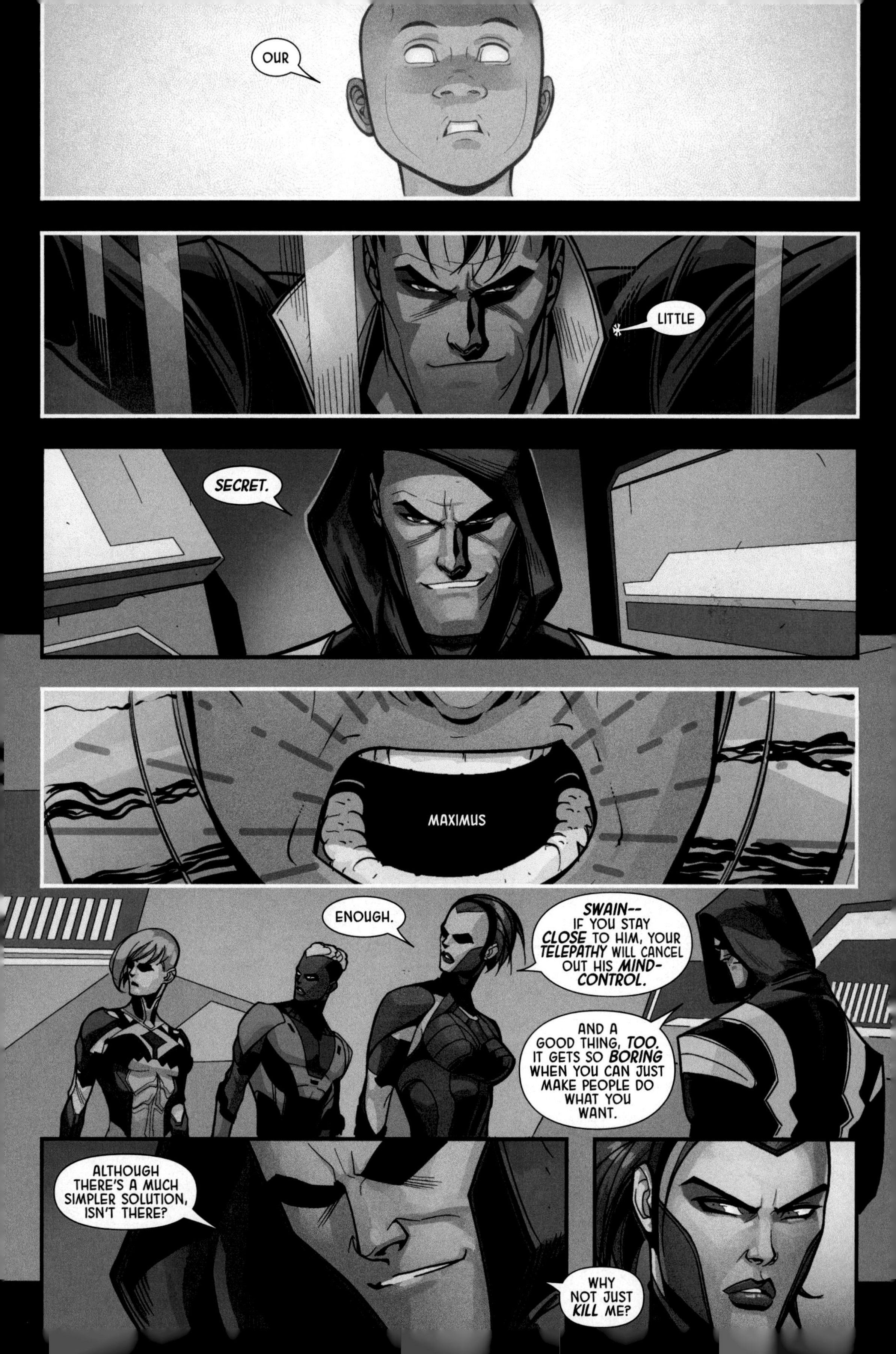
OUR
LITTLE
SECRET.
MAXIMUS
ENOUGH.
SWAIN-- IF YOU STAY CLOSE TO HIM, YOUR TELEPATHY WILL CANCEL OUT HIS MIND-CONTROL.
AND A GOOD THING, TOO. IT GETS SO BORING WHEN YOU CAN JUST MAKE PEOPLE DO WHAT YOU WANT.
ALTHOUGH THERE'S A MUCH SIMPLER SOLUTION, ISN'T THERE?
WHY NOT JUST KILL ME?

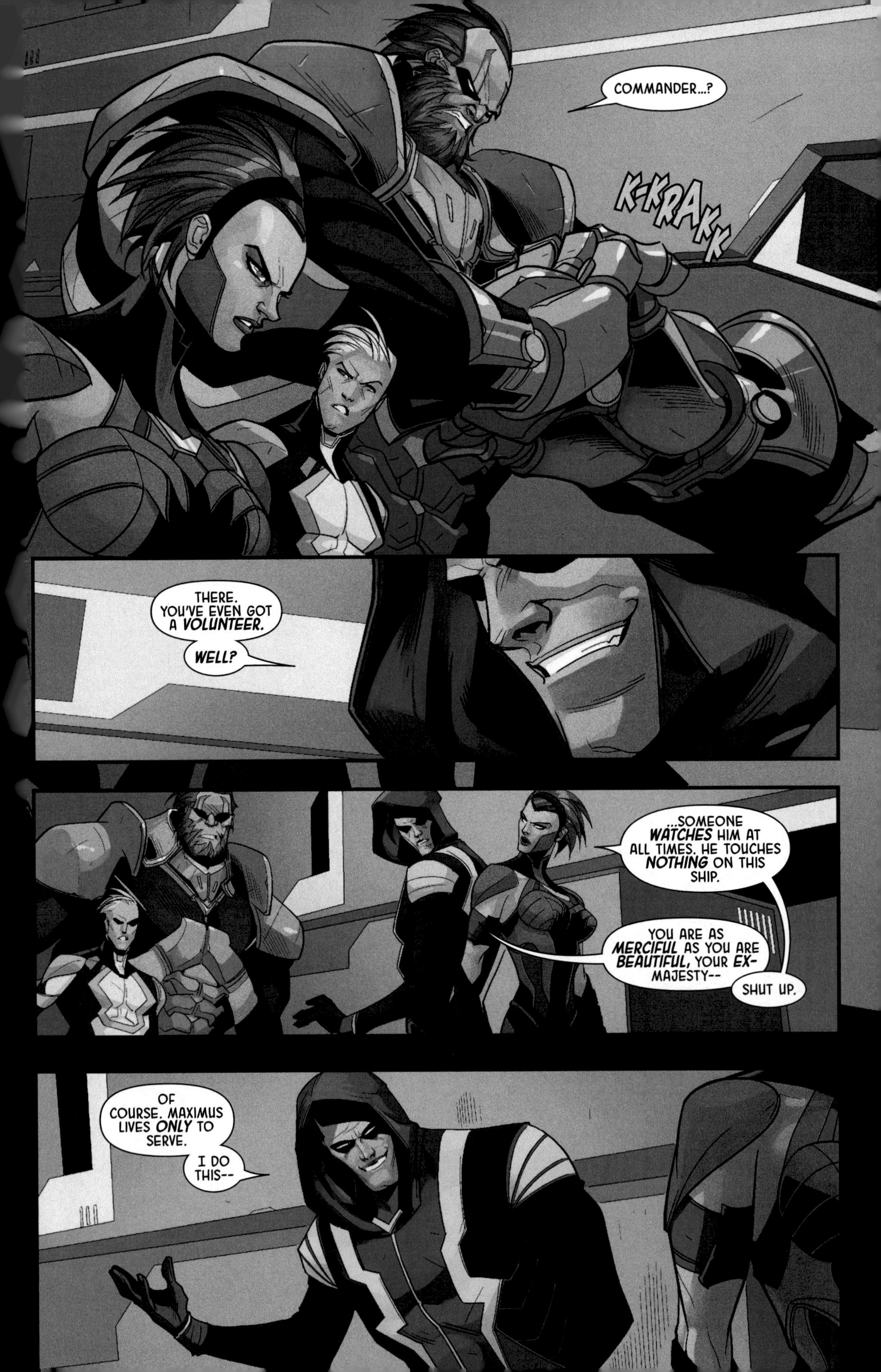
COMMANDER...?
K-KRAKK
THERE. YOU'VE EVEN GOT A VOLUNTEER.
WELL?
...SOMEONE WATCHES HIM AT ALL TIMES. HE TOUCHES NOTHING ON THIS SHIP.
YOU ARE AS MERCIFUL AS YOU ARE BEAUTIFUL, YOUR EX-MAJESTY--
SHUT UP.
OF COURSE. MAXIMUS LIVES ONLY TO SERVE.
I DO THIS--

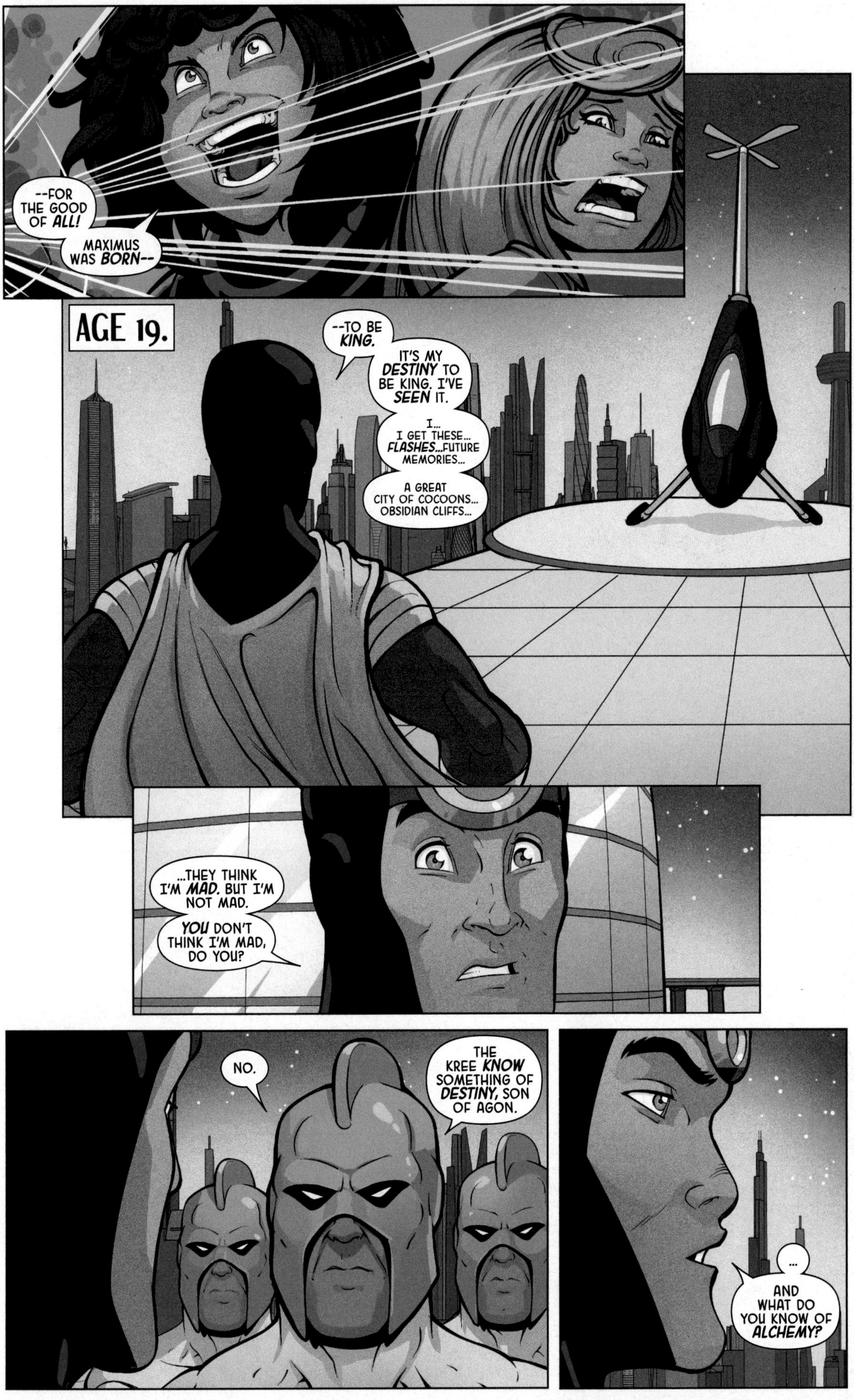
--FOR THE GOOD OF ALL!
MAXIMUS WAS BORN--
AGE 19.
--TO BE KING.
IT'S MY DESTINY TO BE KING. I'VE SEEN IT.
I... I GET THESE... FLASHES...FUTURE MEMORIES...
A GREAT CITY OF COCOONS... OBSIDIAN CLIFFS...
...THEY THINK I'M MAD. BUT I'M NOT MAD.
YOU DON'T THINK I'M MAD, DO YOU?
NO.
THE KREE KNOW SOMETHING OF DESTINY, SON OF AGON.
...
AND WHAT DO YOU KNOW OF ALCHEMY?

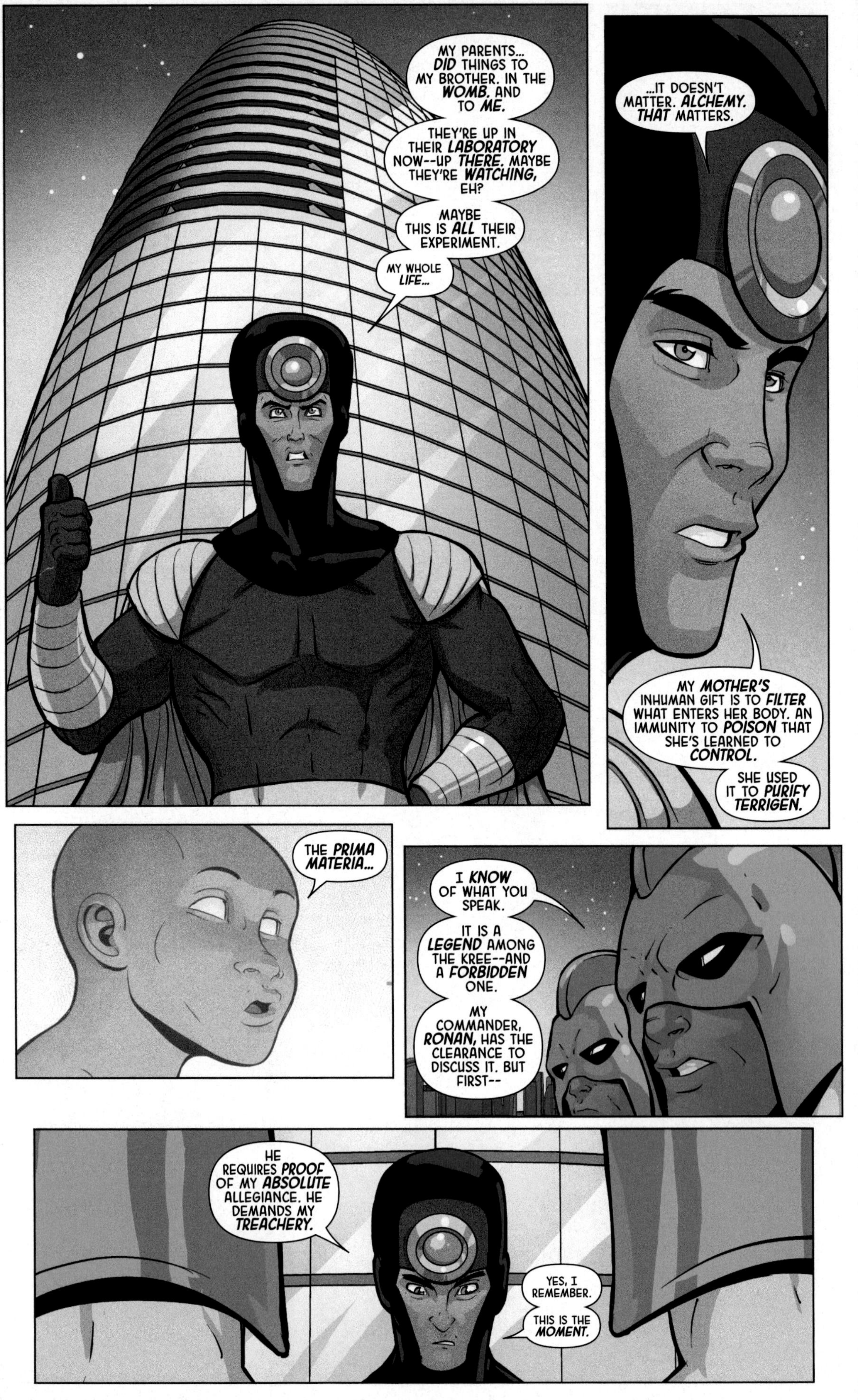

MY PARENTS... DID THINGS TO MY BROTHER. IN THE WOMB. AND TO ME.
THEY'RE UP IN THEIR LABORATORY NOW--UP THERE. MAYBE THEY'RE WATCHING, EH?
MAYBE THIS IS ALL THEIR EXPERIMENT.
MY WHOLE LIFE...
...IT DOESN'T MATTER. ALCHEMY. THAT MATTERS.
MY MOTHER'S INHUMAN GIFT IS TO FILTER WHAT ENTERS HER BODY. AN IMMUNITY TO POISON THAT SHE'S LEARNED TO CONTROL.
SHE USED IT TO PURIFY TERRIGEN.
THE PRIMA MATERIA...
I KNOW OF WHAT YOU SPEAK.
IT IS A LEGEND AMONG THE KREE--AND A FORBIDDEN ONE.
MY COMMANDER, RONAN, HAS THE CLEARANCE TO DISCUSS IT. BUT FIRST--
HE REQUIRES PROOF OF MY ABSOLUTE ALLEGIANCE. HE DEMANDS MY TREACHERY.
YES, I REMEMBER.
THIS IS THE MOMENT.

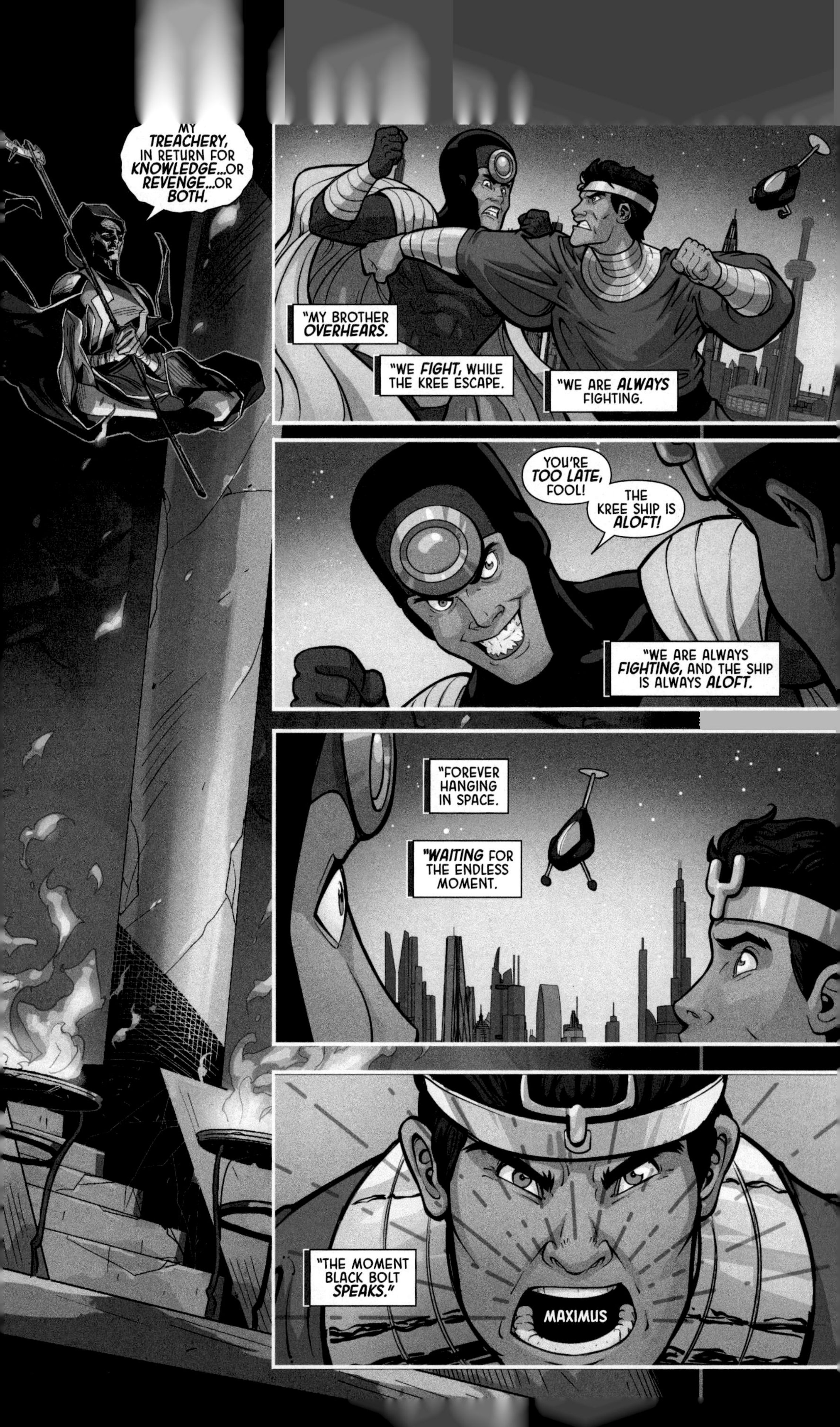

MY TREACHERY, IN RETURN FOR KNOWLEDGE...OR REVENGE...OR BOTH.
"MY BROTHER OVERHEARS.
"WE FIGHT, WHILE THE KREE ESCAPE.
"WE ARE ALWAYS FIGHTING.
YOU'RE TOO LATE, FOOL!
THE KREE SHIP IS ALOFT!
"WE ARE ALWAYS FIGHTING, AND THE SHIP IS ALWAYS ALOFT.
"FOREVER HANGING IN SPACE.
"WAITING FOR THE ENDLESS MOMENT.
"THE MOMENT BLACK BOLT SPEAKS."
MAXIMUS

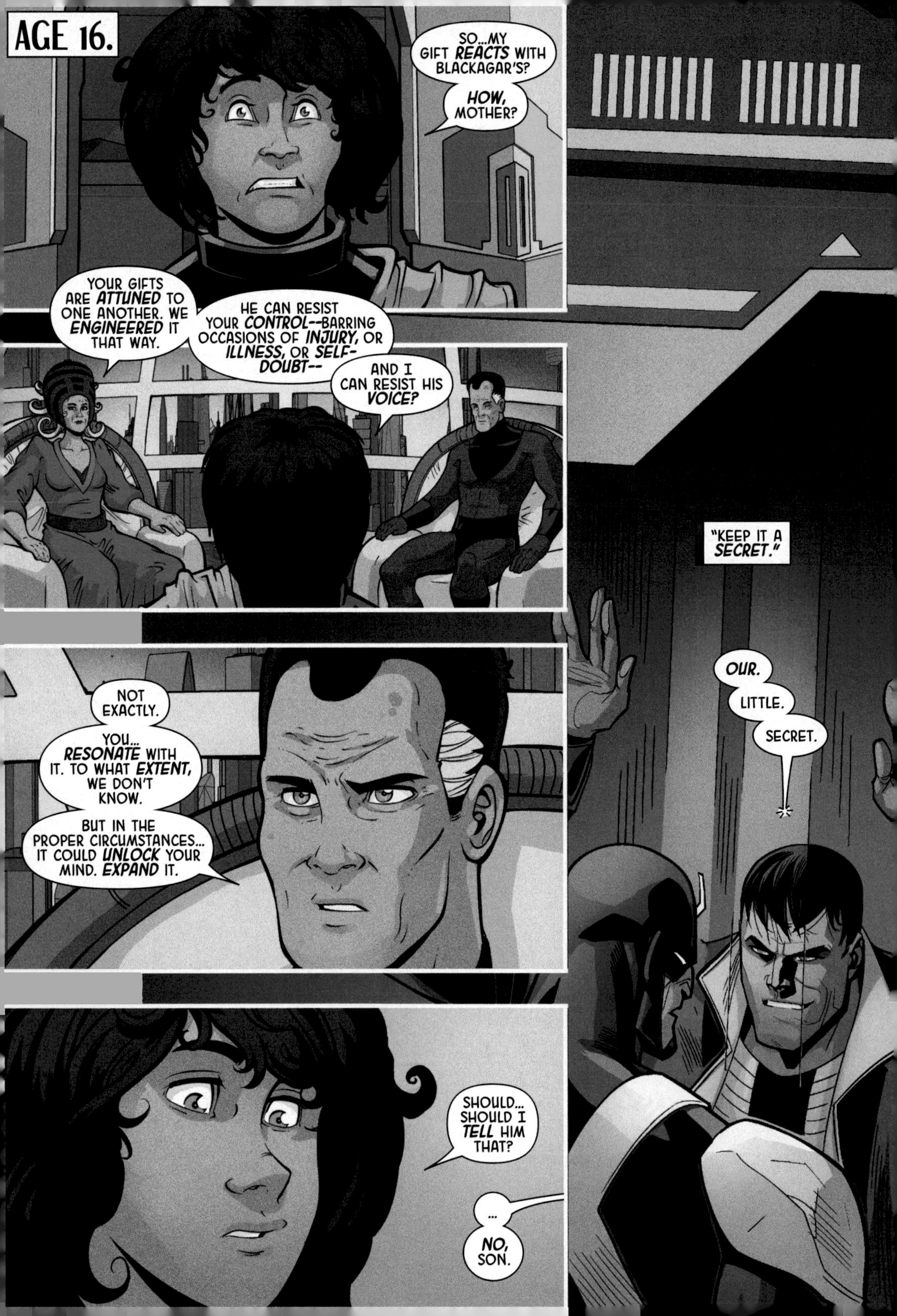
AGE 16.
SO...MY GIFT REACTS WITH BLACKAGAR'S?
HOW, MOTHER?
YOUR GIFTS ARE ATTUNED TO ONE ANOTHER. WE ENGINEERED IT THAT WAY.
HE CAN RESIST YOUR CONTROL--BARRING OCCASIONS OF INJURY, OR ILLNESS, OR SELF-DOUBT--
AND I CAN RESIST HIS VOICE?
NOT EXACTLY.
YOU... RESONATE WITH IT. TO WHAT EXTENT, WE DON'T KNOW.
BUT IN THE PROPER CIRCUMSTANCES... IT COULD UNLOCK YOUR MIND. EXPAND IT.
SHOULD... SHOULD I TELL HIM THAT?
...
NO, SON.
"KEEP IT A SECRET."
OUR.
LITTLE.
SECRET.

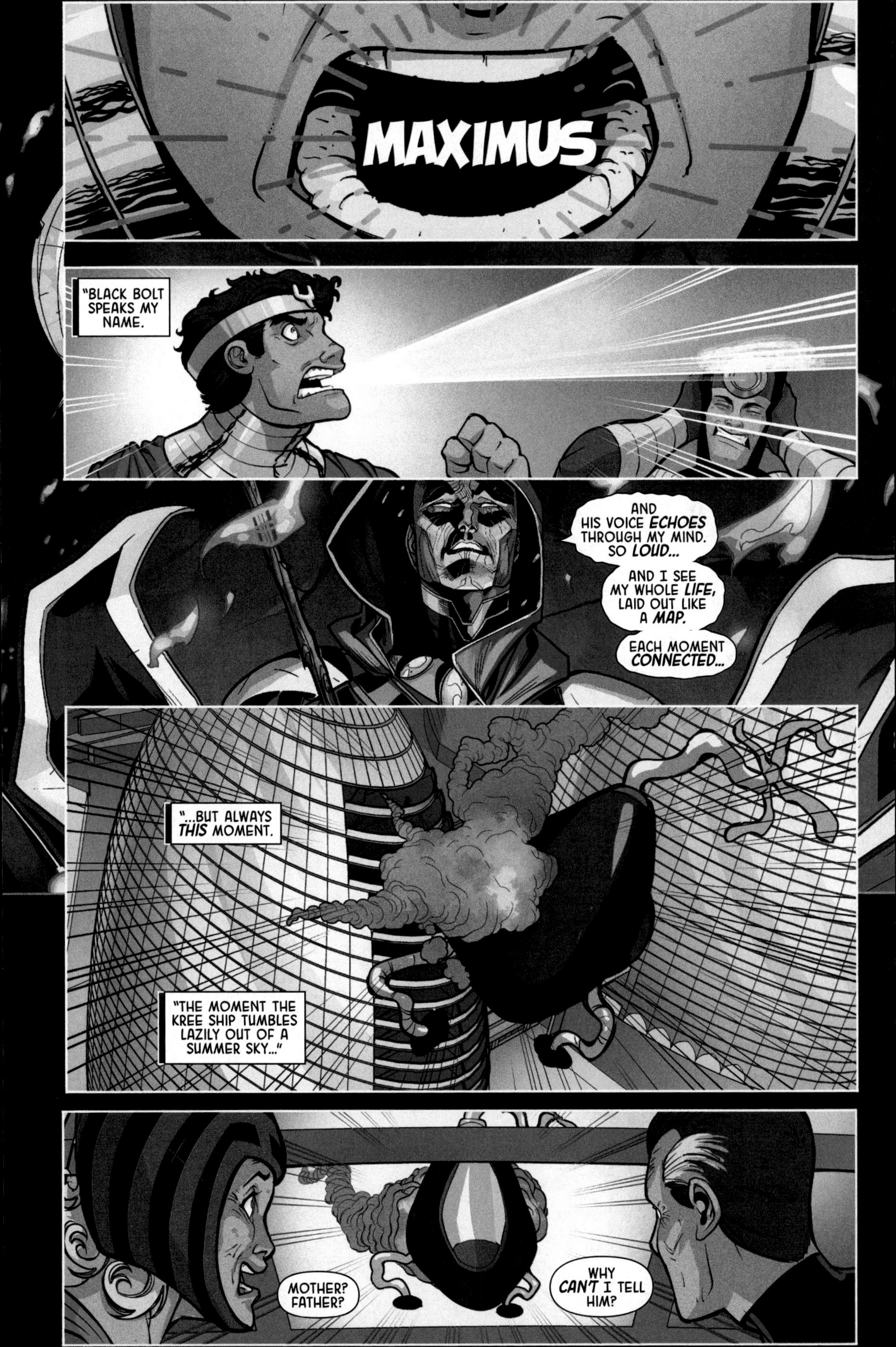
MAXIMUS
"BLACK BOLT SPEAKS MY NAME.
AND HIS VOICE ECHOES THROUGH MY MIND. SO LOUD...
AND I SEE MY WHOLE LIFE, LAID OUT LIKE A MAP.
EACH MOMENT CONNECTED...
"...BUT ALWAYS THIS MOMENT.
"THE MOMENT THE KREE SHIP TUMBLES LAZILY OUT OF A SUMMER SKY..."
MOTHER? FATHER?
WHY CAN'T I TELL HIM?

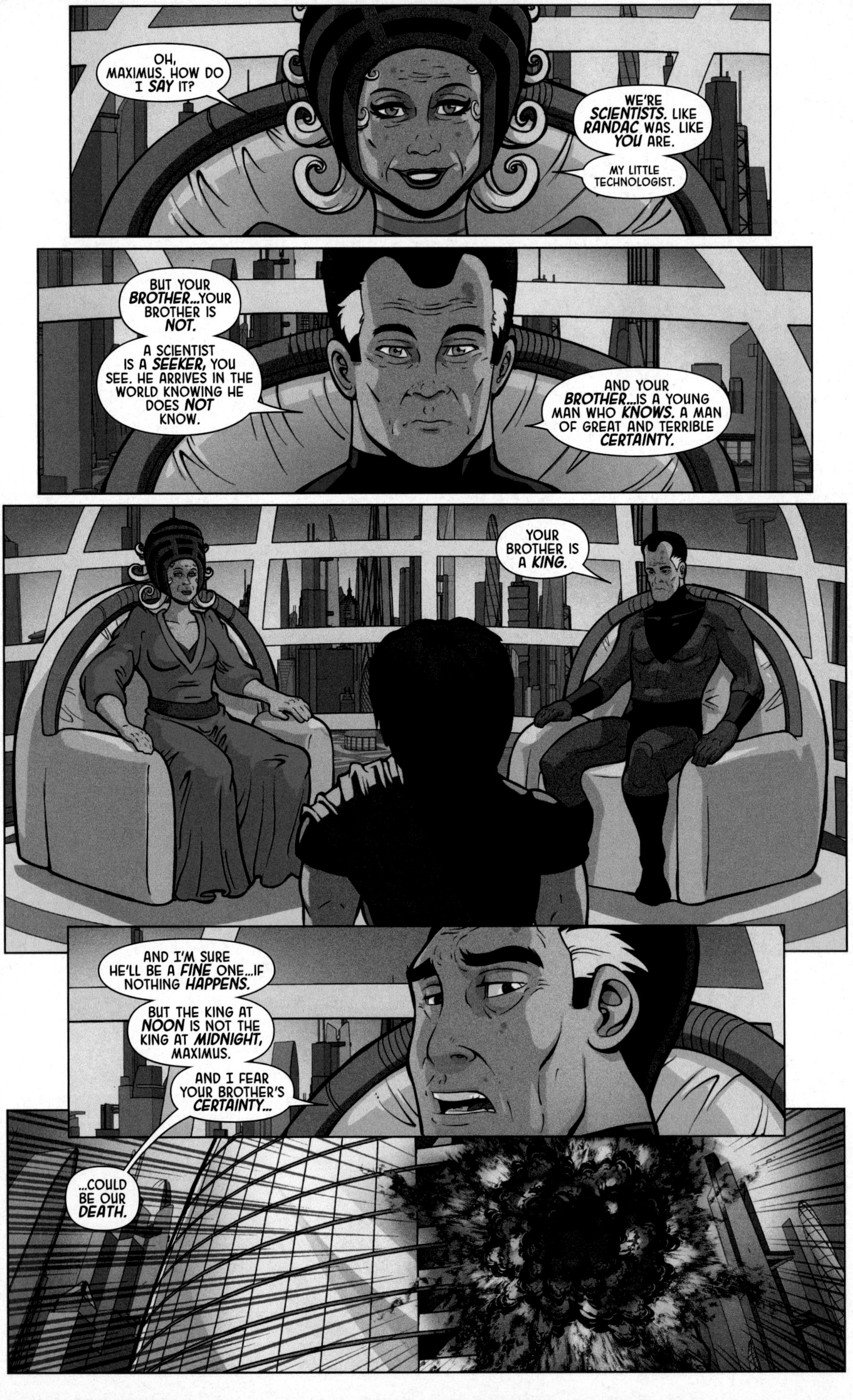
OH, MAXIMUS. HOW DO I SAY IT?
WE'RE SCIENTISTS. LIKE RANDAC WAS. LIKE YOU ARE.
MY LITTLE TECHNOLOGIST.
BUT YOUR BROTHER...YOUR BROTHER IS NOT.
A SCIENTIST IS A SEEKER, YOU SEE. HE ARRIVES IN THE WORLD KNOWING HE DOES NOT KNOW.
AND YOUR BROTHER...IS A YOUNG MAN WHO KNOWS. A MAN OF GREAT AND TERRIBLE CERTAINTY.
YOUR BROTHER IS A KING.
AND I'M SURE HE'LL BE A FINE ONE...IF NOTHING HAPPENS.
BUT THE KING AT NOON IS NOT THE KING AT MIDNIGHT, MAXIMUS.
AND I FEAR YOUR BROTHER'S CERTAINTY...
...COULD BE OUR DEATH.

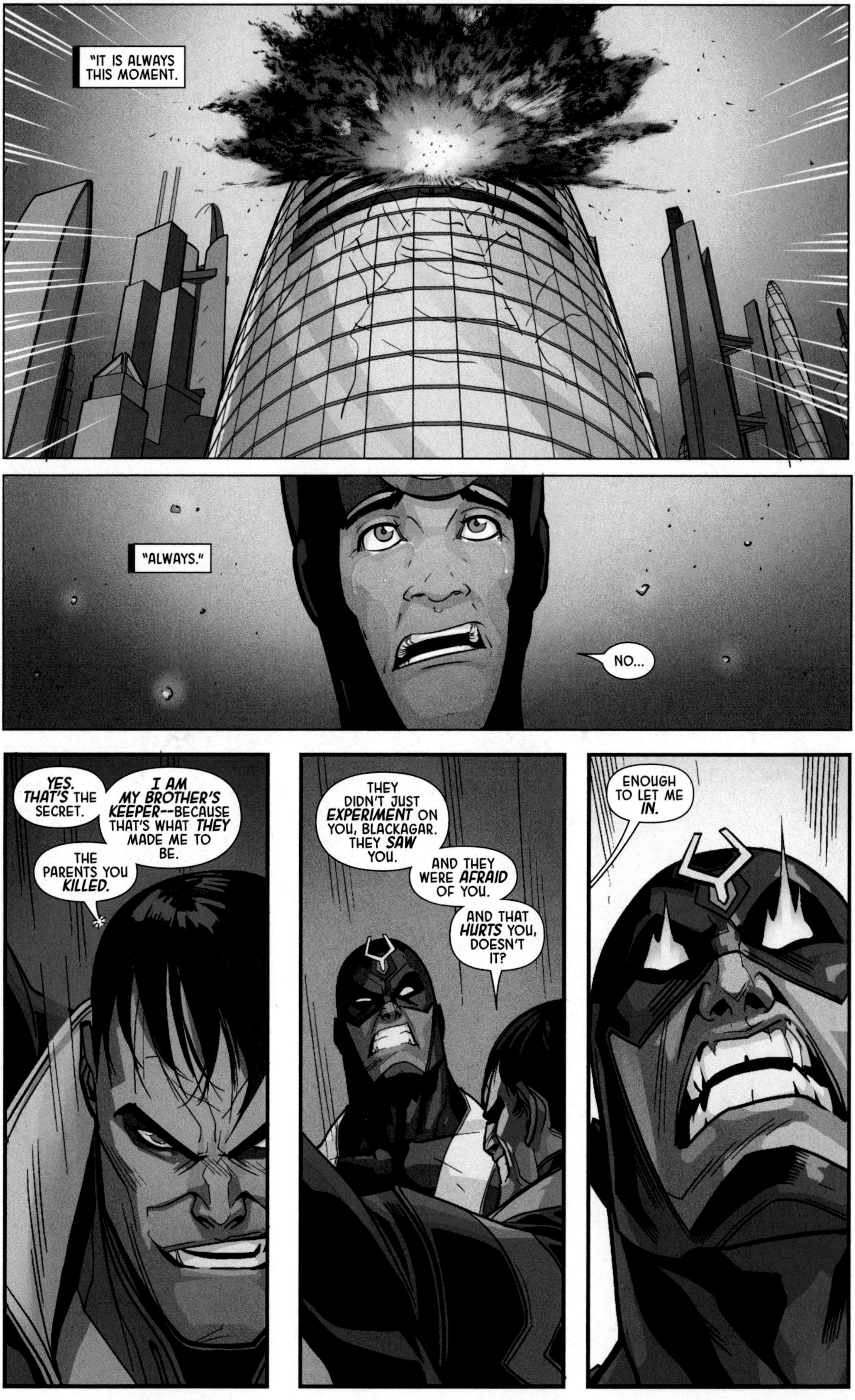
"IT IS ALWAYS THIS MOMENT.
"ALWAYS."
NO...
YES. THAT'S THE SECRET.
I AM MY BROTHER'S KEEPER--BECAUSE THAT'S WHAT THEY MADE ME TO BE.
THE PARENTS YOU KILLED.
THEY DIDN'T JUST EXPERIMENT ON YOU, BLACKAGAR. THEY SAW YOU.
AND THEY WERE AFRAID OF YOU.
AND THAT HURTS YOU, DOESN'T IT?
ENOUGH TO LET ME IN.

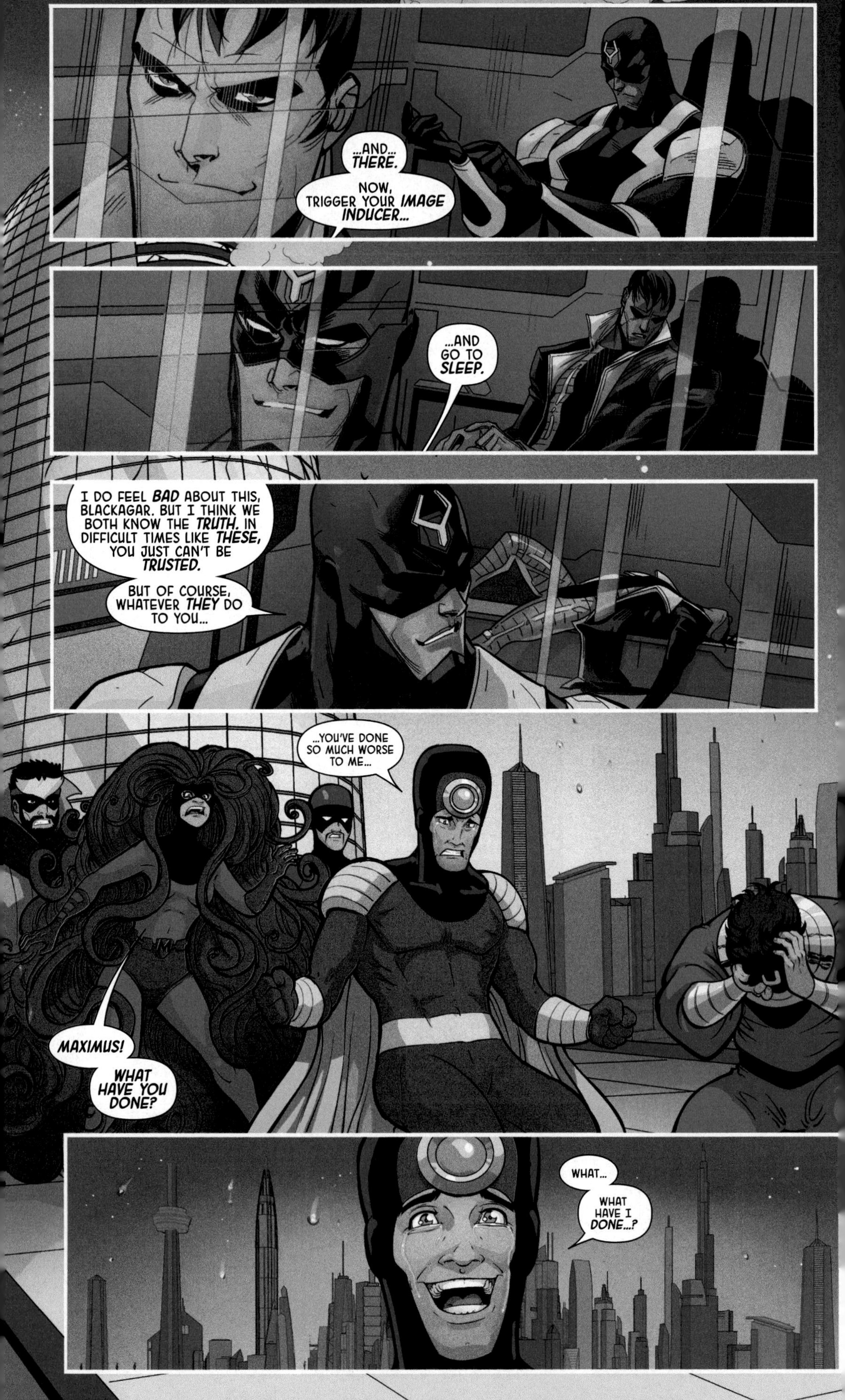

...AND... THERE.
NOW, TRIGGER YOUR IMAGE INDUCER...
...AND GO TO SLEEP.
I DO FEEL BAD ABOUT THIS, BLACKAGAR. BUT I THINK WE BOTH KNOW THE TRUTH. IN DIFFICULT TIMES LIKE THESE, YOU JUST CAN'T BE TRUSTED.
BUT OF COURSE, WHATEVER THEY DO TO YOU...
...YOU'VE DONE SO MUCH WORSE TO ME...
MAXIMUS!
WHAT HAVE YOU DONE?
WHAT...
WHAT HAVE I DONE...?

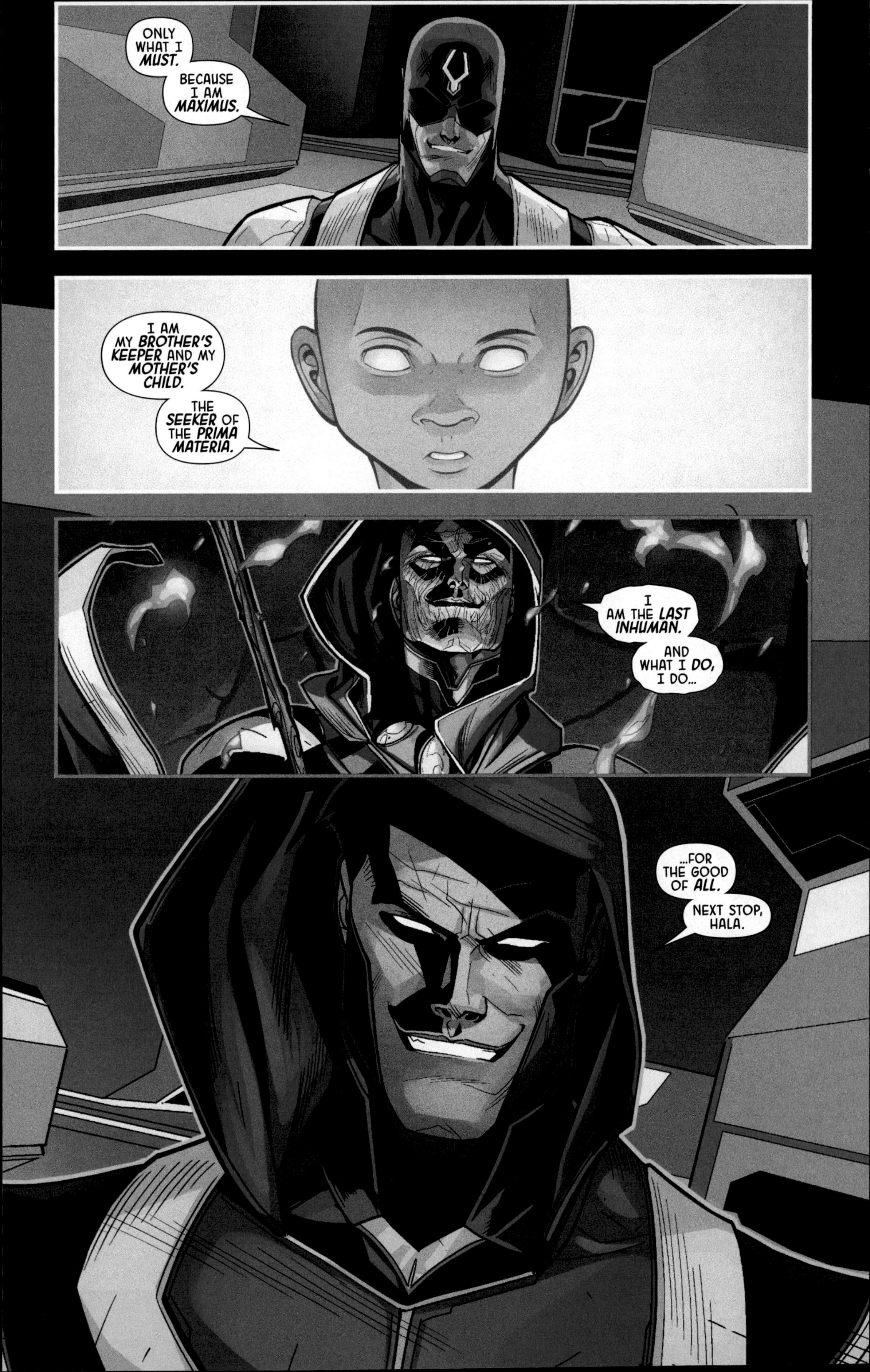
ONLY WHAT I MUST.
BECAUSE I AM MAXIMUS.
I AM MY BROTHER'S KEEPER AND MY MOTHER'S CHILD.
THE SEEKER OF THE PRIMA MATERIA.
I AM THE LAST INHUMAN.
AND WHAT I DO, I DO...
...FOR THE GOOD OF ALL.
NEXT STOP, HALA.

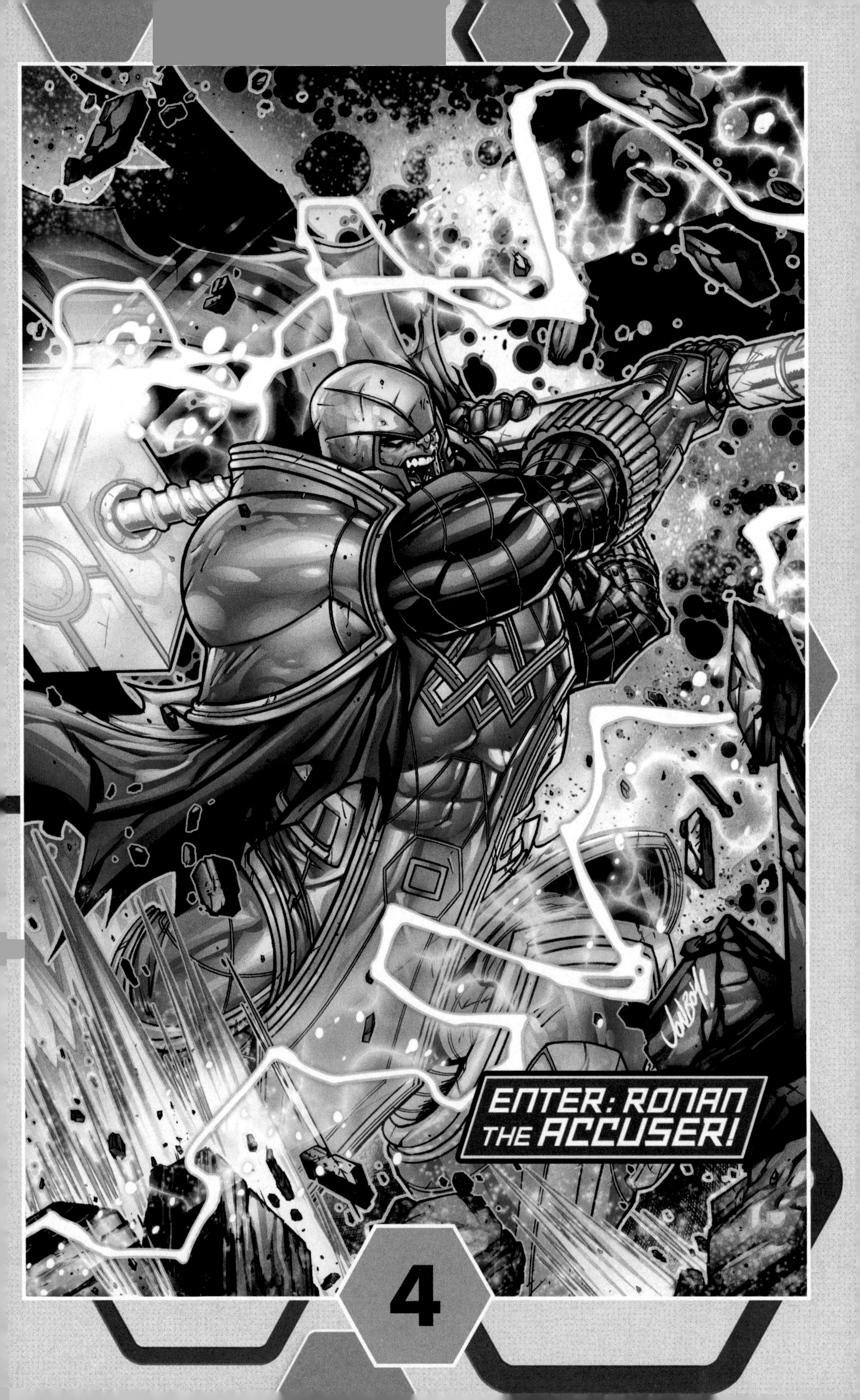
ENTER: RONAN THE ACCUSER!
4

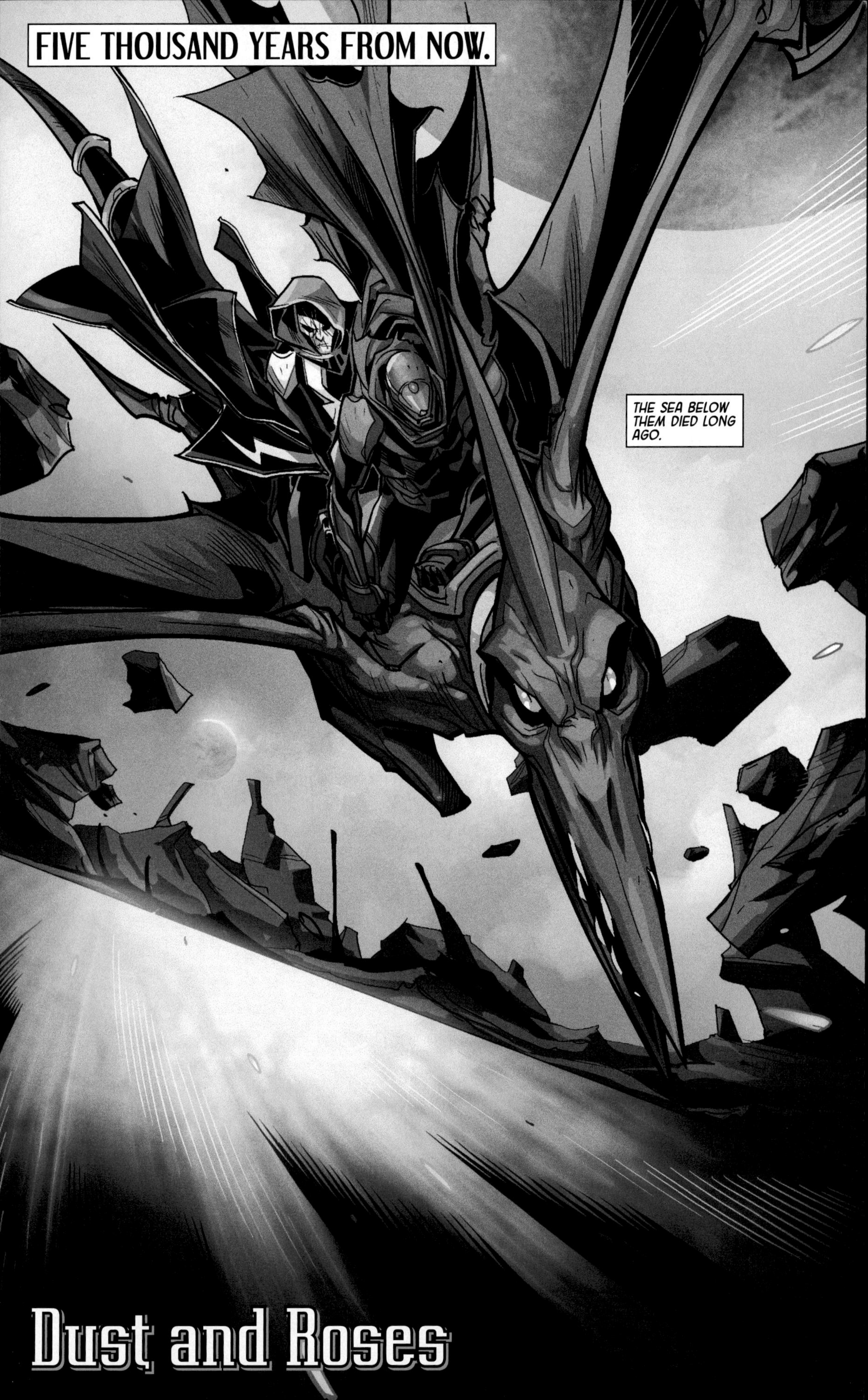
FIVE THOUSAND YEARS FROM NOW.
THE SEA BELOW THEM DIED LONG AGO.
Dust and Roses

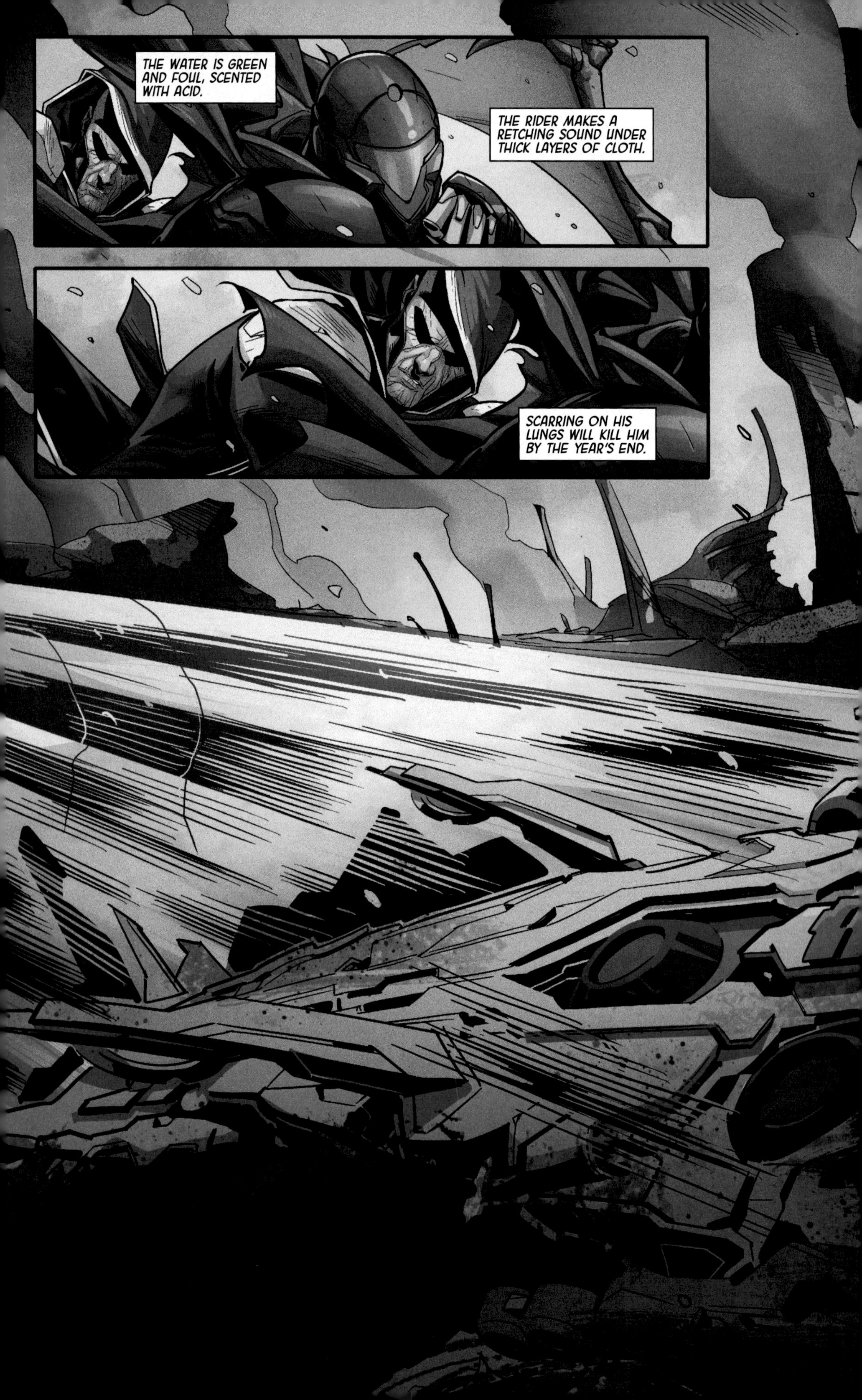
THE WATER IS GREEN AND FOUL, SCENTED WITH ACID.
THE RIDER MAKES A RETCHING SOUND UNDER THICK LAYERS OF CLOTH.
SCARRING ON HIS LUNGS WILL KILL HIM BY THE YEAR'S END.

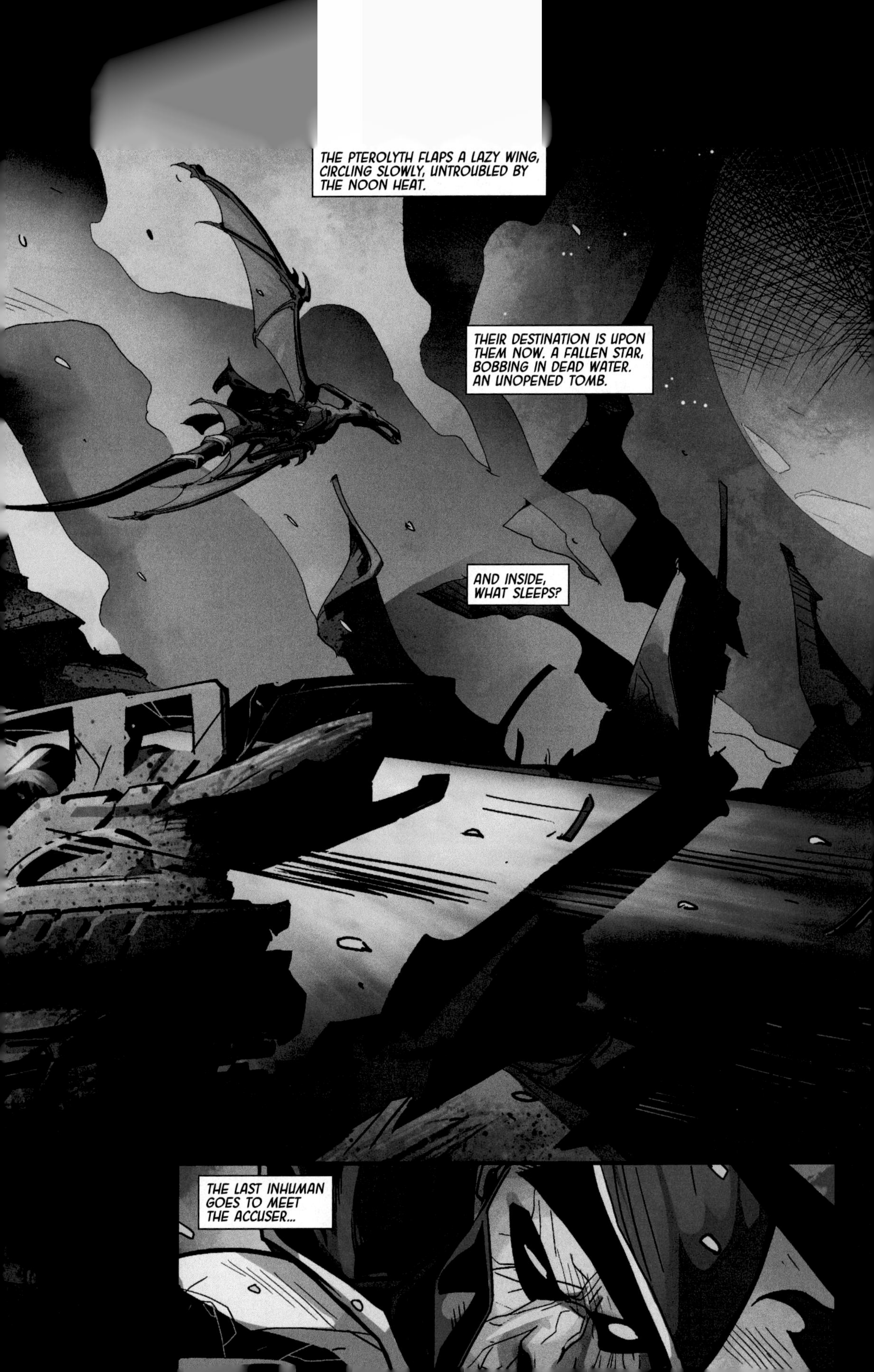
THE PTEROLYTH FLAPS A LAZY WING, CIRCLING SLOWLY, UNTROUBLED BY THE NOON HEAT.
THEIR DESTINATION IS UPON THEM NOW. A FALLEN STAR, BOBBING IN DEAD WATER. AN UNOPENED TOMB.
AND INSIDE, WHAT SLEEPS?
THE LAST INHUMAN GOES TO MEET THE ACCUSER...

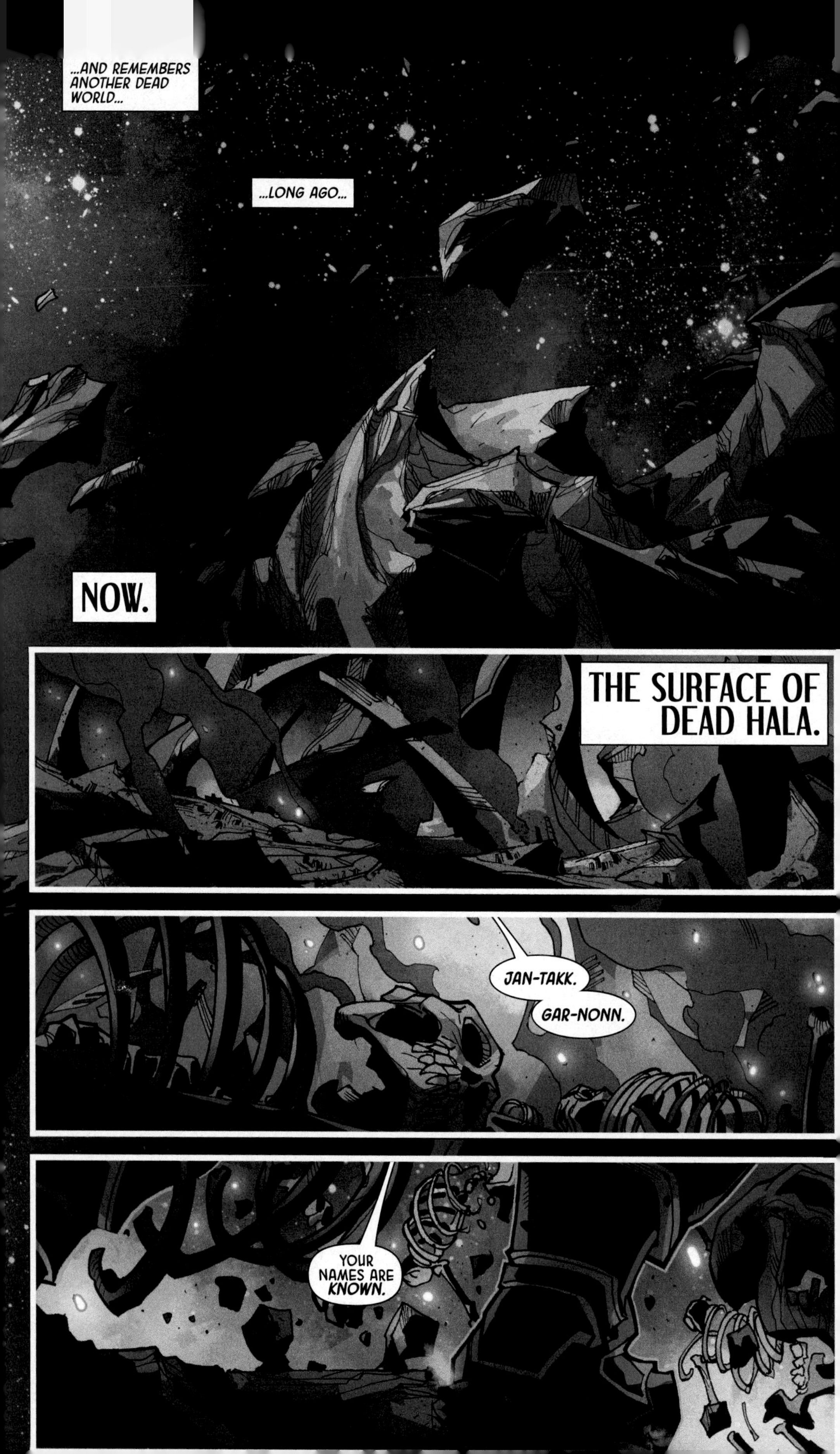

...AND REMEMBERS ANOTHER DEAD WORLD...
...LONG AGO...
NOW.
THE SURFACE OF DEAD HALA.
JAN-TAKK.
GAR-NONN.
YOUR NAMES ARE KNOWN.

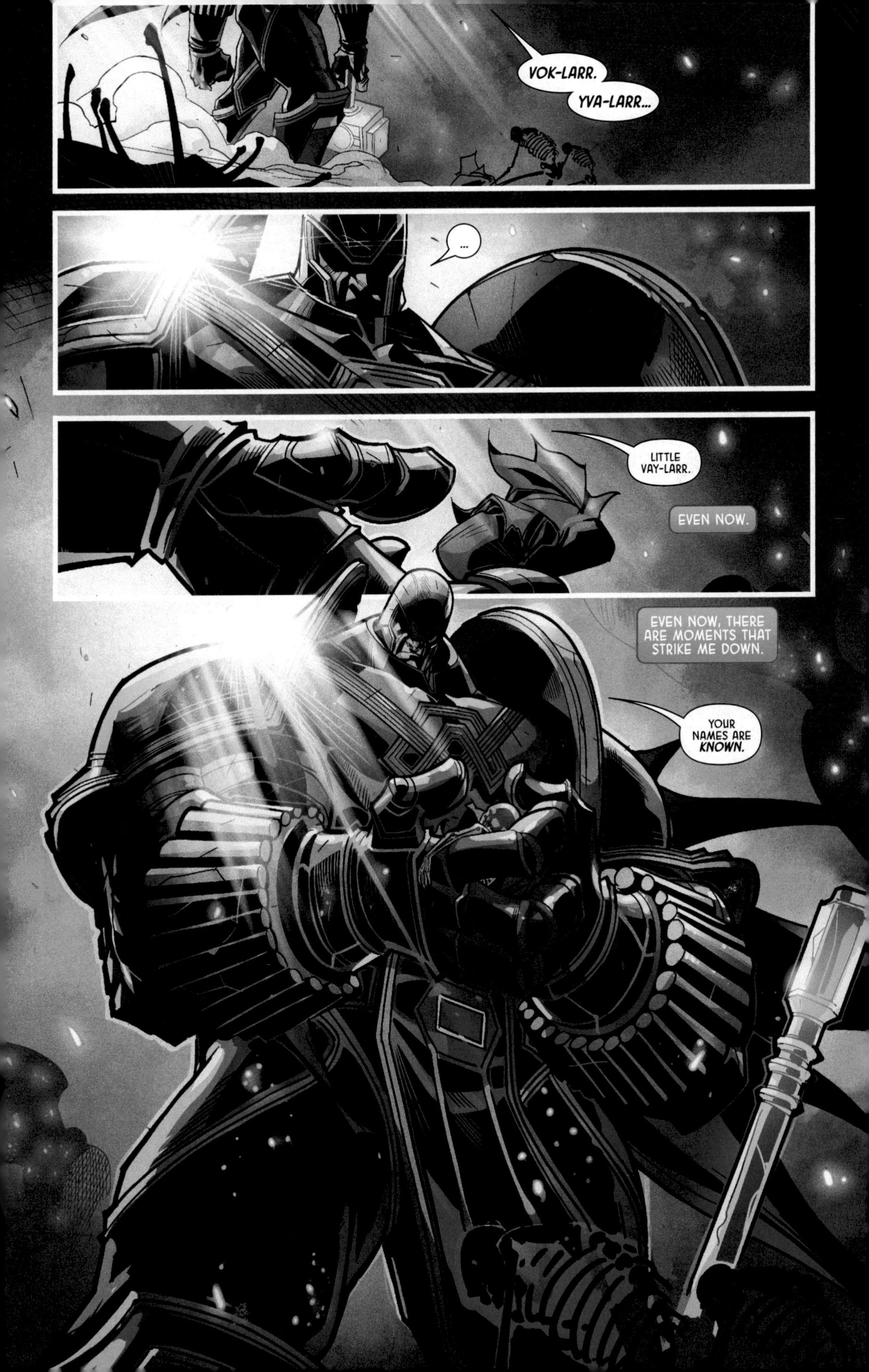
VOK-LARR.
YVA-LARR...
...
LITTLE VAY-LARR.
EVEN NOW.
EVEN NOW, THERE ARE MOMENTS THAT STRIKE ME DOWN.
YOUR NAMES ARE KNOWN.

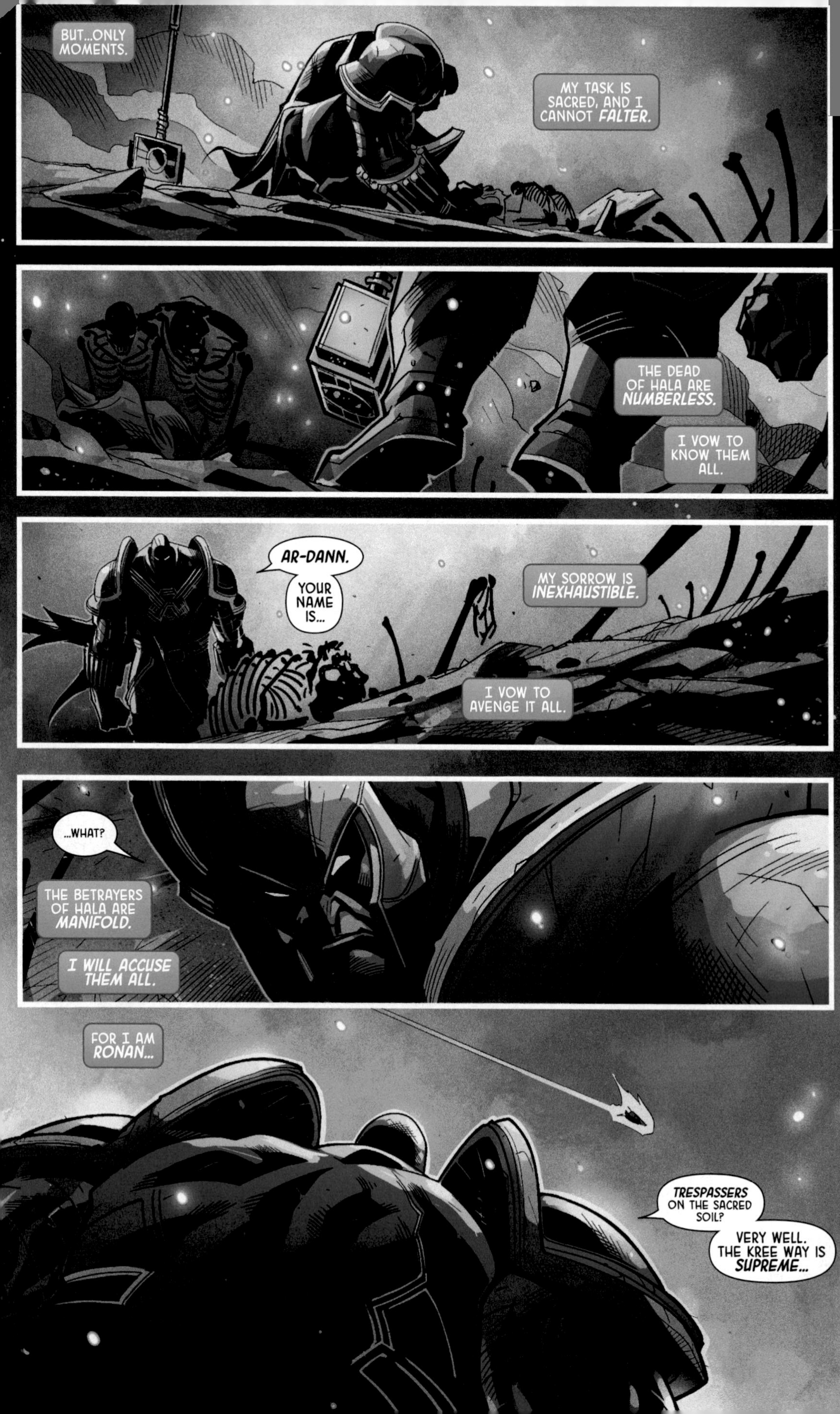
BUT...ONLY MOMENTS.
MY TASK IS SACRED, AND I CANNOT FALTER.
THE DEAD OF HALA ARE NUMBERLESS.
I VOW TO KNOW THEM ALL.
AR-DANN.
YOUR NAME IS...
MY SORROW IS INEXHAUSTIBLE.
I VOW TO AVENGE IT ALL.
...WHAT?
THE BETRAYERS OF HALA ARE MANIFOLD.
I WILL ACCUSE THEM ALL.
FOR I AM RONAN...
TRESPASSERS ON THE SACRED SOIL?
VERY WELL. THE KREE WAY IS SUPREME...

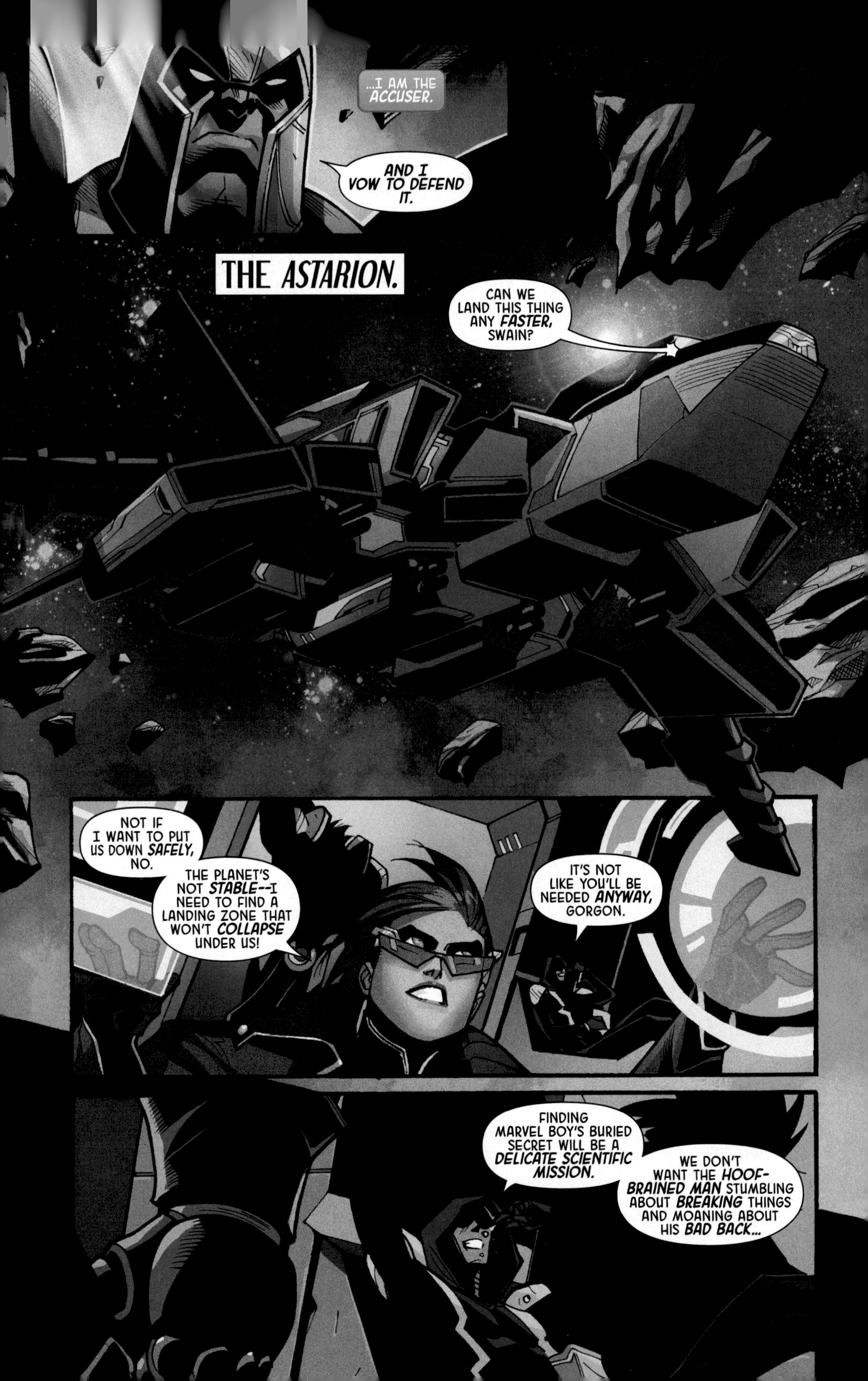
...I AM THE ACCUSER.
AND I VOW TO DEFEND IT.
THE ASTARION.
CAN WE LAND THIS THING ANY FASTER, SWAIN?
NOT IF I WANT TO PUT US DOWN SAFELY, NO.
THE PLANET'S NOT STABLE--I NEED TO FIND A LANDING ZONE THAT WON'T COLLAPSE UNDER US!
IT'S NOT LIKE YOU'LL BE NEEDED ANYWAY, GORGON.
FINDING MARVEL BOY'S BURIED SECRET WILL BE A DELICATE SCIENTIFIC MISSION.
WE DON'T WANT THE HOOF-BRAINED MAN STUMBLING ABOUT BREAKING THINGS AND MOANING ABOUT HIS BAD BACK...

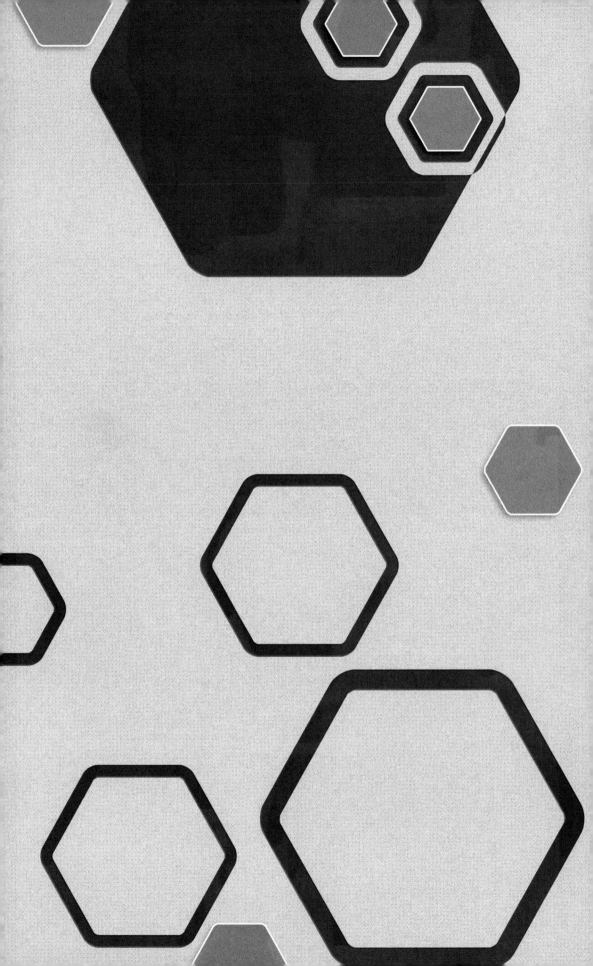

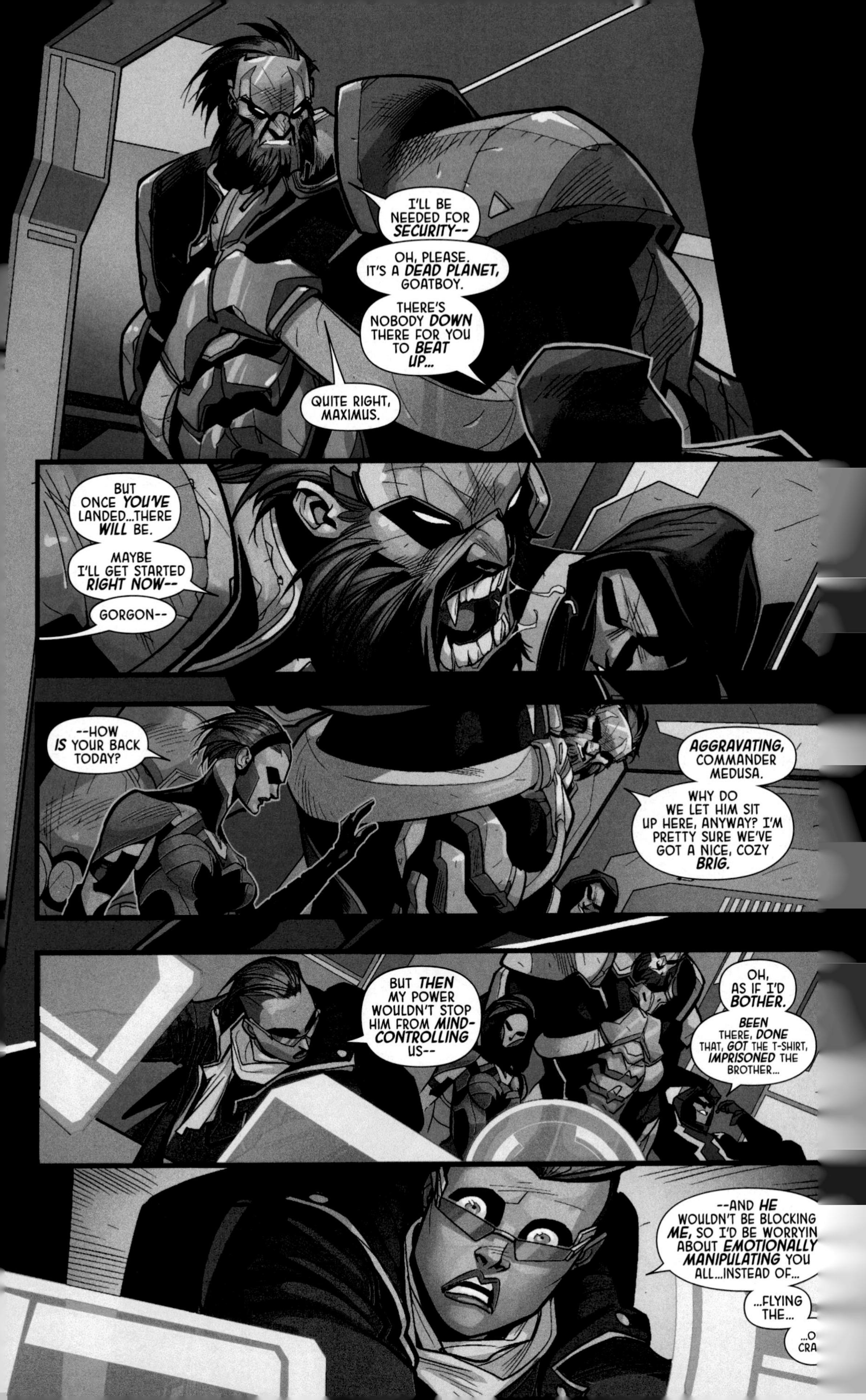
I'LL BE NEEDED FOR SECURITY--
OH, PLEASE. IT'S A DEAD PLANET, GOATBOY.
THERE'S NOBODY DOWN THERE FOR YOU TO BEAT UP...
QUITE RIGHT, MAXIMUS.
BUT ONCE YOU'VE LANDED...THERE WILL BE.
MAYBE I'LL GET STARTED RIGHT NOW--
GORGON--
--HOW IS YOUR BACK TODAY?
AGGRAVATING, COMMANDER MEDUSA.
WHY DO WE LET HIM SIT UP HERE, ANYWAY? I'M PRETTY SURE WE'VE GOT A NICE, COZY BRIG.
BUT THEN MY POWER WOULDN'T STOP HIM FROM MIND-CONTROLLING US--
OH, AS IF I'D BOTHER.
BEEN THERE, DONE THAT, GOT THE T-SHIRT, IMPRISONED THE BROTHER...
--AND HE WOULDN'T BE BLOCKING ME, SO I'D BE WORRYIN ABOUT EMOTIONALLY MANIPULATING YOU ALL...INSTEAD OF...
...FLYING THE...
...O CRA

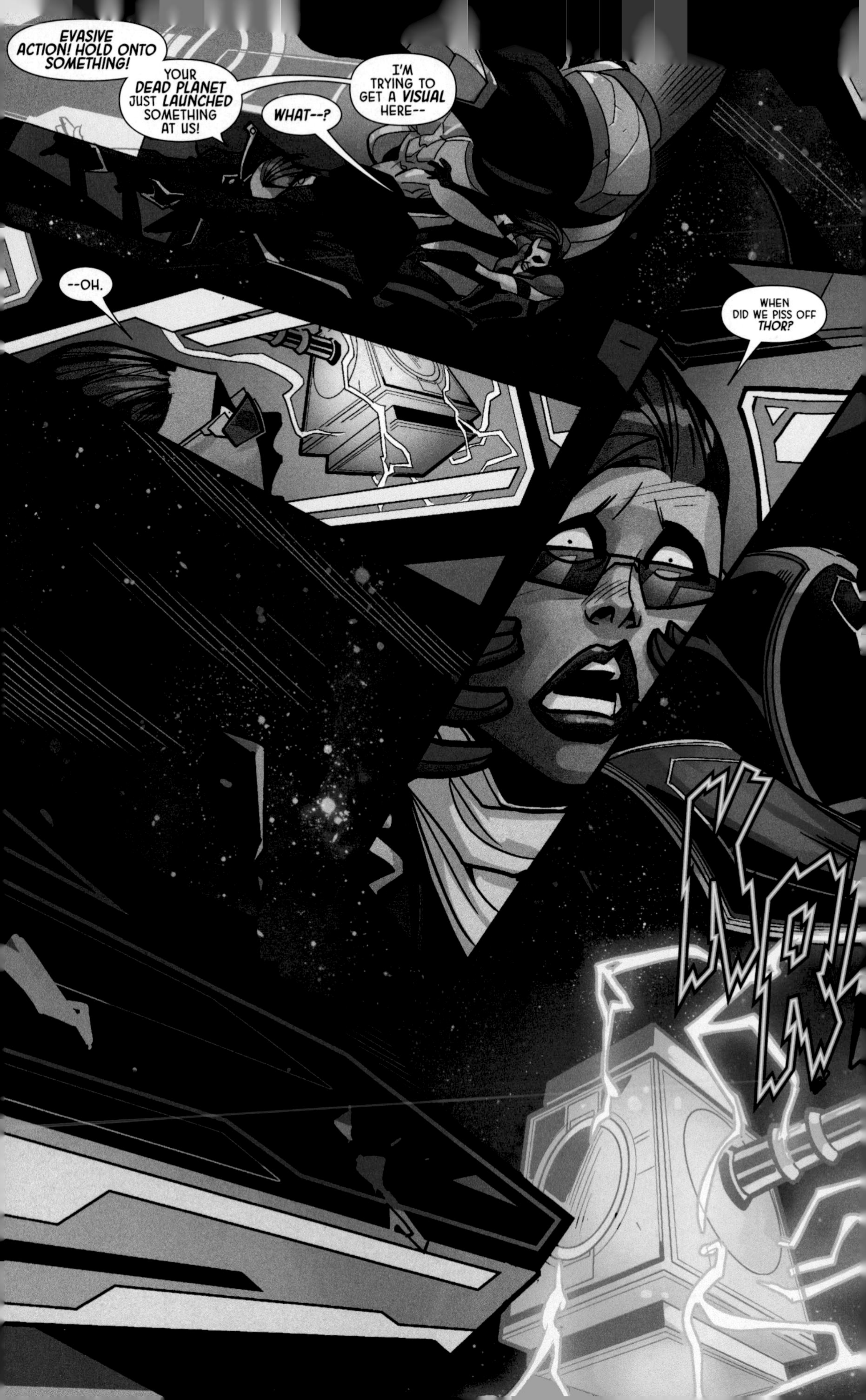
EVASIVE ACTION! HOLD ONTO SOMETHING!
YOUR DEAD PLANET JUST LAUNCHED SOMETHING AT US!
WHAT--?
I'M TRYING TO GET A VISUAL HERE--
--OH.
WHEN DID WE PISS OFF THOR?

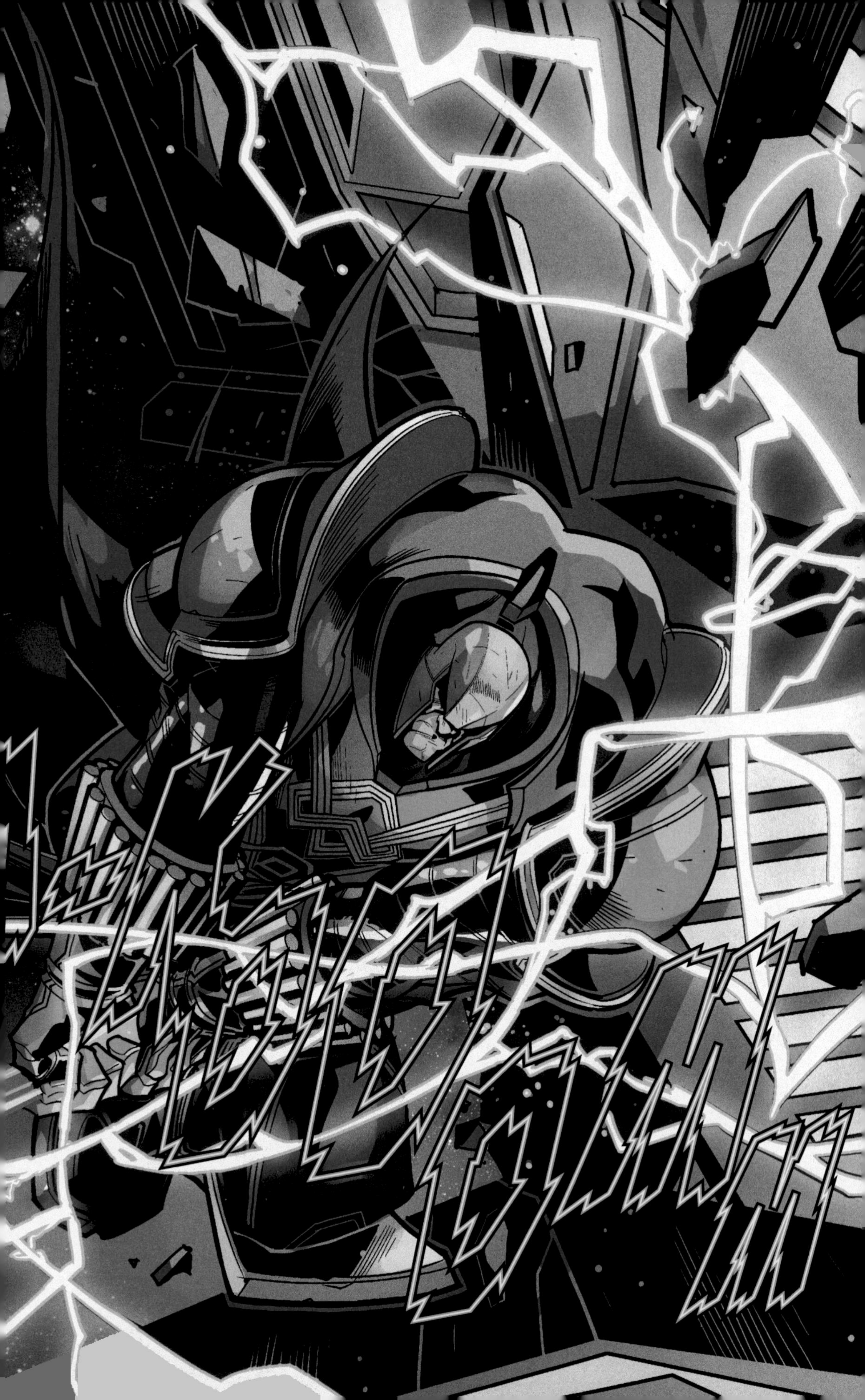

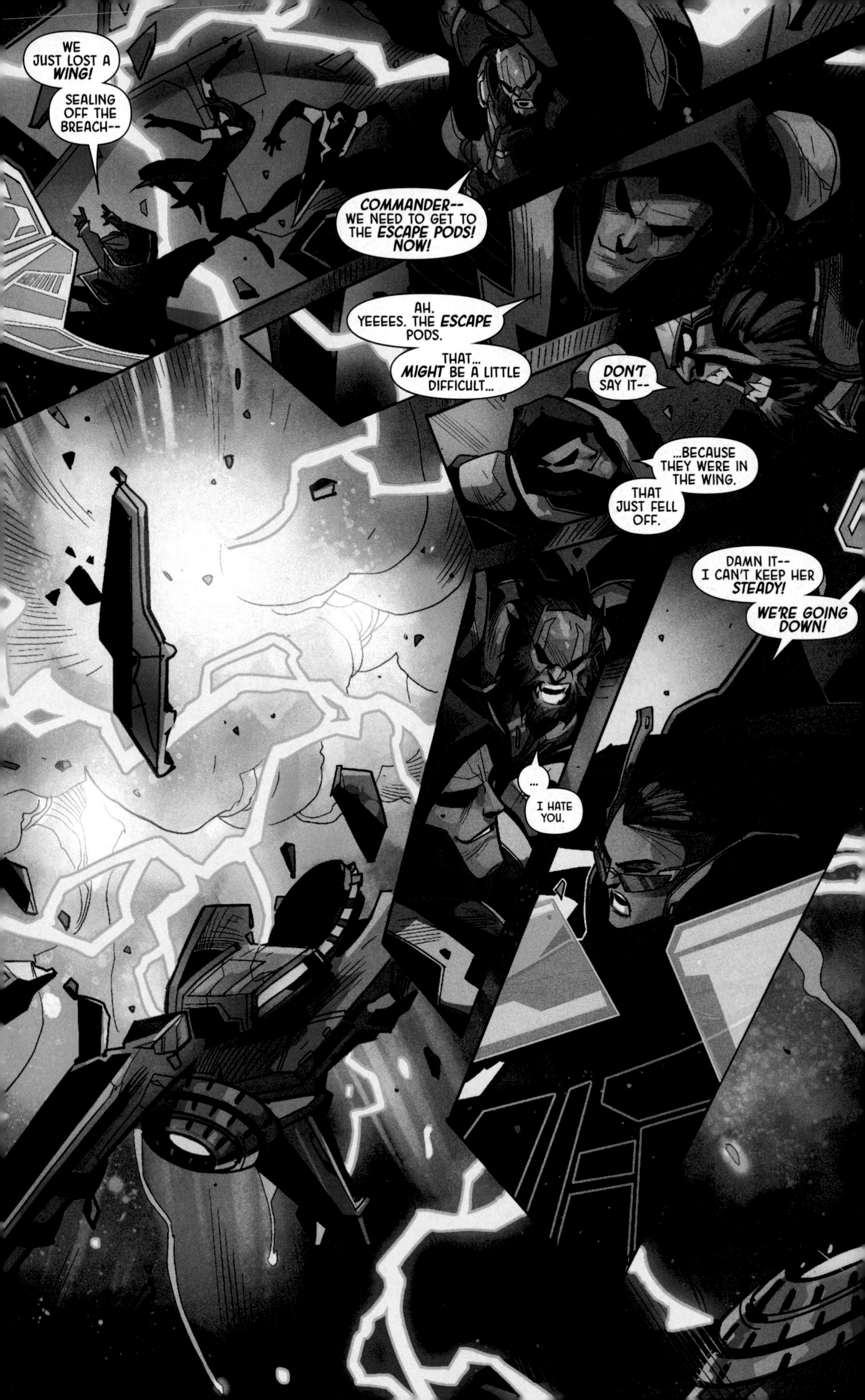
WE JUST LOST A WING!
SEALING OFF THE BREACH--
COMMANDER-- WE NEED TO GET TO THE ESCAPE PODS! NOW!
AH. YEEEES. THE ESCAPE PODS.
THAT... MIGHT BE A LITTLE DIFFICULT...
DON'T SAY IT--
...BECAUSE THEY WERE IN THE WING.
THAT JUST FELL OFF.
DAMN IT-- I CAN'T KEEP HER STEADY!
WE'RE GOING DOWN!
...
I HATE YOU.

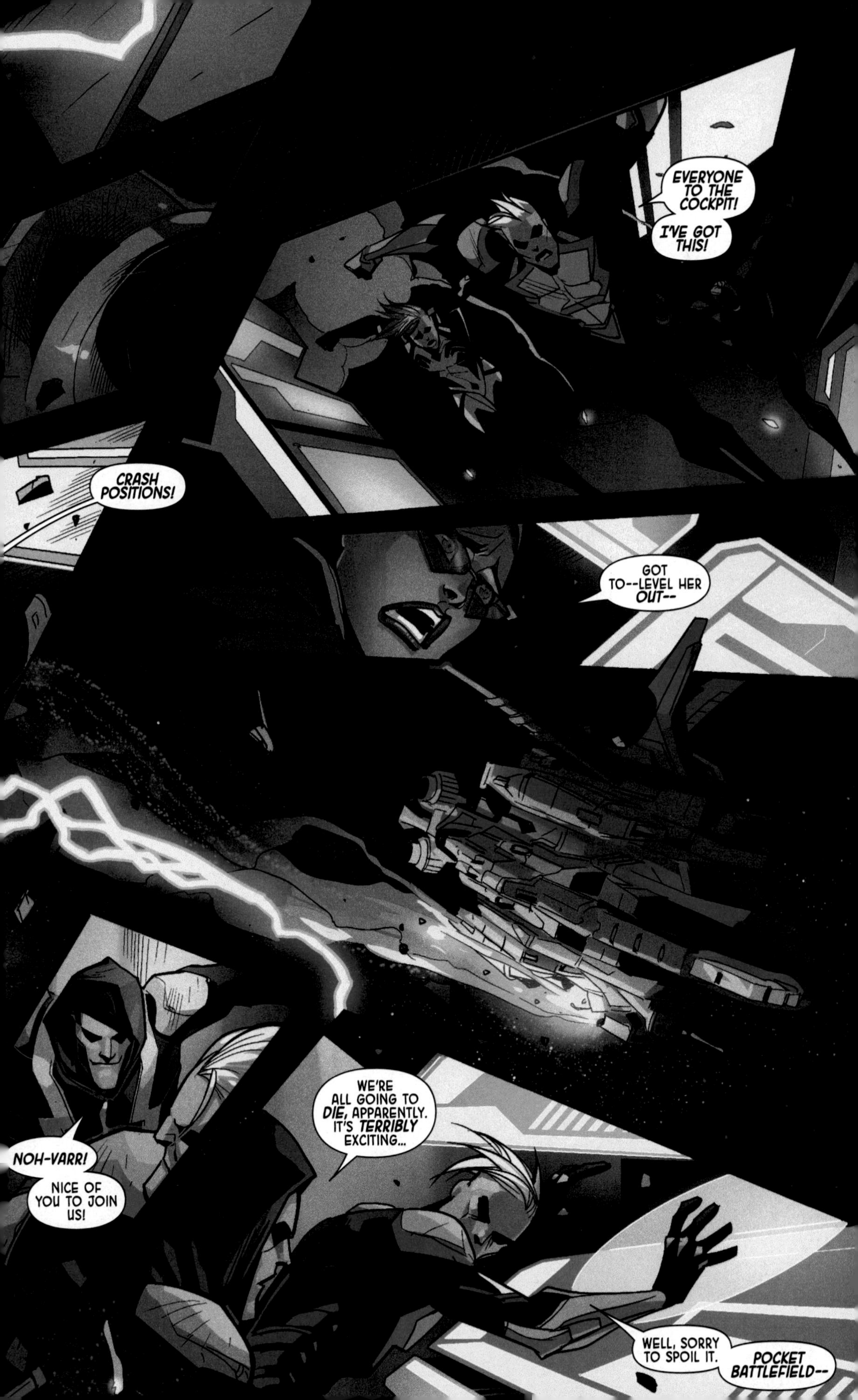
EVERYONE TO THE COCKPIT!
I'VE GOT THIS!
CRASH POSITIONS!
GOT TO--LEVEL HER OUT--
WE'RE ALL GOING TO DIE, APPARENTLY. IT'S TERRIBLY EXCITING...
NOH-VARR!
NICE OF YOU TO JOIN US!
WELL, SORRY TO SPOIL IT.
POCKET BATTLEFIELD--

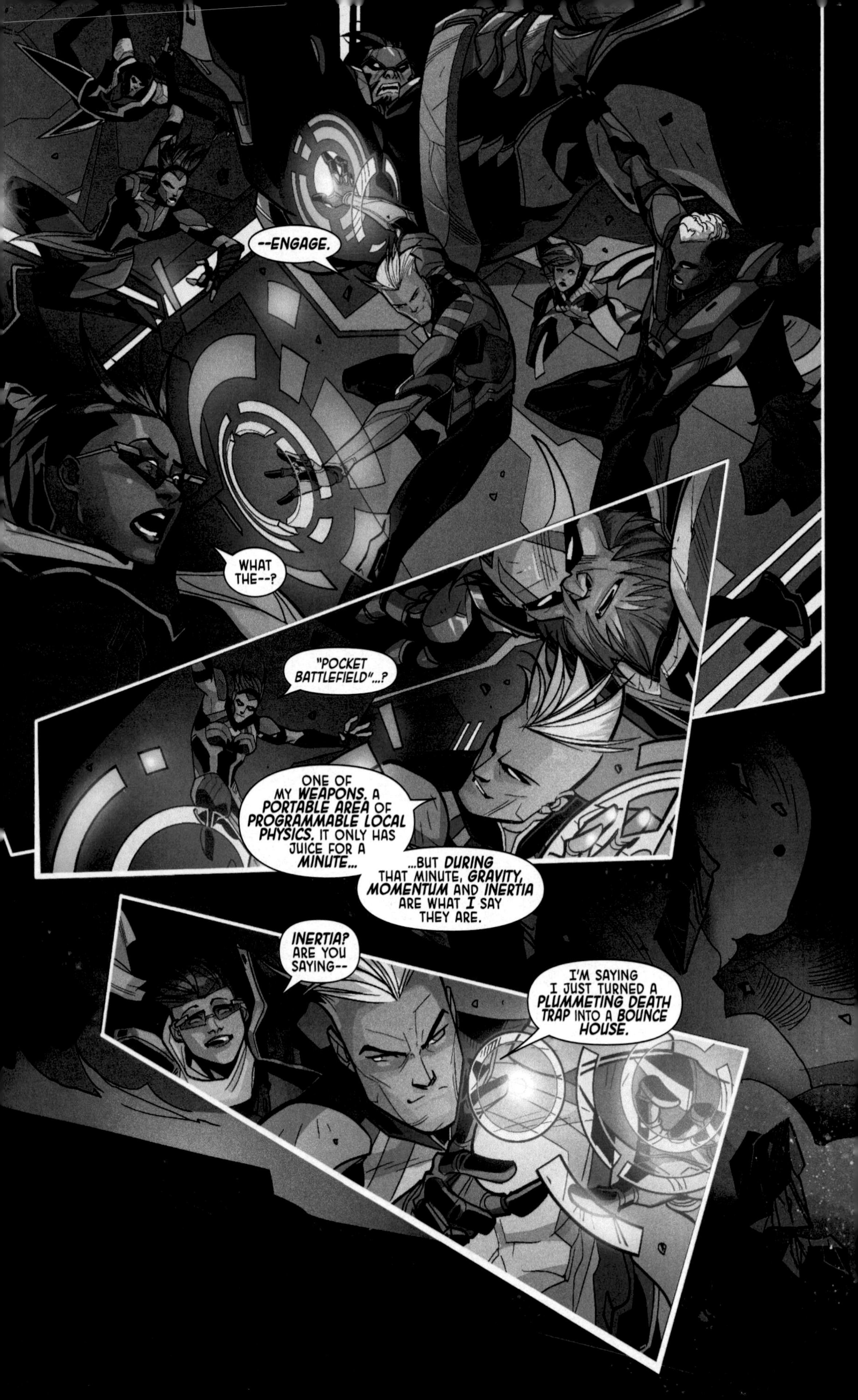
--ENGAGE.
WHAT THE--?
"POCKET BATTLEFIELD"...?
ONE OF MY WEAPONS. A PORTABLE AREA OF PROGRAMMABLE LOCAL PHYSICS. IT ONLY HAS JUICE FOR A MINUTE...
...BUT DURING THAT MINUTE, GRAVITY, MOMENTUM AND INERTIA ARE WHAT I SAY THEY ARE.
INERTIA? ARE YOU SAYING--
I'M SAYING I JUST TURNED A PLUMMETING DEATH TRAP INTO A BOUNCE HOUSE.

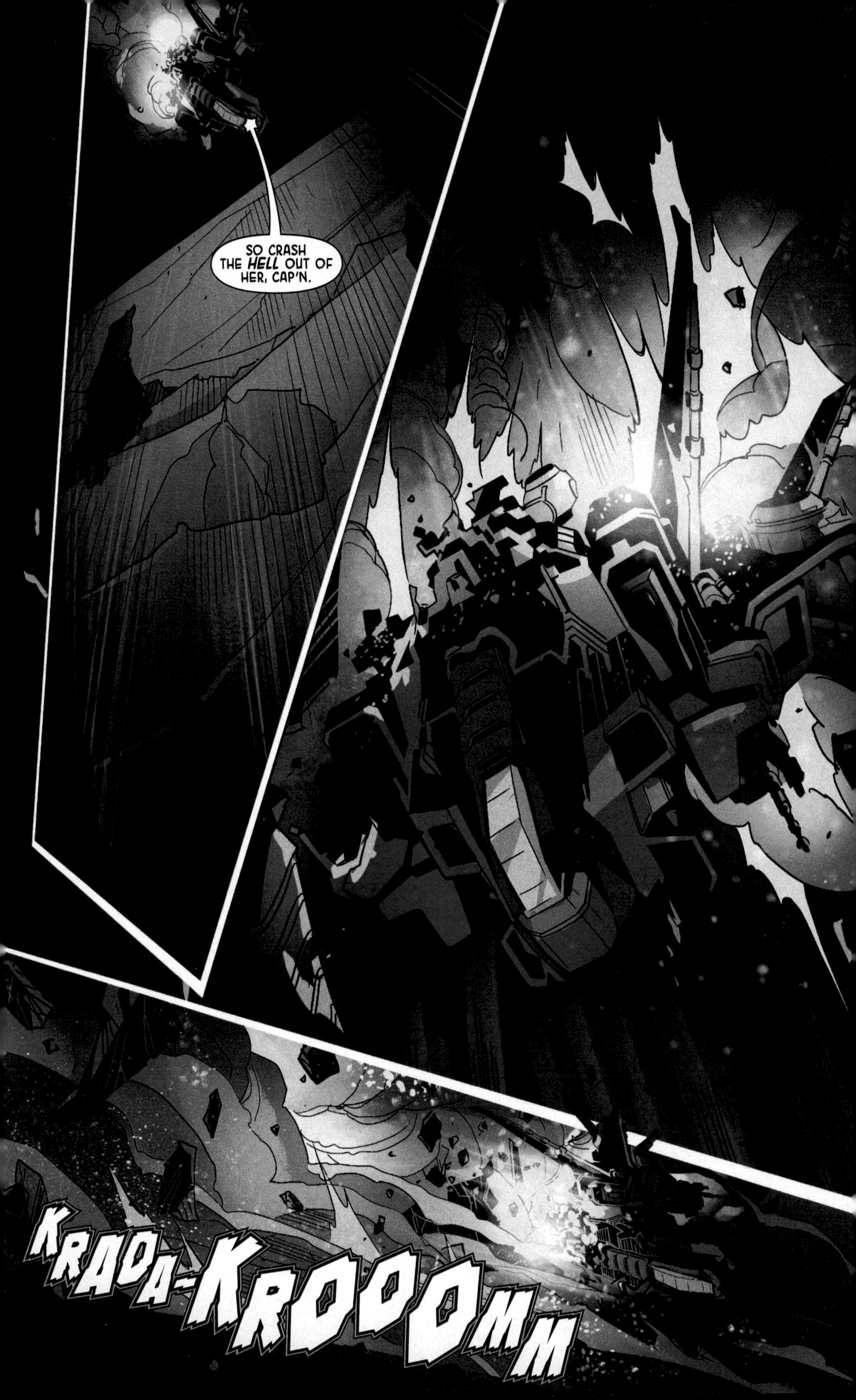
SO CRASH THE HELL OUT OF HER, CAP'N.
KRADA-KROOOMM

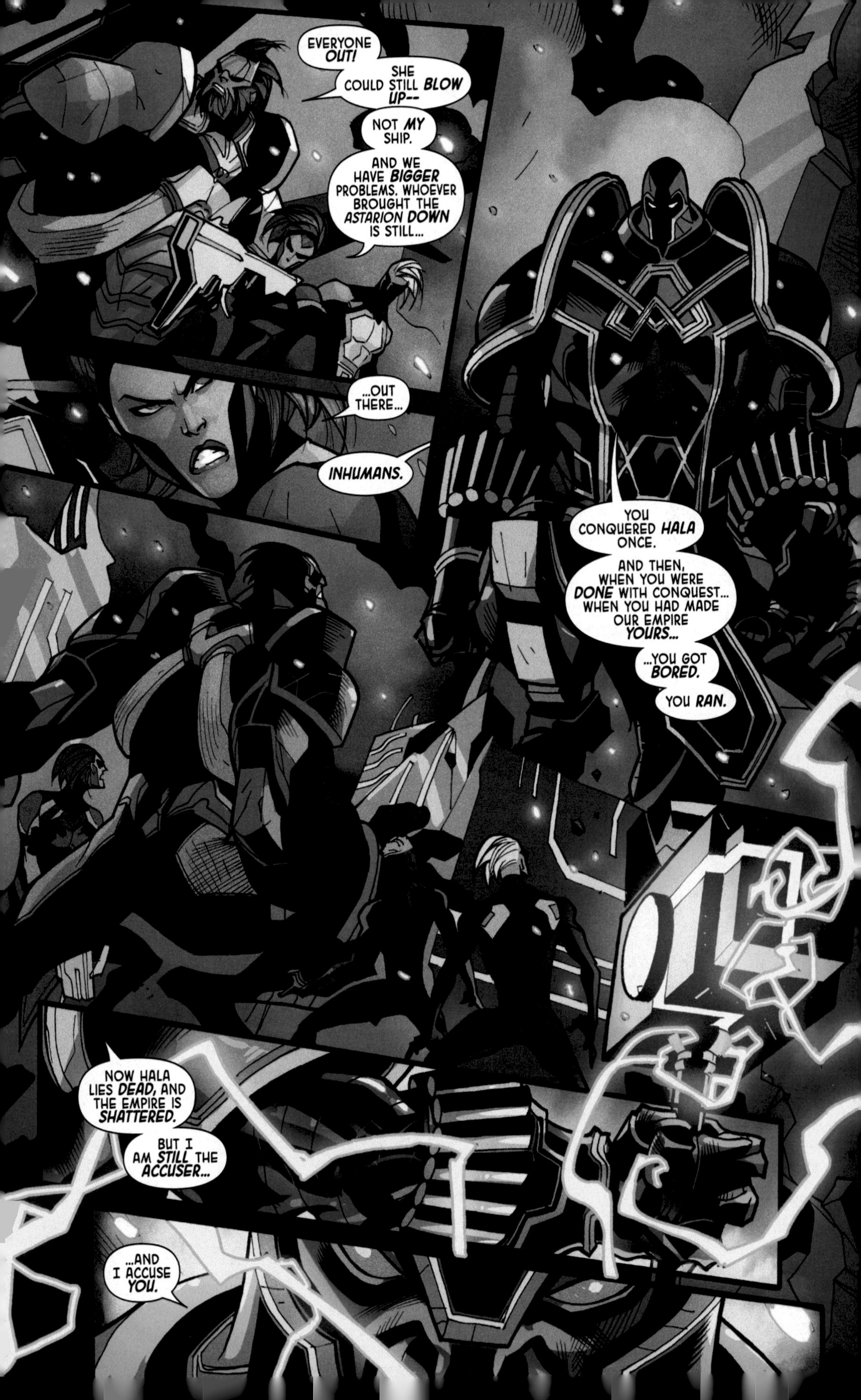
EVERYONE OUT!
SHE COULD STILL BLOW UP--
NOT MY SHIP.
AND WE HAVE BIGGER PROBLEMS. WHOEVER BROUGHT THE ASTARION DOWN IS STILL...
...OUT THERE...
INHUMANS.
YOU CONQUERED HALA ONCE.
AND THEN, WHEN YOU WERE DONE WITH CONQUEST... WHEN YOU HAD MADE OUR EMPIRE YOURS...
...YOU GOT BORED.
YOU RAN.
NOW HALA LIES DEAD, AND THE EMPIRE IS SHATTERED.
BUT I AM STILL THE ACCUSER...
...AND I ACCUSE YOU.

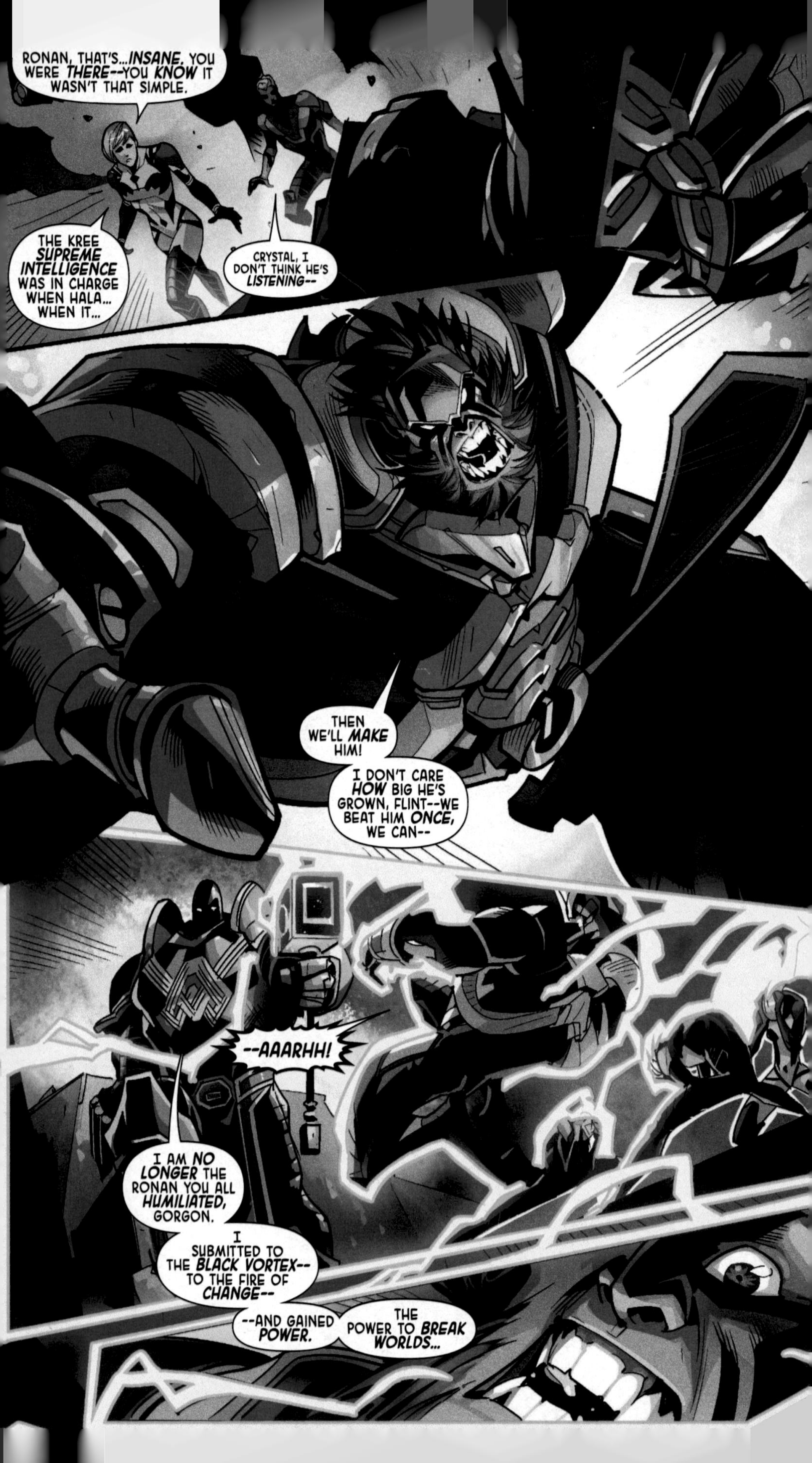
RONAN, THAT'S...INSANE. YOU WERE THERE--YOU KNOW IT WASN'T THAT SIMPLE.
THE KREE SUPREME INTELLIGENCE WAS IN CHARGE WHEN HALA... WHEN IT...
CRYSTAL, I DON'T THINK HE'S LISTENING--
THEN WE'LL MAKE HIM!
I DON'T CARE HOW BIG HE'S GROWN, FLINT--WE BEAT HIM ONCE, WE CAN--
--AAARHH!
I AM NO LONGER THE RONAN YOU ALL HUMILIATED, GORGON.
I SUBMITTED TO THE BLACK VORTEX--TO THE FIRE OF CHANGE--
--AND GAINED POWER.
THE POWER TO BREAK WORLDS...

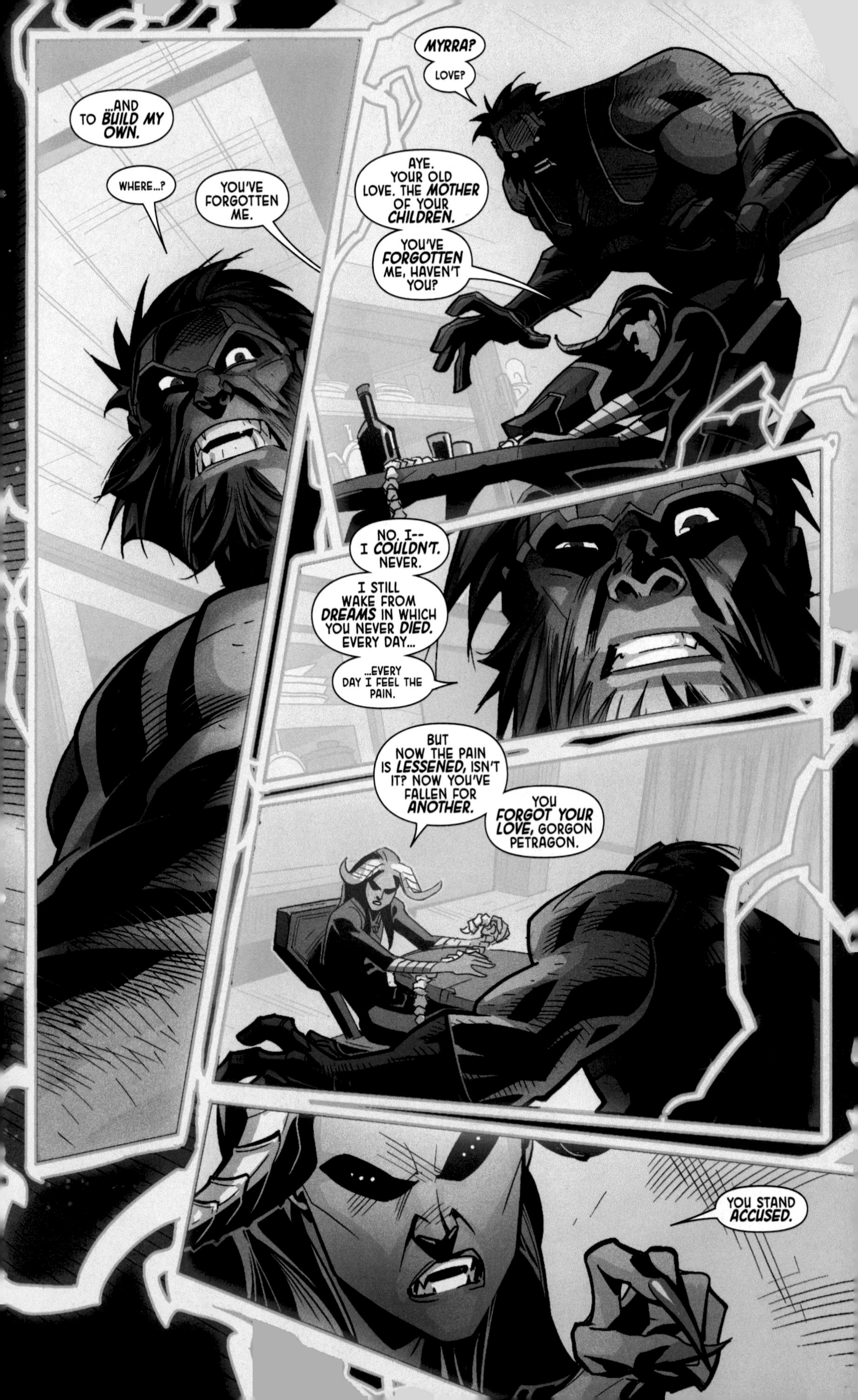
...AND TO BUILD MY OWN.
WHERE...?
YOU'VE FORGOTTEN ME.
MYRRA?
LOVE?
AYE. YOUR OLD LOVE. THE MOTHER OF YOUR CHILDREN.
YOU'VE FORGOTTEN ME, HAVEN'T YOU?
NO. I-- I COULDN'T. NEVER.
I STILL WAKE FROM DREAMS IN WHICH YOU NEVER DIED. EVERY DAY...
...EVERY DAY I FEEL THE PAIN.
BUT NOW THE PAIN IS LESSENED, ISN'T IT? NOW YOU'VE FALLEN FOR ANOTHER.
YOU FORGOT YOUR LOVE, GORGON PETRAGON.
YOU STAND ACCUSED.

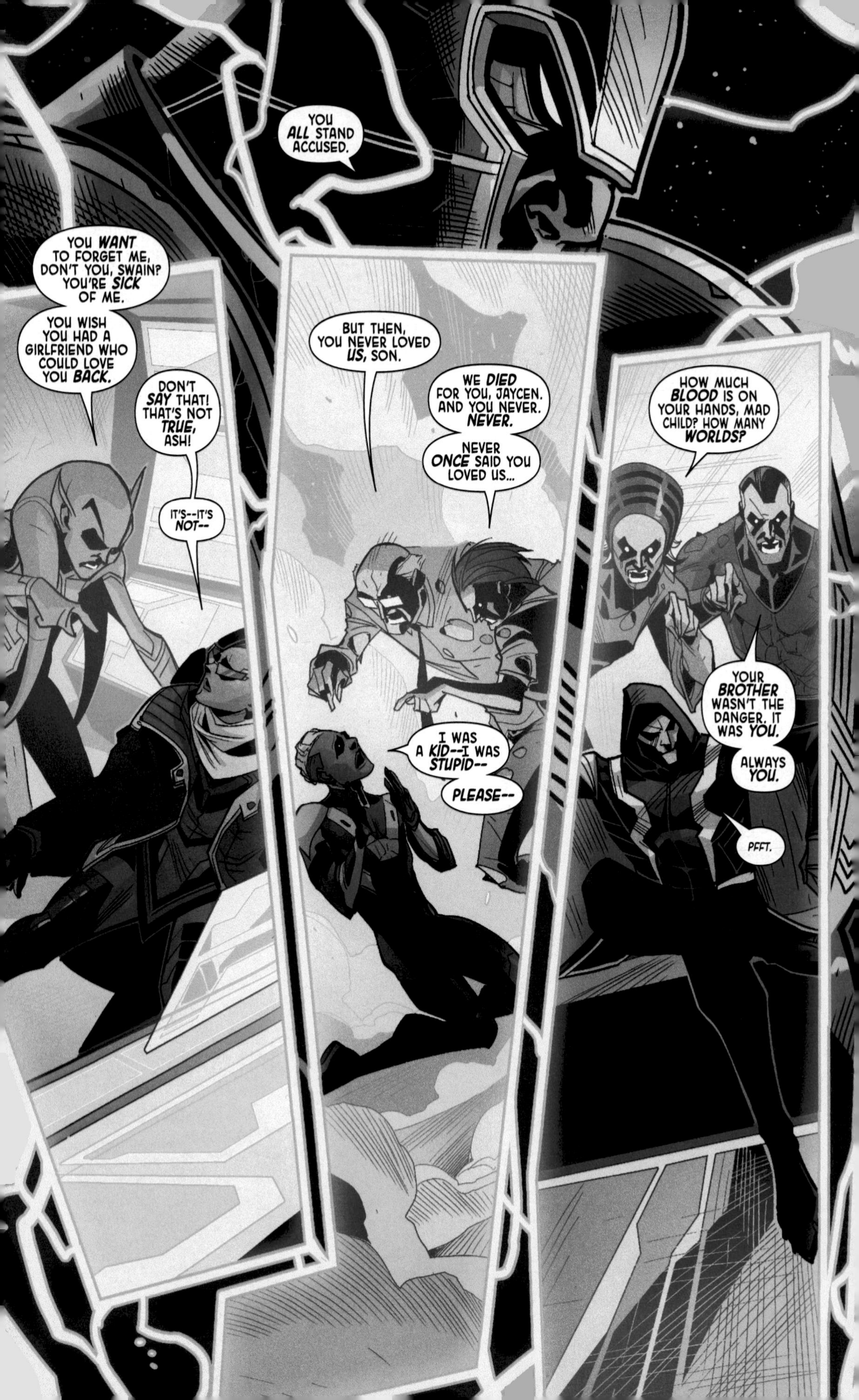
YOU ALL STAND ACCUSED.
YOU WANT TO FORGET ME, DON'T YOU, SWAIN? YOU'RE SICK OF ME.
YOU WISH YOU HAD A GIRLFRIEND WHO COULD LOVE YOU BACK.
DON'T SAY THAT! THAT'S NOT TRUE, ASH!
IT'S--IT'S NOT--
BUT THEN, YOU NEVER LOVED US, SON.
WE DIED FOR YOU, JAYCEN. AND YOU NEVER. NEVER.
NEVER ONCE SAID YOU LOVED US...
I WAS A KID--I WAS STUPID--
PLEASE--
HOW MUCH BLOOD IS ON YOUR HANDS, MAD CHILD? HOW MANY WORLDS?
YOUR BROTHER WASN'T THE DANGER. IT WAS YOU.
ALWAYS YOU.
PFFT.

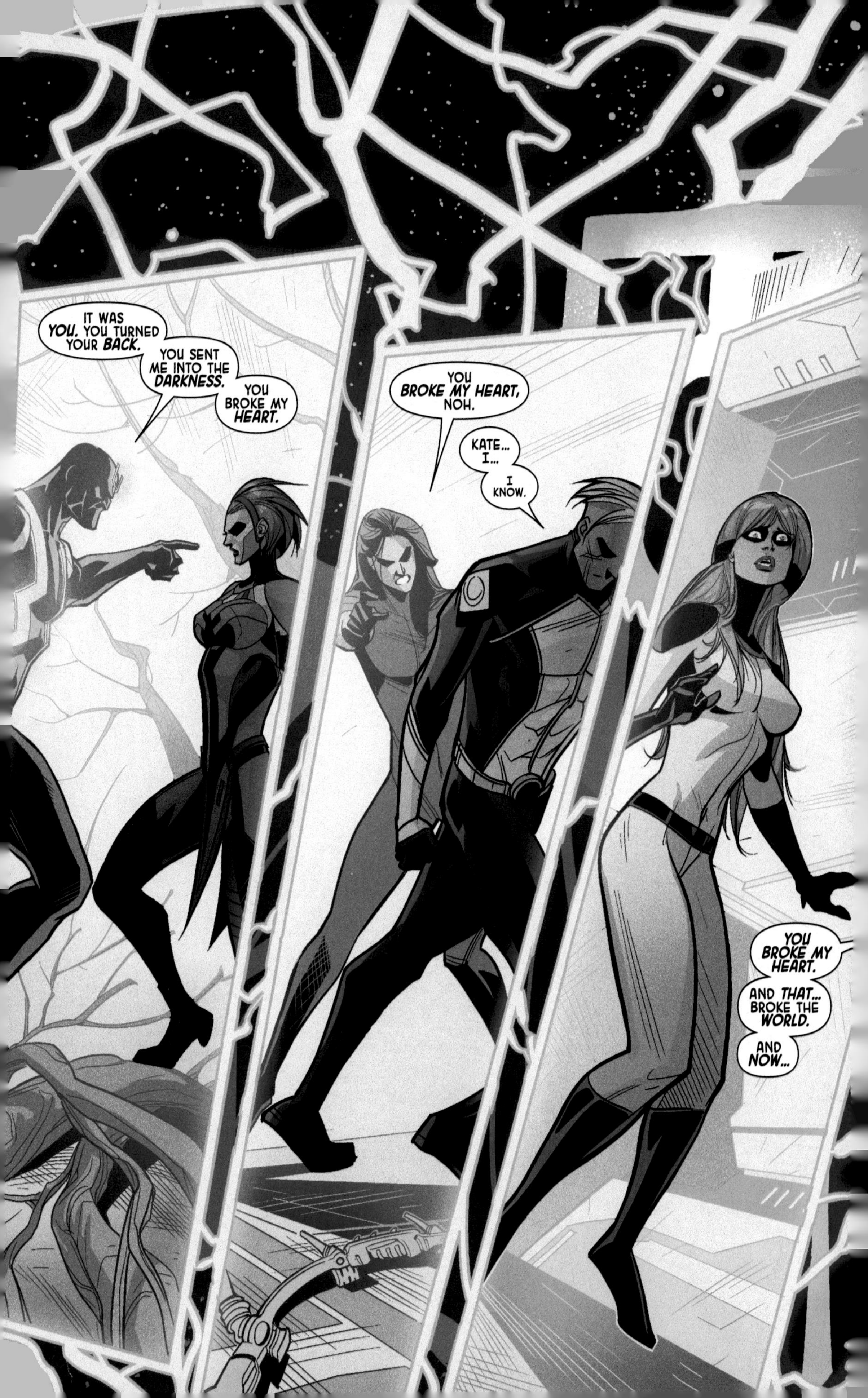
IT WAS YOU. YOU TURNED YOUR BACK.
YOU SENT ME INTO THE DARKNESS.
YOU BROKE MY HEART.
YOU BROKE MY HEART, NOH.
KATE... I...
I KNOW.
YOU BROKE MY HEART.
AND THAT... BROKE THE WORLD.
AND NOW...

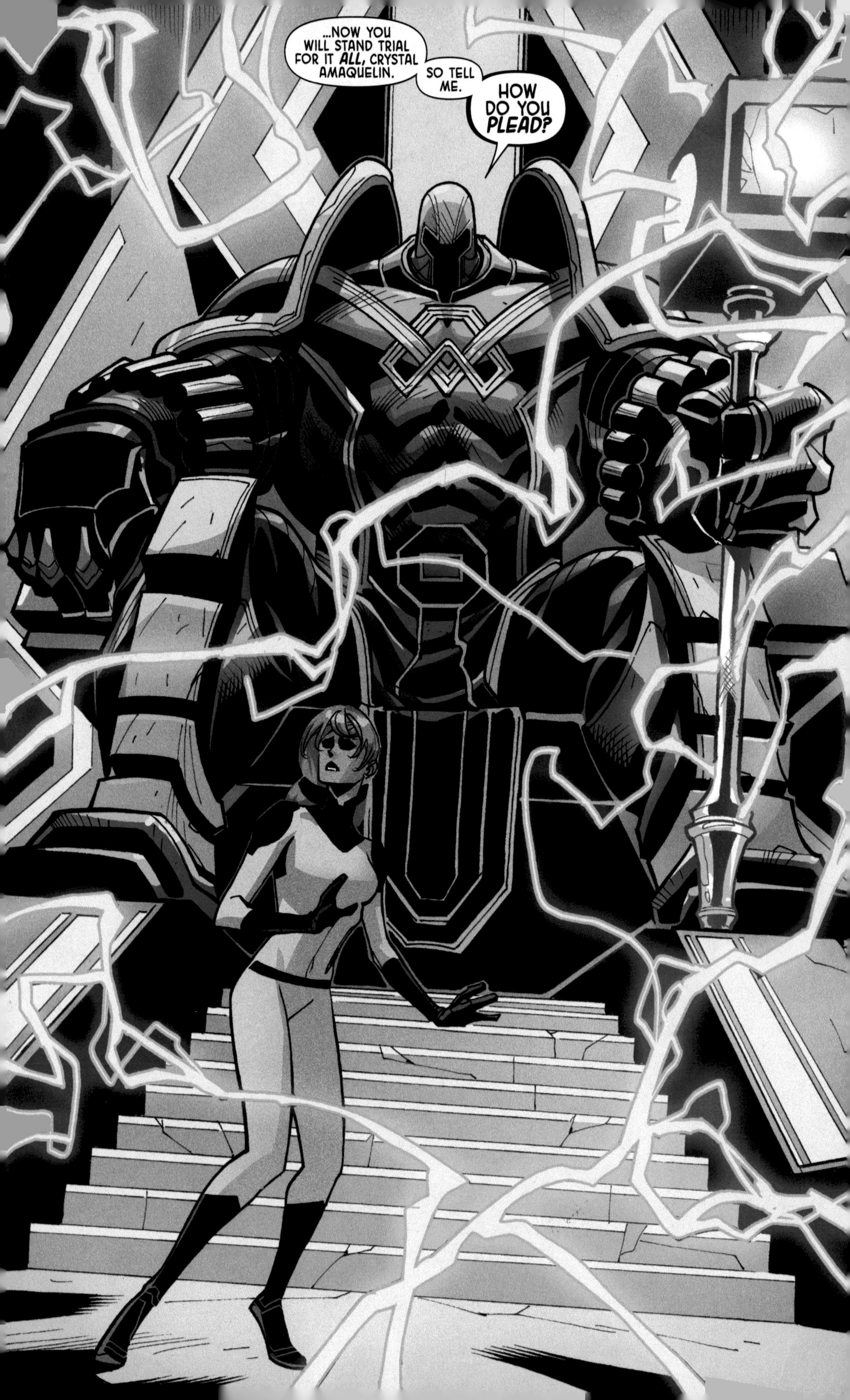
...NOW YOU WILL STAND TRIAL FOR IT ALL, CRYSTAL AMAQUELIN.
SO TELL ME.
HOW DO YOU PLEAD?

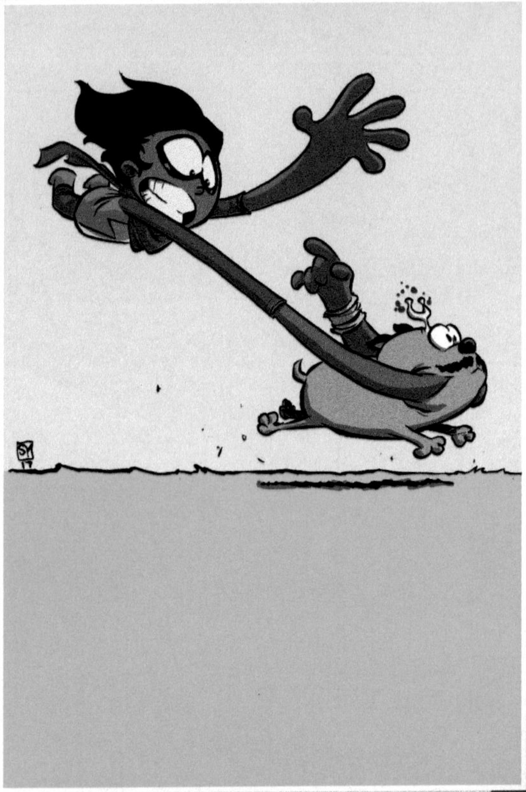

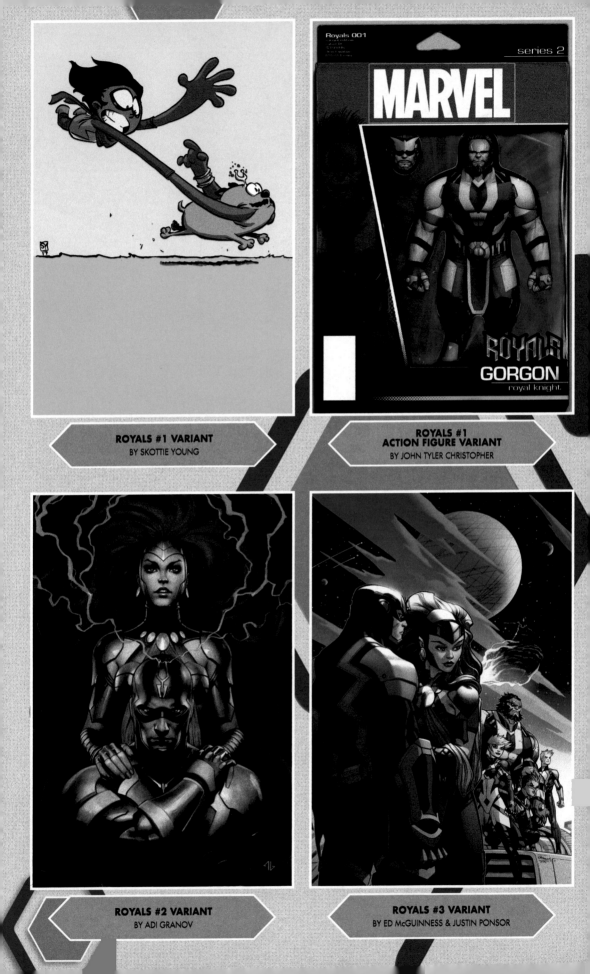

ROYALS #1 VARIANT
BY SKOTTIE YOUNG

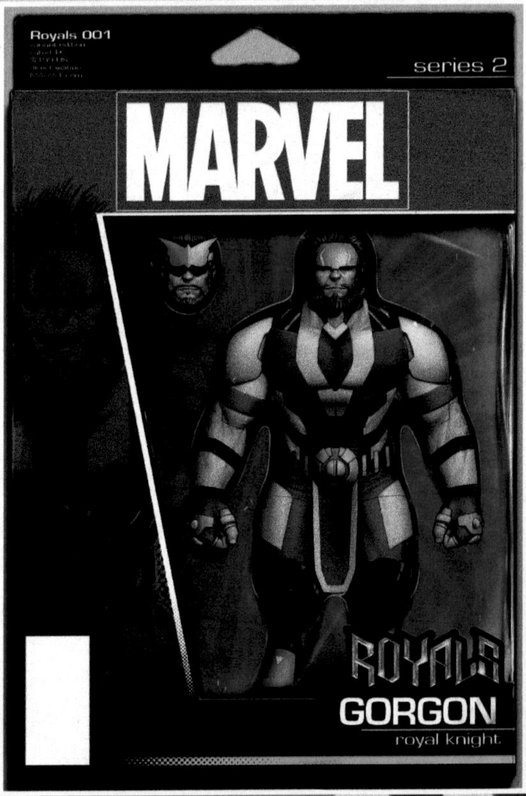
Royals 001
series 2
MARVEL
ROYALS
GORGON
royal knight

ROYALS #1
ACTION FIGURE VARIANT
BY JOHN TYLER CHRISTOPHER

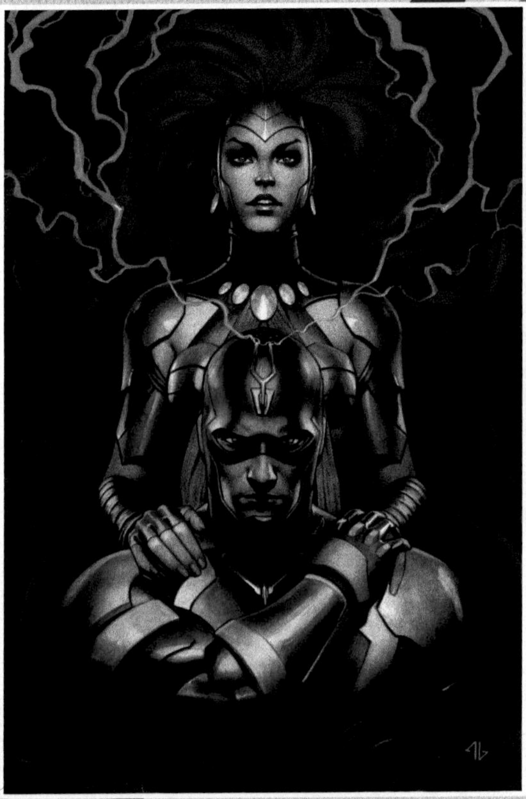

ROYALS #2 VARIANT
BY ADI GRANOV

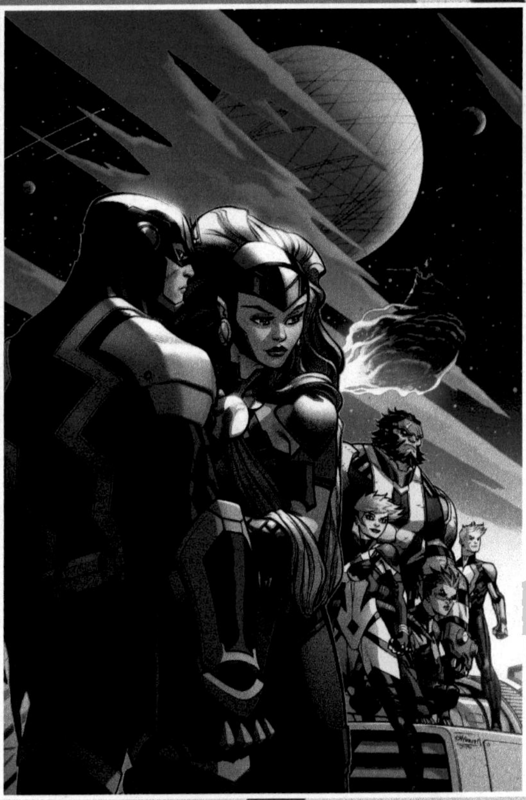

ROYALS #3 VARIANT
BY ED McGUINNESS & JUSTIN PONSOR

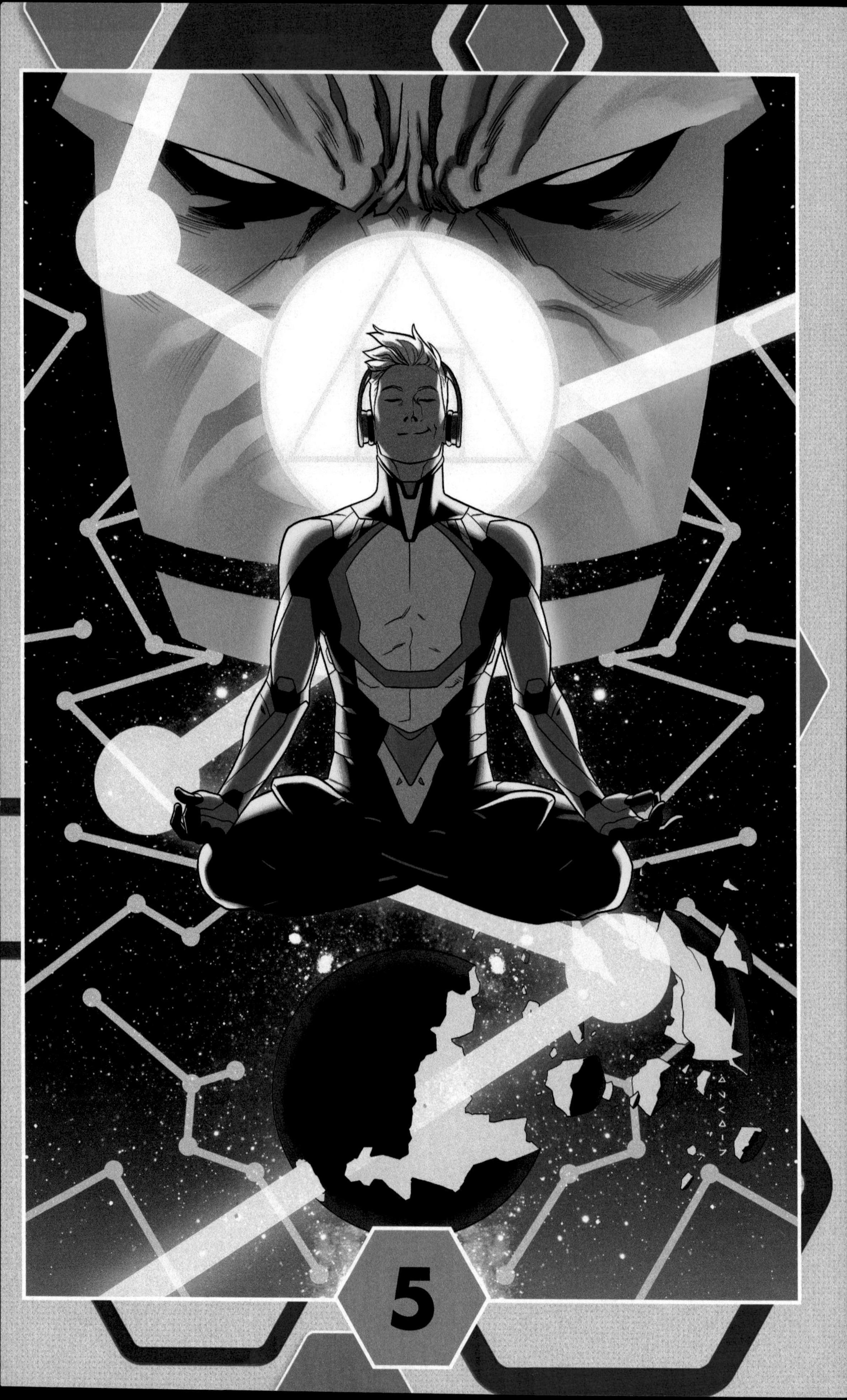
5

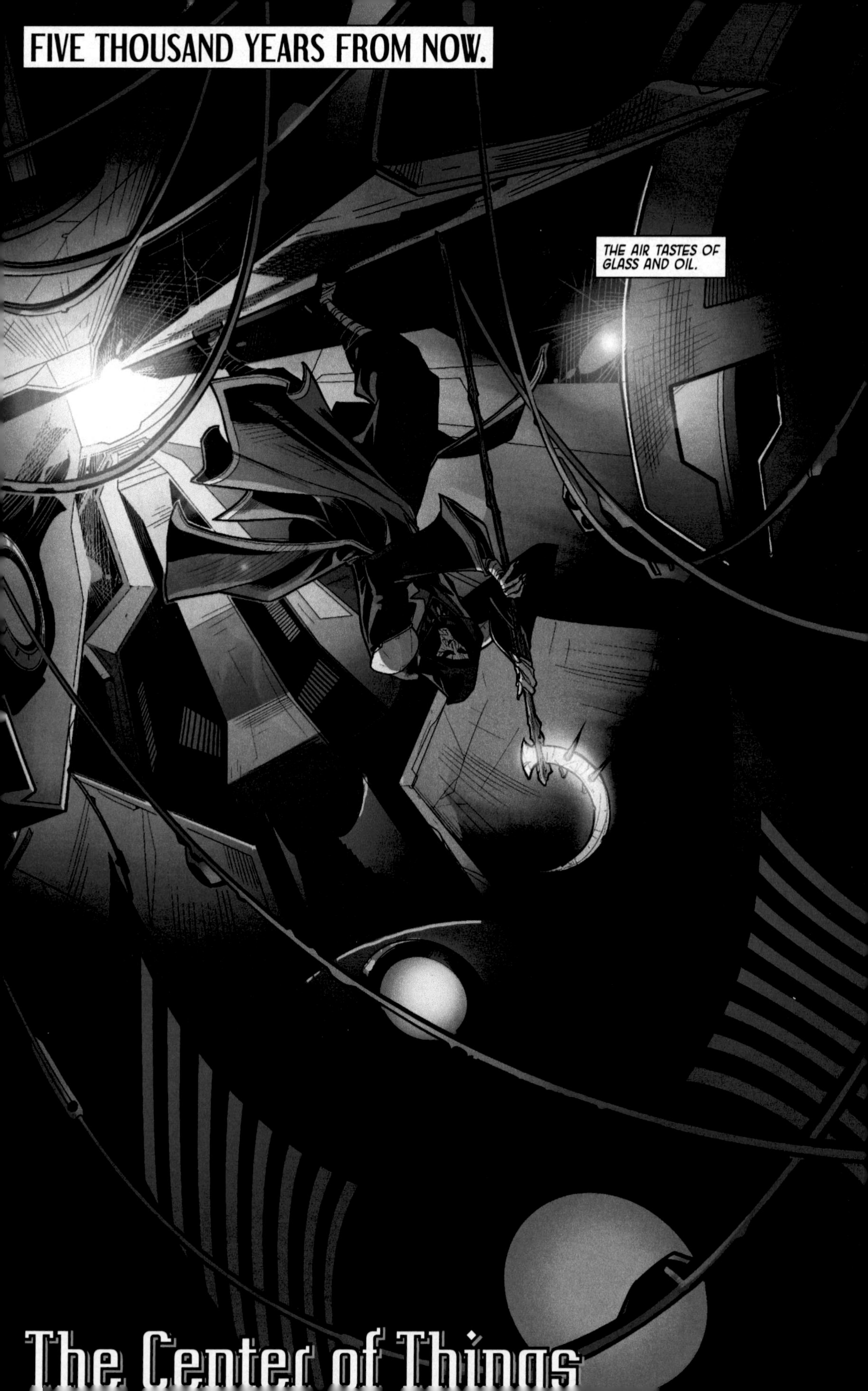
FIVE THOUSAND YEARS FROM NOW.
THE AIR TASTES OF GLASS AND OIL.
The Center of Things

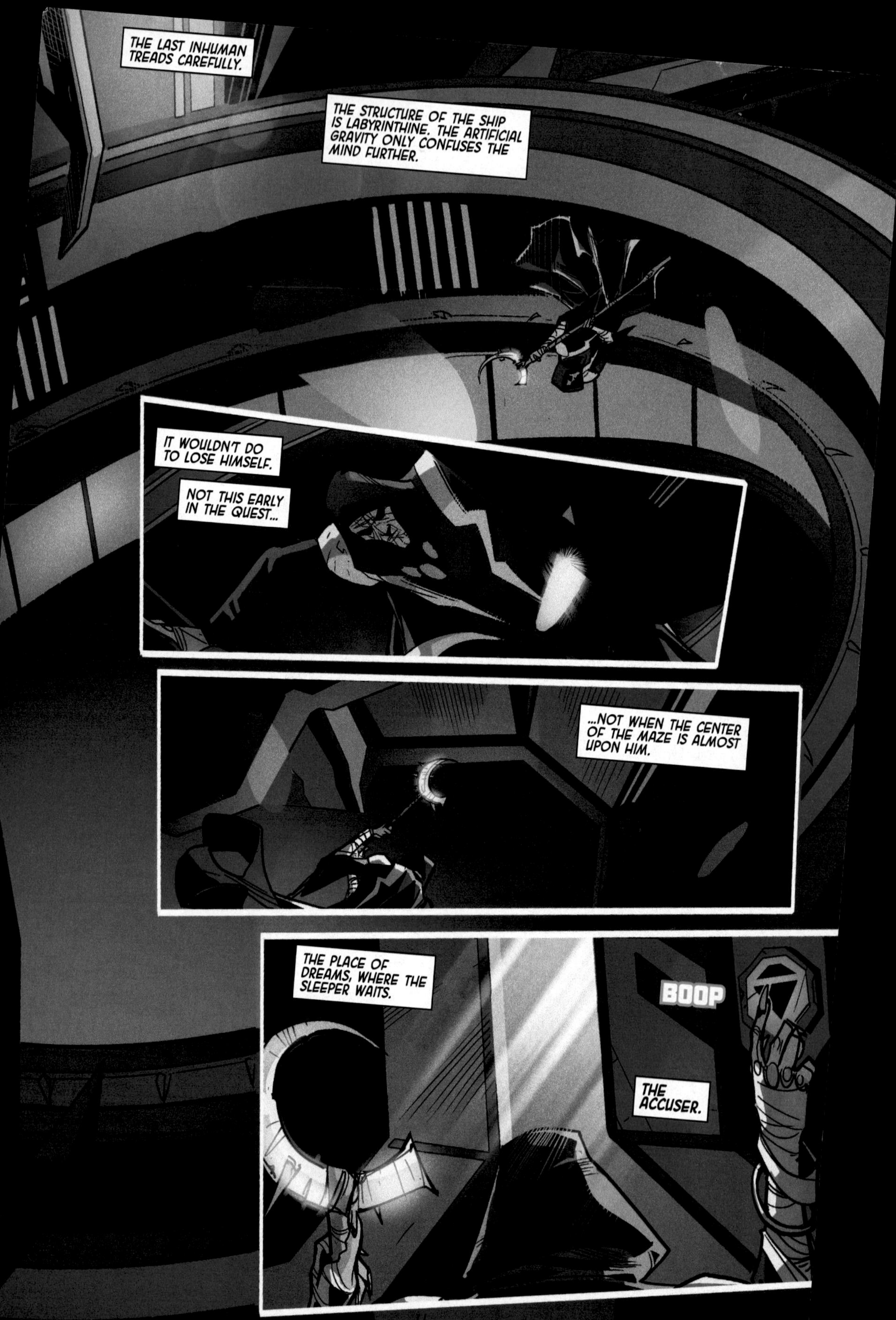

THE LAST INHUMAN TREADS CAREFULLY.
THE STRUCTURE OF THE SHIP IS LABYRINTHINE. THE ARTIFICIAL GRAVITY ONLY CONFUSES THE MIND FURTHER.
IT WOULDN'T DO TO LOSE HIMSELF.
NOT THIS EARLY IN THE QUEST...
...NOT WHEN THE CENTER OF THE MAZE IS ALMOST UPON HIM.
THE PLACE OF DREAMS, WHERE THE SLEEPER WAITS.
BOOP
THE ACCUSER.

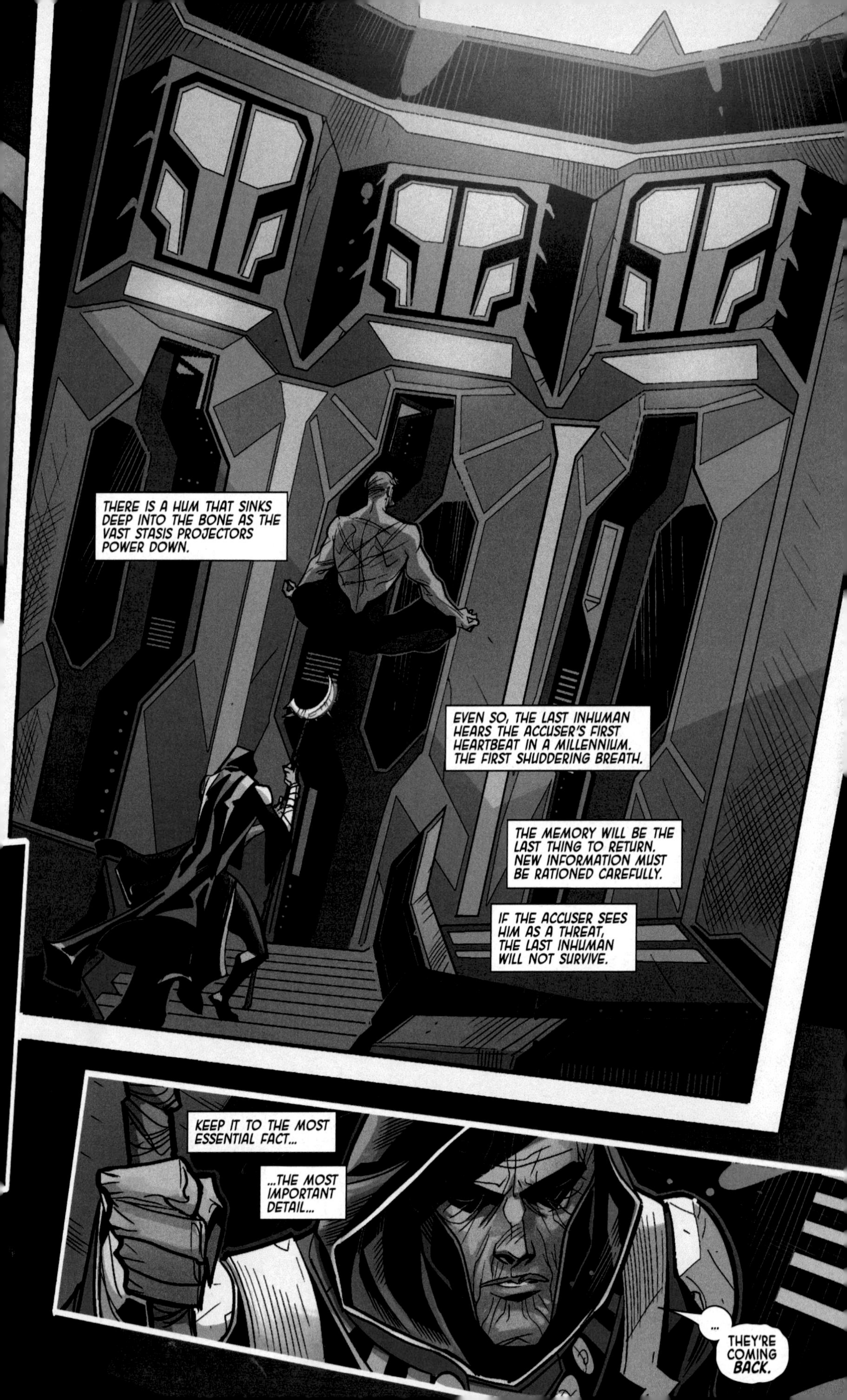
THERE IS A HUM THAT SINKS DEEP INTO THE BONE AS THE VAST STASIS PROJECTORS POWER DOWN.
EVEN SO, THE LAST INHUMAN HEARS THE ACCUSER'S FIRST HEARTBEAT IN A MILLENNIUM. THE FIRST SHUDDERING BREATH.
THE MEMORY WILL BE THE LAST THING TO RETURN. NEW INFORMATION MUST BE RATIONED CAREFULLY.
IF THE ACCUSER SEES HIM AS A THREAT, THE LAST INHUMAN WILL NOT SURVIVE.
KEEP IT TO THE MOST ESSENTIAL FACT...
...THE MOST IMPORTANT DETAIL...
... THEY'RE COMING BACK.

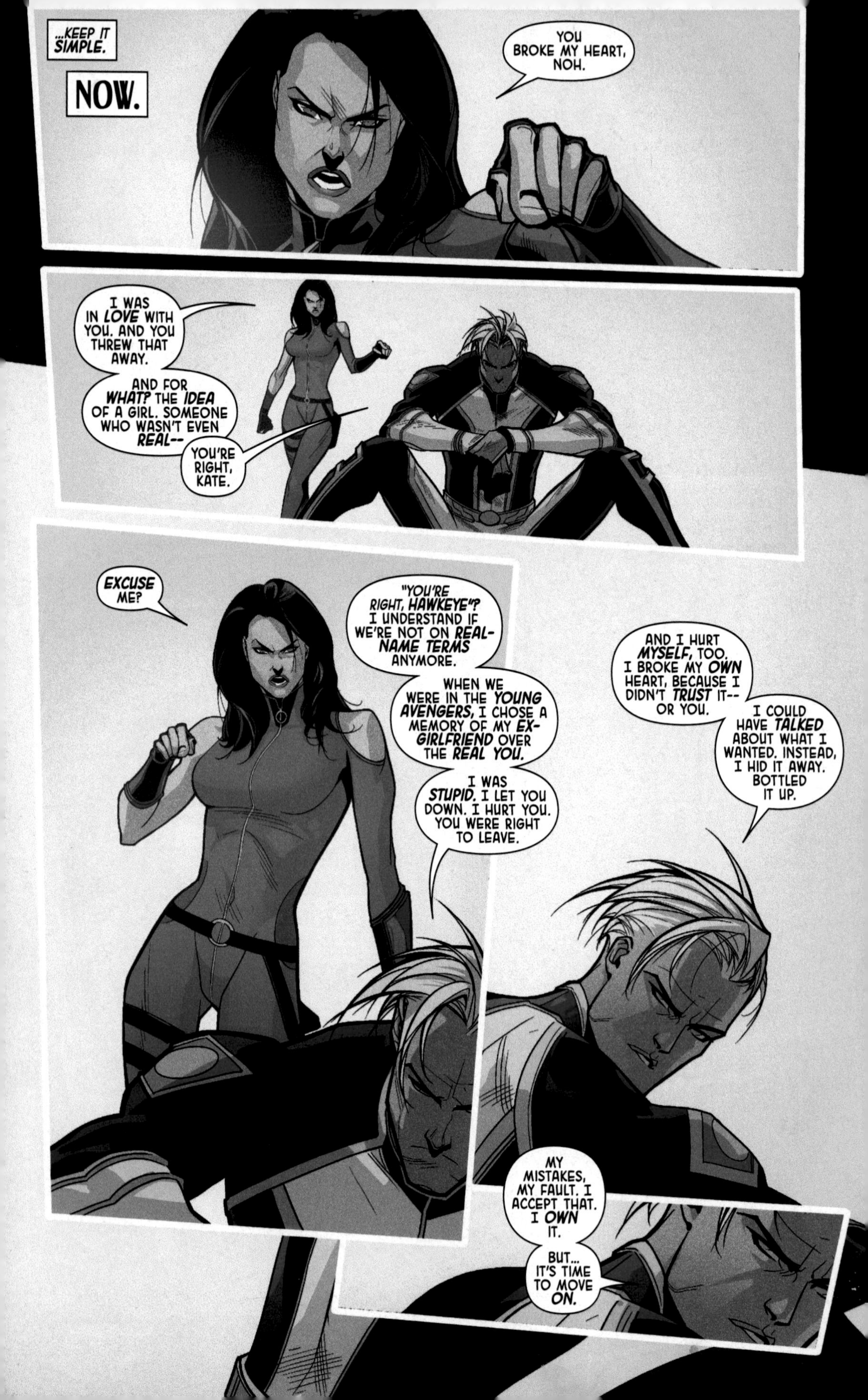
...KEEP IT SIMPLE.
NOW.
YOU BROKE MY HEART, NOH.
I WAS IN LOVE WITH YOU. AND YOU THREW THAT AWAY.
AND FOR WHAT? THE IDEA OF A GIRL. SOMEONE WHO WASN'T EVEN REAL--
YOU'RE RIGHT, KATE.
EXCUSE ME?
"YOU'RE RIGHT, HAWKEYE"? I UNDERSTAND IF WE'RE NOT ON REAL-NAME TERMS ANYMORE.
WHEN WE WERE IN THE YOUNG AVENGERS, I CHOSE A MEMORY OF MY EX-GIRLFRIEND OVER THE REAL YOU.
I WAS STUPID. I LET YOU DOWN. I HURT YOU. YOU WERE RIGHT TO LEAVE.
AND I HURT MYSELF, TOO. I BROKE MY OWN HEART, BECAUSE I DIDN'T TRUST IT-- OR YOU.
I COULD HAVE TALKED ABOUT WHAT I WANTED. INSTEAD, I HID IT AWAY. BOTTLED IT UP.
MY MISTAKES, MY FAULT. I ACCEPT THAT. I OWN IT.
BUT... IT'S TIME TO MOVE ON.

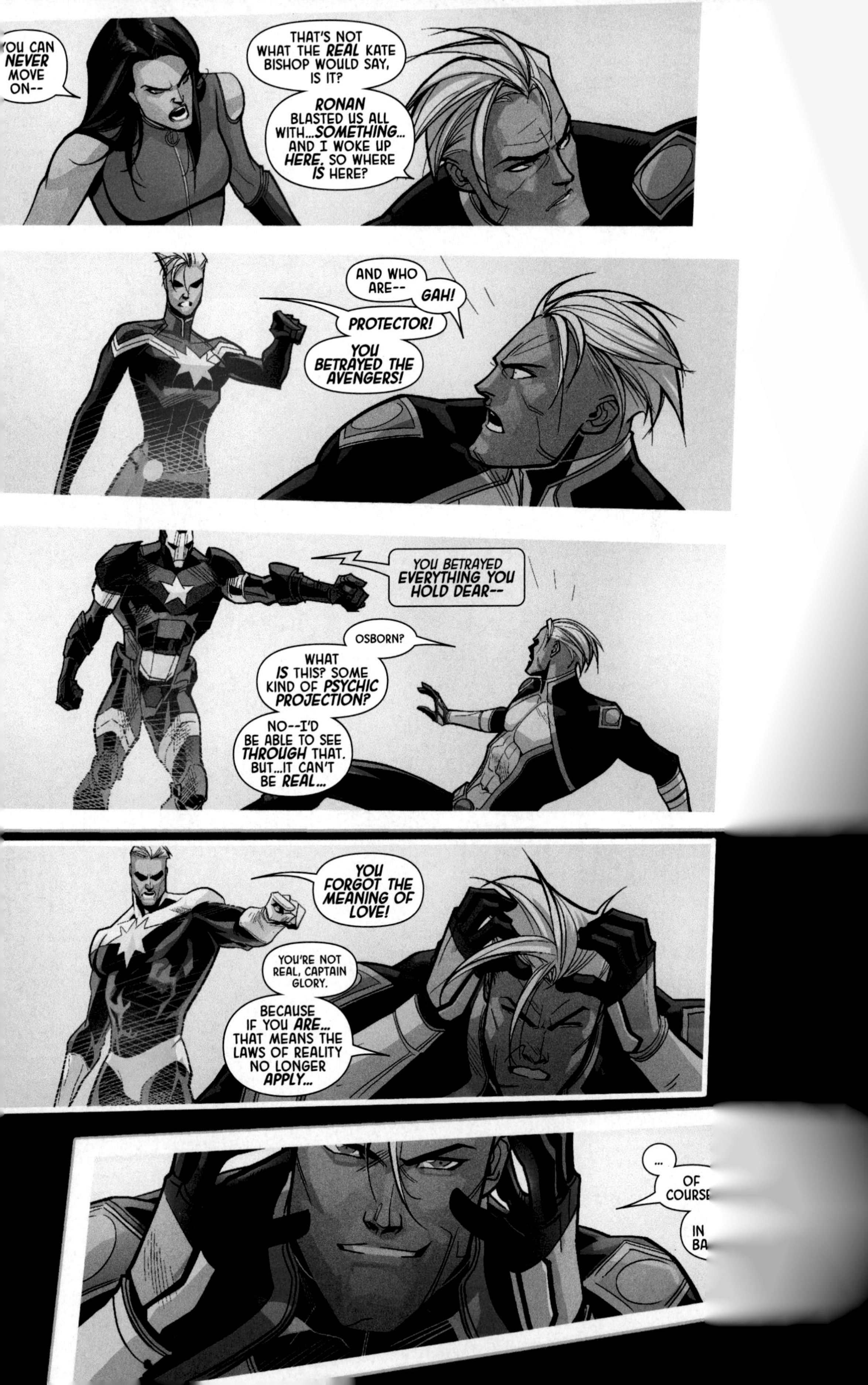
YOU CAN NEVER MOVE ON--
THAT'S NOT WHAT THE REAL KATE BISHOP WOULD SAY, IS IT?
RONAN BLASTED US ALL WITH...SOMETHING... AND I WOKE UP HERE. SO WHERE IS HERE?
AND WHO ARE-- GAH!
PROTECTOR!
YOU BETRAYED THE AVENGERS!
YOU BETRAYED EVERYTHING YOU HOLD DEAR--
OSBORN?
WHAT IS THIS? SOME KIND OF PSYCHIC PROJECTION?
NO--I'D BE ABLE TO SEE THROUGH THAT. BUT...IT CAN'T BE REAL...
YOU FORGOT THE MEANING OF LOVE!
YOU'RE NOT REAL, CAPTAIN GLORY.
BECAUSE IF YOU ARE... THAT MEANS THE LAWS OF REALITY NO LONGER APPLY...
...
OF COURSE

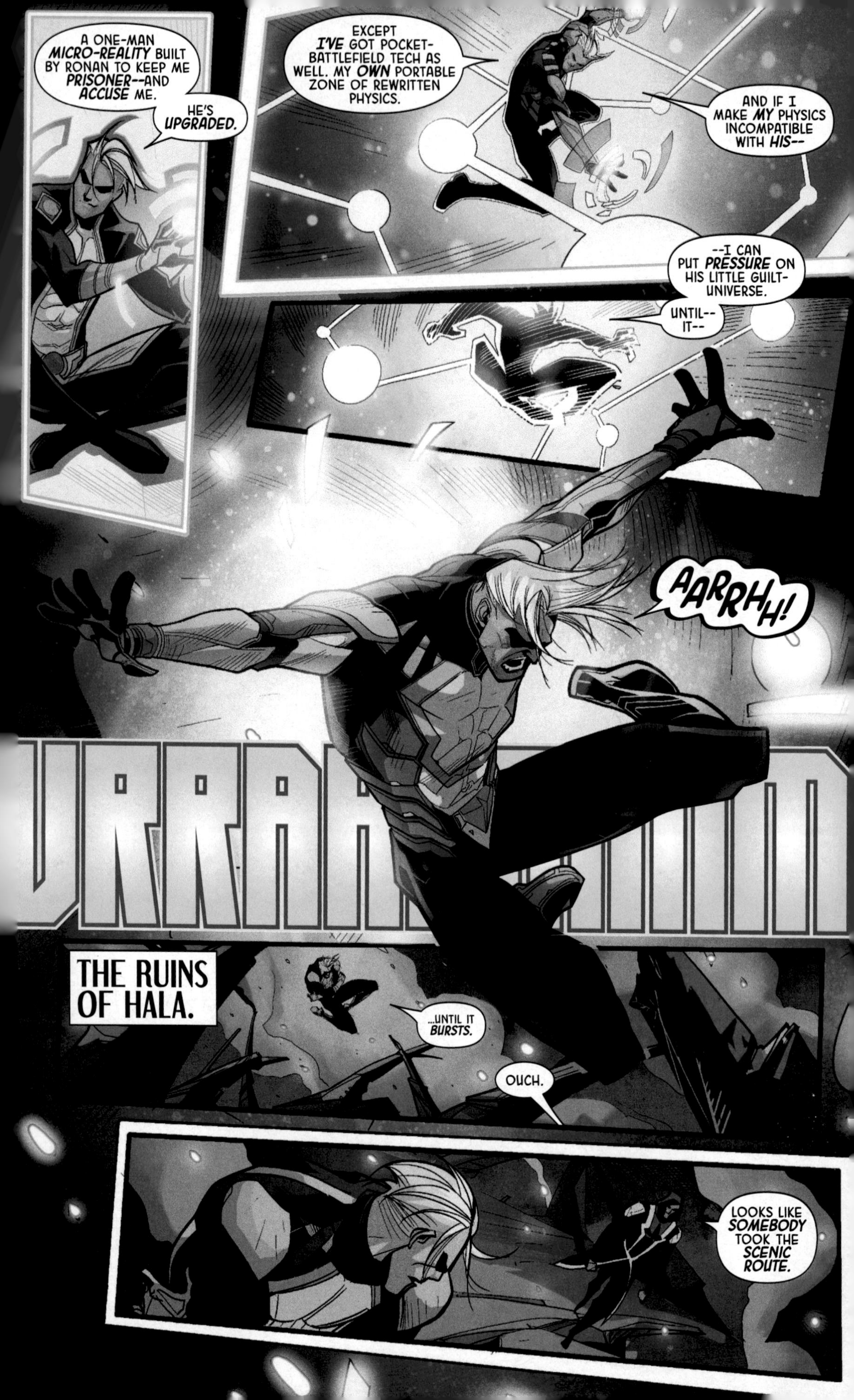

A ONE-MAN MICRO-REALITY BUILT BY RONAN TO KEEP ME PRISONER--AND ACCUSE ME.
HE'S UPGRADED.
EXCEPT I'VE GOT POCKET-BATTLEFIELD TECH AS WELL. MY OWN PORTABLE ZONE OF REWRITTEN PHYSICS.
AND IF I MAKE MY PHYSICS INCOMPATIBLE WITH HIS--
--I CAN PUT PRESSURE ON HIS LITTLE GUILT-UNIVERSE.
UNTIL-- IT--
AARRHH!
URRAAAAMM
THE RUINS OF HALA.
...UNTIL IT BURSTS.
OUCH.
LOOKS LIKE SOMEBODY TOOK THE SCENIC ROUTE.

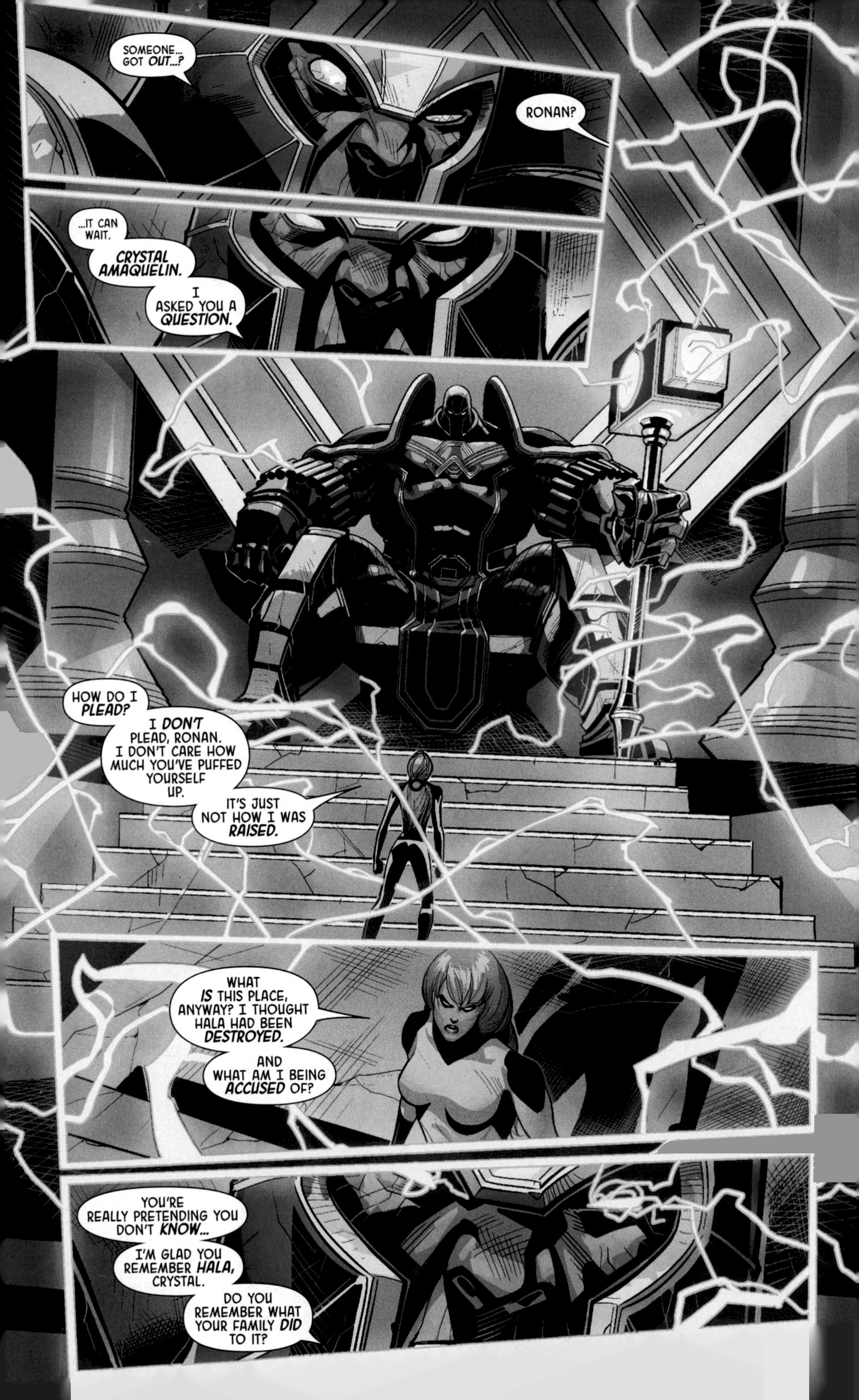
SOMEONE... GOT OUT...?
RONAN?
...IT CAN WAIT.
CRYSTAL AMAQUELIN.
I ASKED YOU A QUESTION.
HOW DO I PLEAD?
I DON'T PLEAD, RONAN. I DON'T CARE HOW MUCH YOU'VE PUFFED YOURSELF UP.
IT'S JUST NOT HOW I WAS RAISED.
WHAT IS THIS PLACE, ANYWAY? I THOUGHT HALA HAD BEEN DESTROYED.
AND WHAT AM I BEING ACCUSED OF?
YOU'RE REALLY PRETENDING YOU DON'T KNOW...
I'M GLAD YOU REMEMBER HALA, CRYSTAL.
DO YOU REMEMBER WHAT YOUR FAMILY DID TO IT?

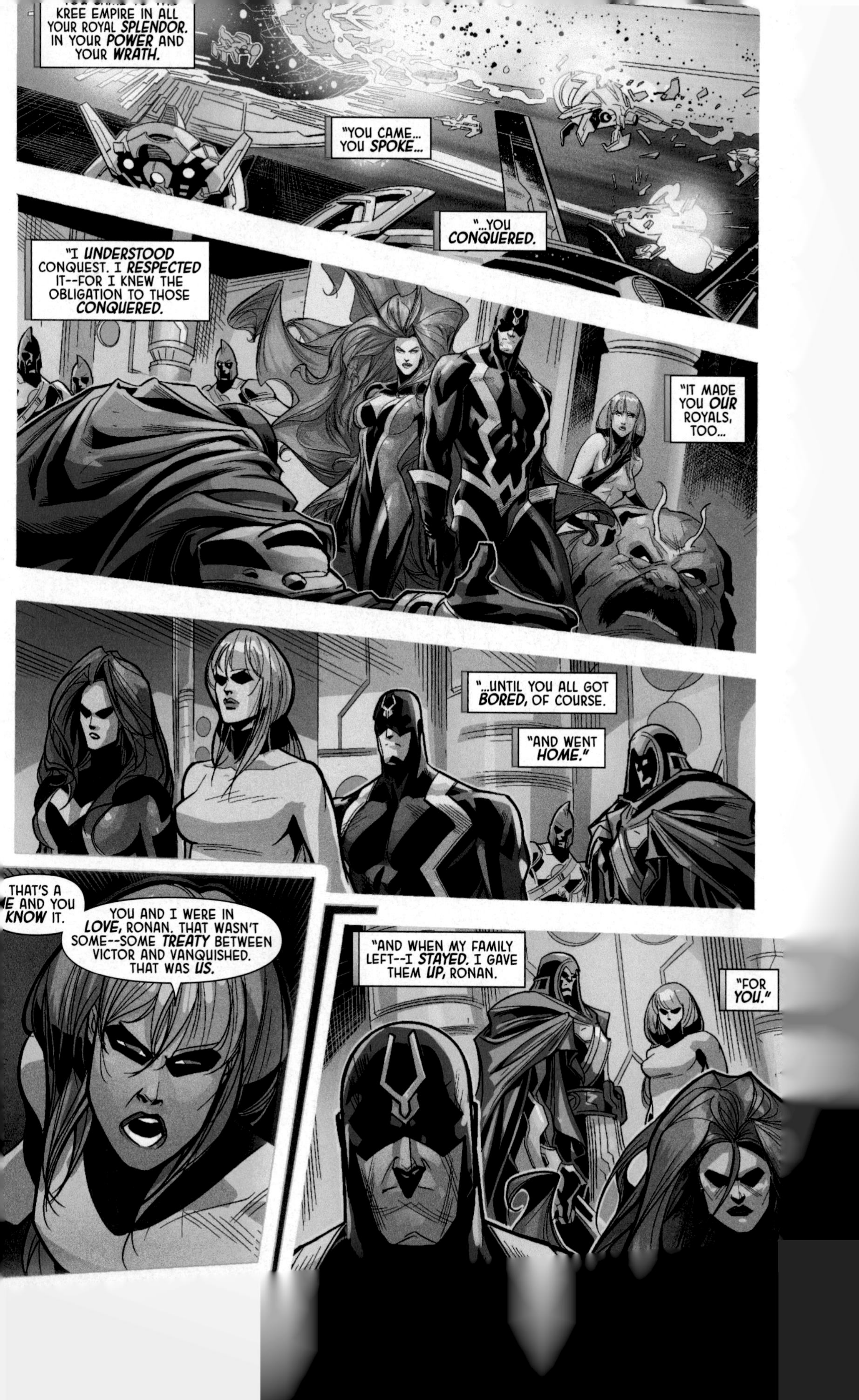
KREE EMPIRE IN ALL YOUR ROYAL SPLENDOR. IN YOUR POWER AND YOUR WRATH.
"YOU CAME... YOU SPOKE...
"...YOU CONQUERED.
"I UNDERSTOOD CONQUEST. I RESPECTED IT--FOR I KNEW THE OBLIGATION TO THOSE CONQUERED.
"IT MADE YOU OUR ROYALS, TOO...
"...UNTIL YOU ALL GOT BORED, OF COURSE.
"AND WENT HOME."
THAT'S A E AND YOU KNOW IT.
YOU AND I WERE IN LOVE, RONAN. THAT WASN'T SOME--SOME TREATY BETWEEN VICTOR AND VANQUISHED. THAT WAS US.
"AND WHEN MY FAMILY LEFT--I STAYED. I GAVE THEM UP, RONAN.
"FOR YOU."

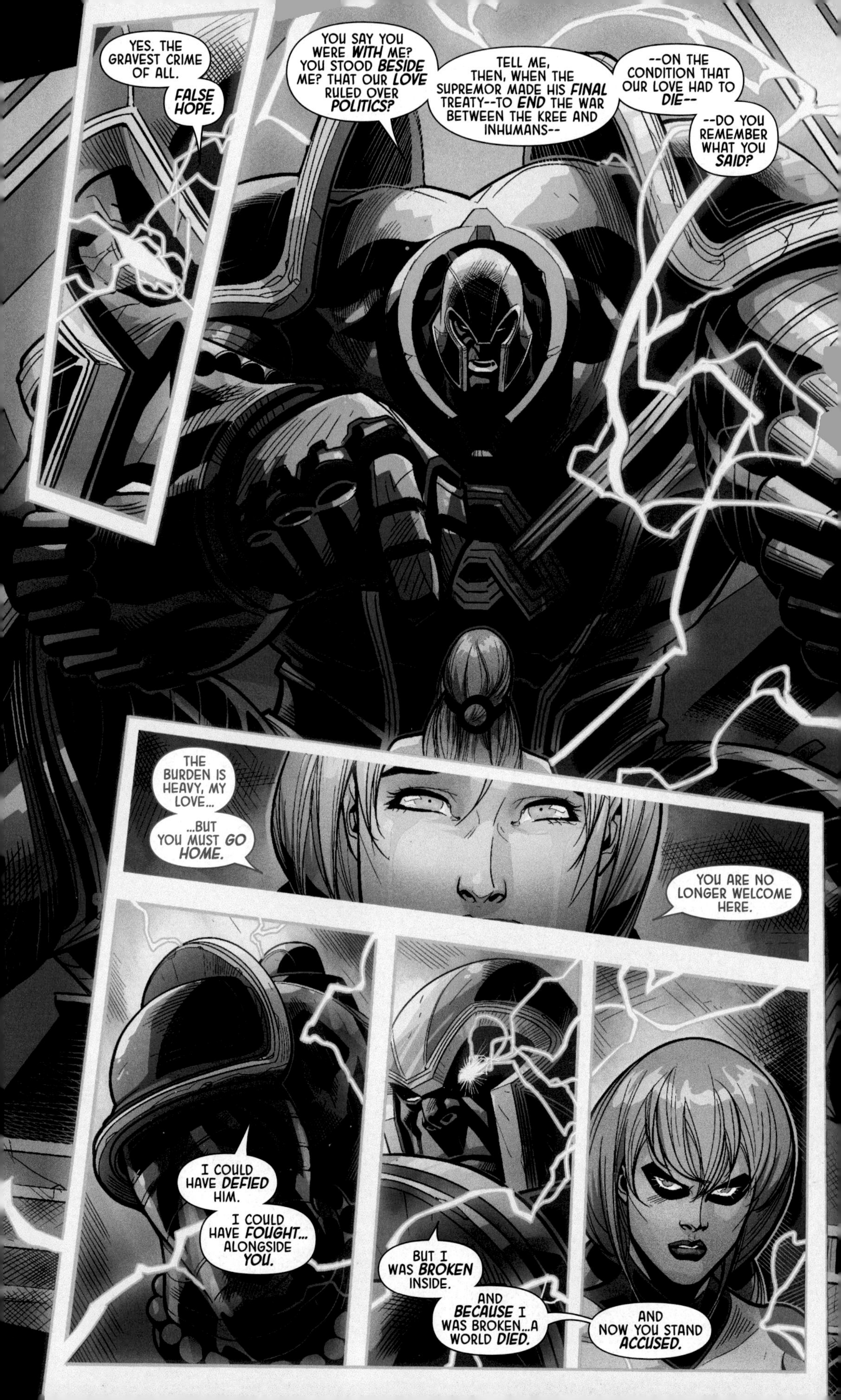
YES. THE GRAVEST CRIME OF ALL.
FALSE HOPE.
YOU SAY YOU WERE WITH ME? YOU STOOD BESIDE ME? THAT OUR LOVE RULED OVER POLITICS?
TELL ME, THEN, WHEN THE SUPREMOR MADE HIS FINAL TREATY--TO END THE WAR BETWEEN THE KREE AND INHUMANS--
--ON THE CONDITION THAT OUR LOVE HAD TO DIE--
--DO YOU REMEMBER WHAT YOU SAID?
THE BURDEN IS HEAVY, MY LOVE...
...BUT YOU MUST GO HOME.
YOU ARE NO LONGER WELCOME HERE.
I COULD HAVE DEFIED HIM.
I COULD HAVE FOUGHT... ALONGSIDE YOU.
BUT I WAS BROKEN INSIDE.
AND BECAUSE I WAS BROKEN...A WORLD DIED.
AND NOW YOU STAND ACCUSED.

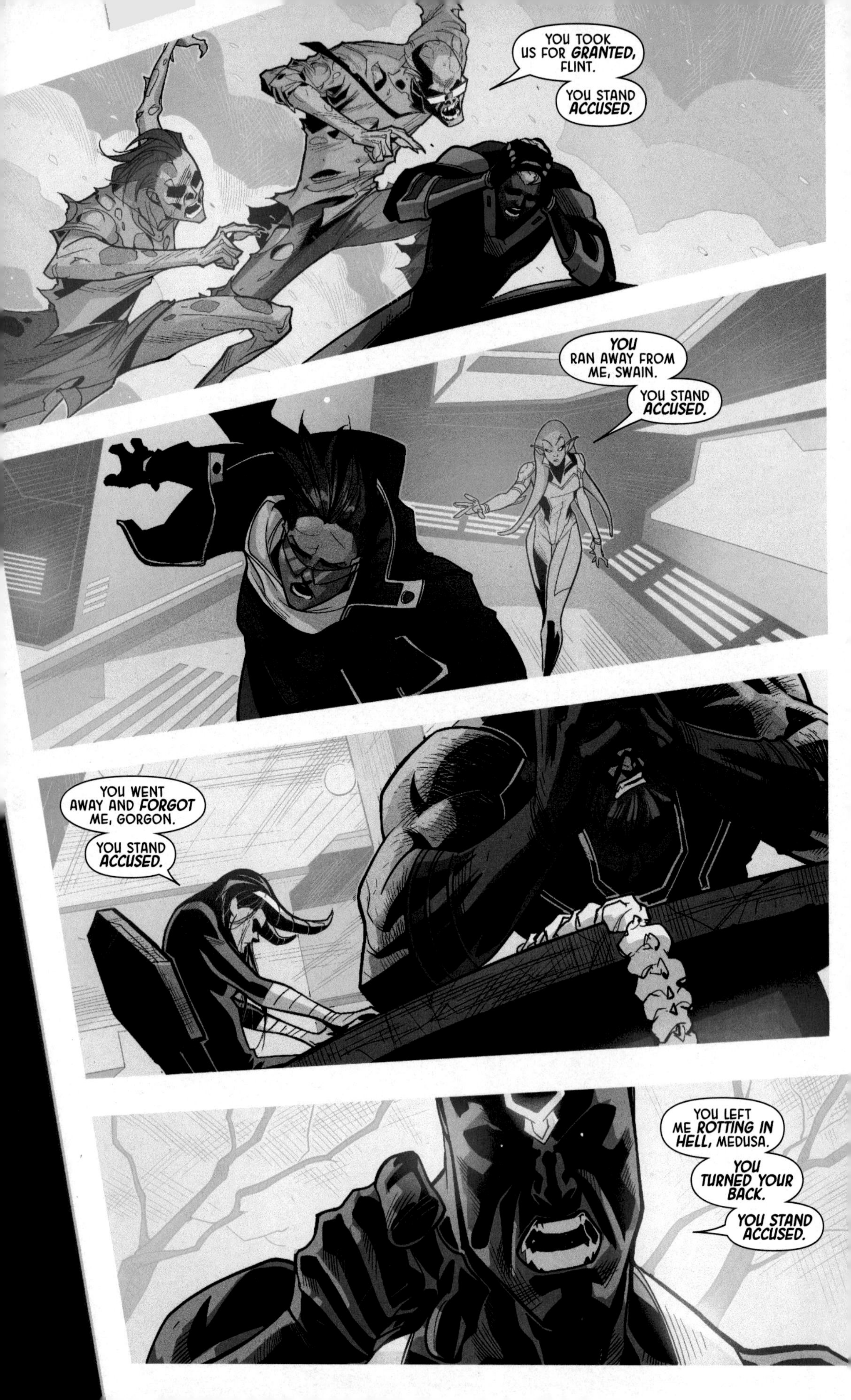
YOU TOOK US FOR GRANTED, FLINT.
YOU STAND ACCUSED.
YOU RAN AWAY FROM ME, SWAIN.
YOU STAND ACCUSED.
YOU WENT AWAY AND FORGOT ME, GORGON.
YOU STAND ACCUSED.
YOU LEFT ME ROTTING IN HELL, MEDUSA.
YOU TURNED YOUR BACK.
YOU STAND ACCUSED.

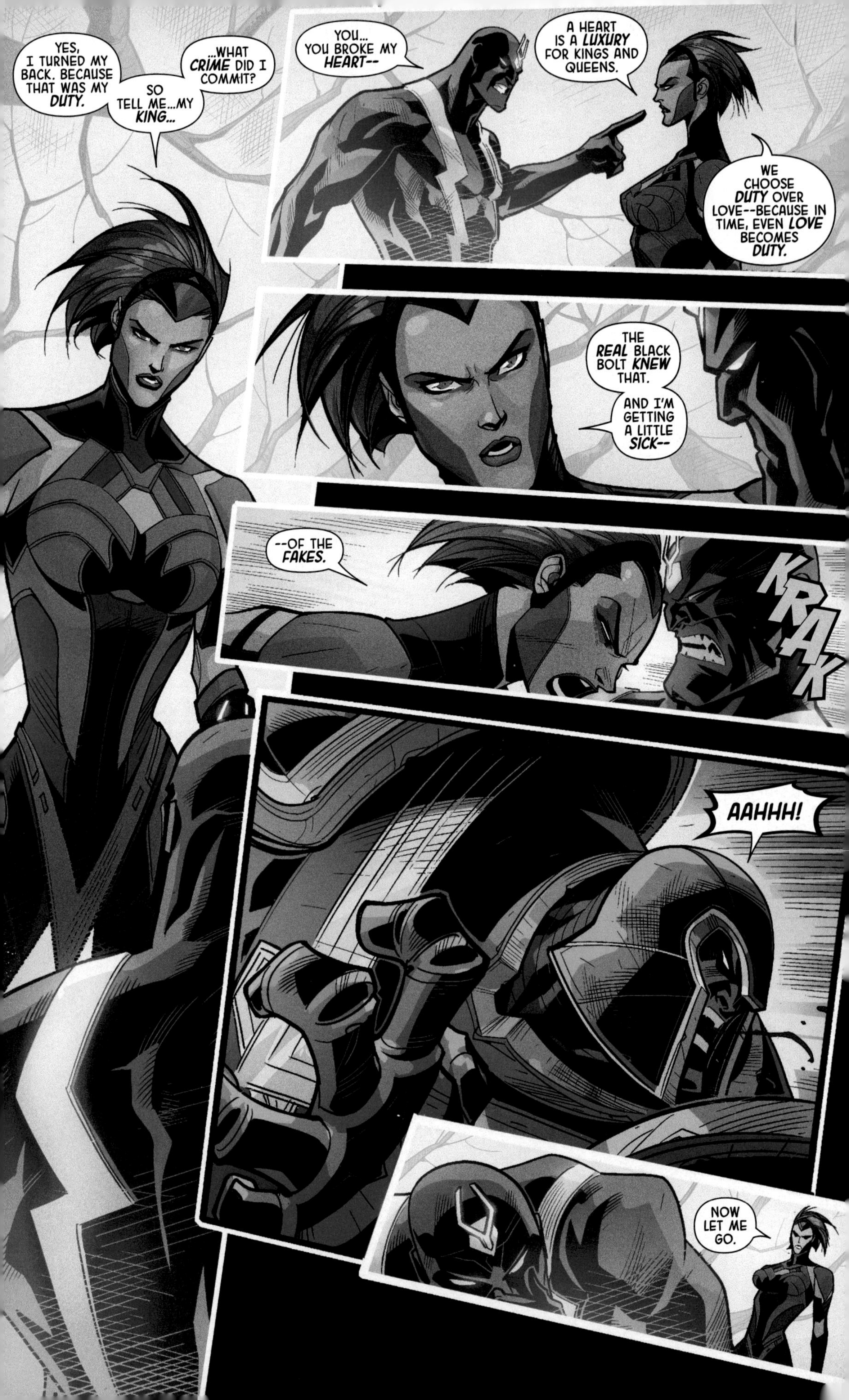
YES, I TURNED MY BACK. BECAUSE THAT WAS MY DUTY.
SO TELL ME...MY KING...
...WHAT CRIME DID I COMMIT?
YOU... YOU BROKE MY HEART--
A HEART IS A LUXURY FOR KINGS AND QUEENS.
WE CHOOSE DUTY OVER LOVE--BECAUSE IN TIME, EVEN LOVE BECOMES DUTY.
THE REAL BLACK BOLT KNEW THAT.
AND I'M GETTING A LITTLE SICK--
--OF THE FAKES.
KRAK
AAHHH!
NOW LET ME GO.

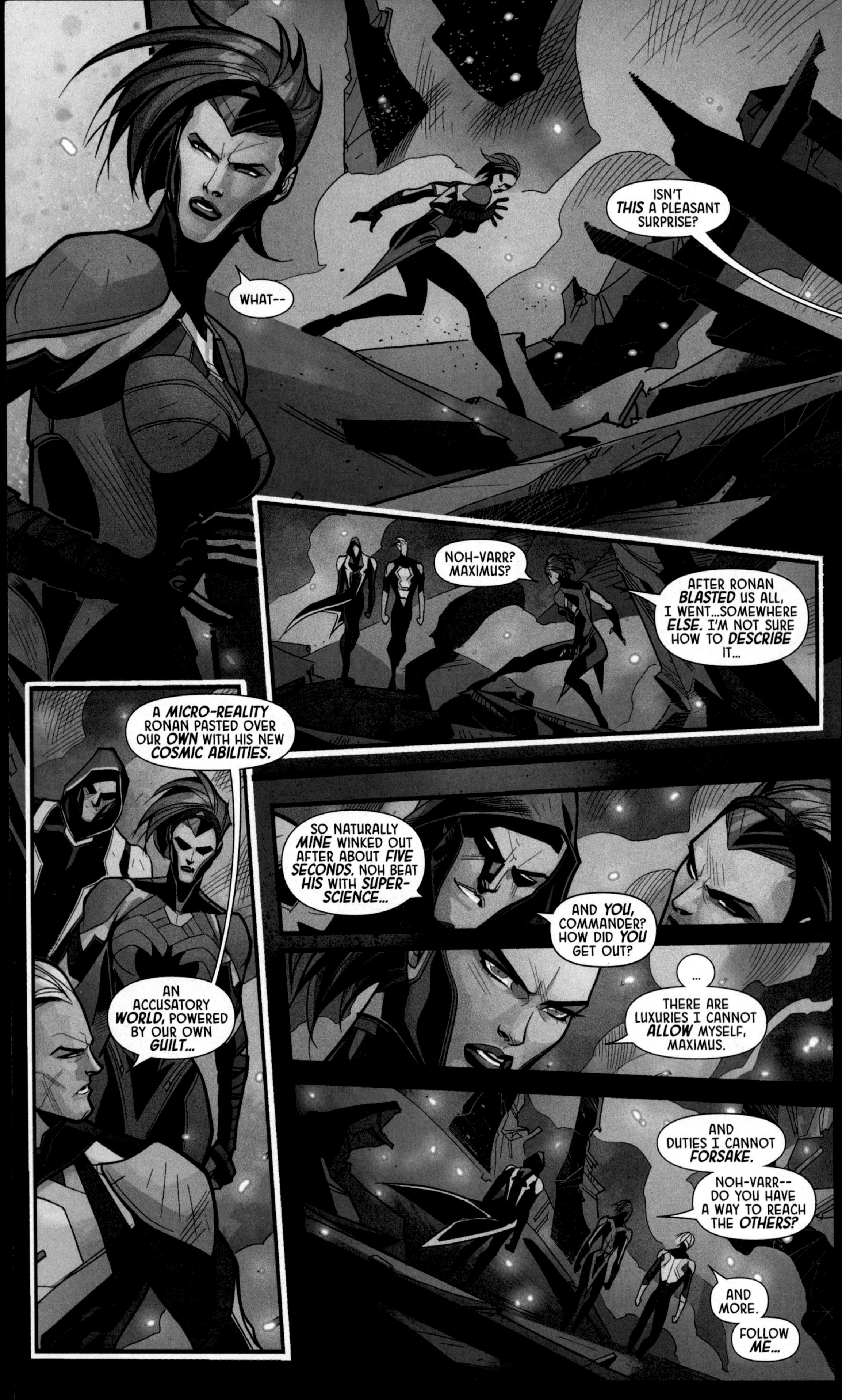
ISN'T THIS A PLEASANT SURPRISE?
WHAT--
NOH-VARR? MAXIMUS?
AFTER RONAN BLASTED US ALL, I WENT...SOMEWHERE ELSE. I'M NOT SURE HOW TO DESCRIBE IT...
A MICRO-REALITY RONAN PASTED OVER OUR OWN WITH HIS NEW COSMIC ABILITIES.
AN ACCUSATORY WORLD, POWERED BY OUR OWN GUILT...
SO NATURALLY MINE WINKED OUT AFTER ABOUT FIVE SECONDS. NOH BEAT HIS WITH SUPER-SCIENCE...
AND YOU, COMMANDER? HOW DID YOU GET OUT?
...
THERE ARE LUXURIES I CANNOT ALLOW MYSELF, MAXIMUS.
AND DUTIES I CANNOT FORSAKE.
NOH-VARR-- DO YOU HAVE A WAY TO REACH THE OTHERS?
AND MORE.
FOLLOW ME...

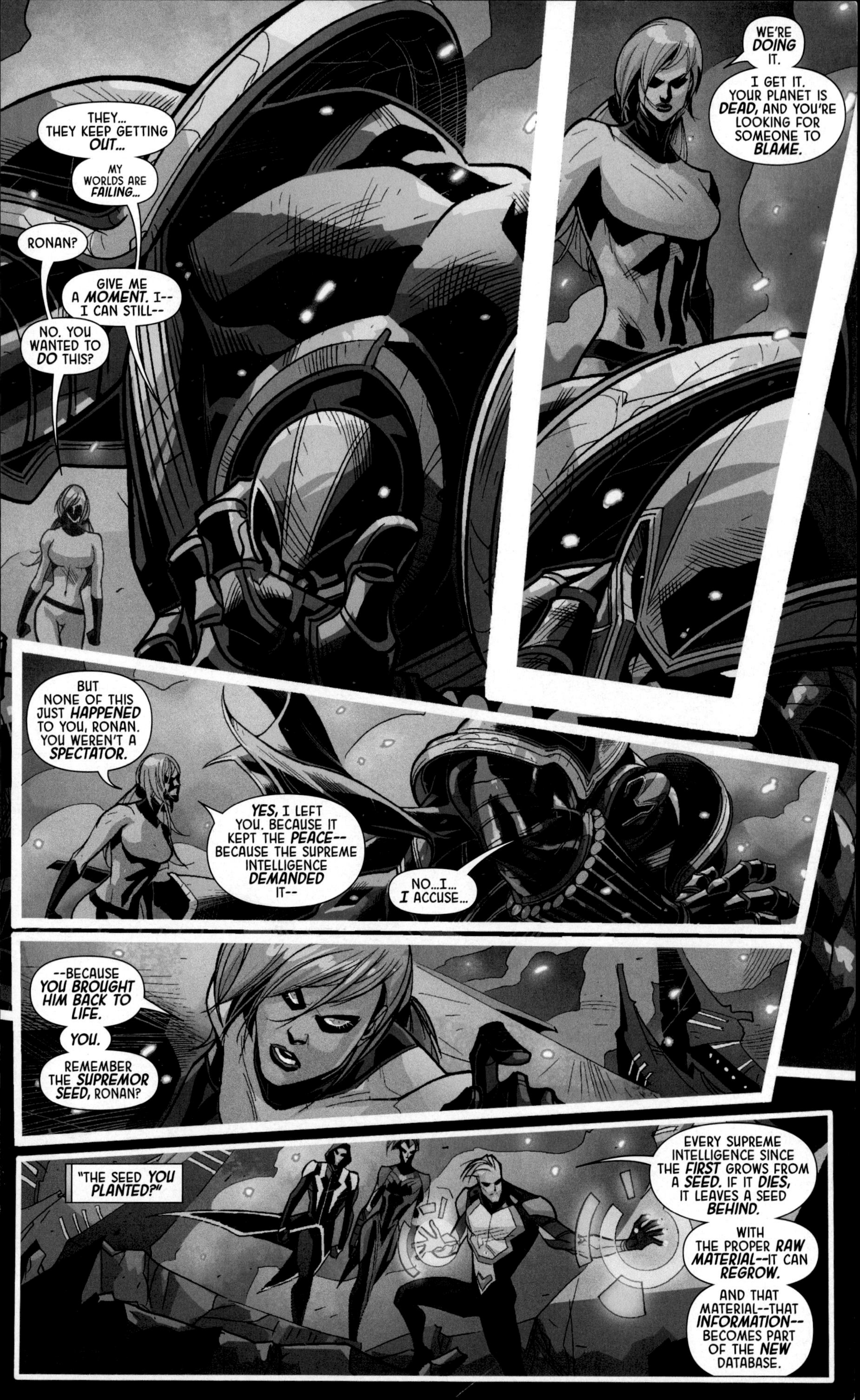
THEY... THEY KEEP GETTING OUT...
MY WORLDS ARE FAILING...
RONAN?
GIVE ME A MOMENT. I-- I CAN STILL--
NO. YOU WANTED TO DO THIS?
WE'RE DOING IT.
I GET IT. YOUR PLANET IS DEAD, AND YOU'RE LOOKING FOR SOMEONE TO BLAME.
BUT NONE OF THIS JUST HAPPENED TO YOU, RONAN. YOU WEREN'T A SPECTATOR.
YES, I LEFT YOU. BECAUSE IT KEPT THE PEACE--BECAUSE THE SUPREME INTELLIGENCE DEMANDED IT--
NO...I... I ACCUSE...
--BECAUSE YOU BROUGHT HIM BACK TO LIFE.
YOU.
REMEMBER THE SUPREMOR SEED, RONAN?
"THE SEED YOU PLANTED?"
EVERY SUPREME INTELLIGENCE SINCE THE FIRST GROWS FROM A SEED. IF IT DIES, IT LEAVES A SEED BEHIND.
WITH THE PROPER RAW MATERIAL--IT CAN REGROW.
AND THAT MATERIAL--THAT INFORMATION--BECOMES PART OF THE NEW DATABASE.

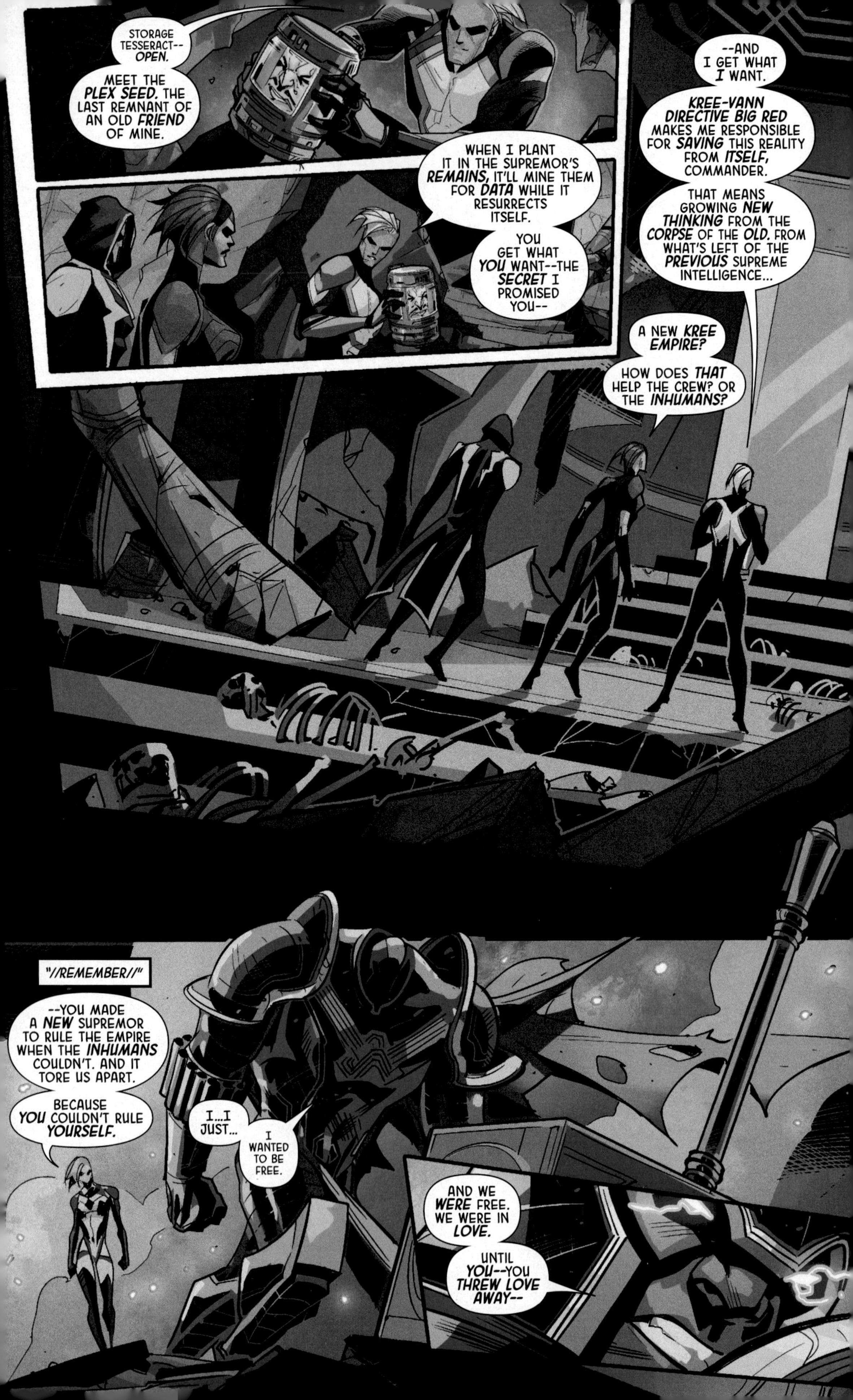
STORAGE TESSERACT-- OPEN.
MEET THE PLEX SEED. THE LAST REMNANT OF AN OLD FRIEND OF MINE.
WHEN I PLANT IT IN THE SUPREMOR'S REMAINS, IT'LL MINE THEM FOR DATA WHILE IT RESURRECTS ITSELF.
YOU GET WHAT YOU WANT--THE SECRET I PROMISED YOU--
--AND I GET WHAT I WANT.
KREE-VANN DIRECTIVE BIG RED MAKES ME RESPONSIBLE FOR SAVING THIS REALITY FROM ITSELF, COMMANDER.
THAT MEANS GROWING NEW THINKING FROM THE CORPSE OF THE OLD. FROM WHAT'S LEFT OF THE PREVIOUS SUPREME INTELLIGENCE...
A NEW KREE EMPIRE?
HOW DOES THAT HELP THE CREW? OR THE INHUMANS?
"//REMEMBER//"
--YOU MADE A NEW SUPREMOR TO RULE THE EMPIRE WHEN THE INHUMANS COULDN'T. AND IT TORE US APART.
BECAUSE YOU COULDN'T RULE YOURSELF.
I...I JUST...
I WANTED TO BE FREE.
AND WE WERE FREE. WE WERE IN LOVE.
UNTIL YOU--YOU THREW LOVE AWAY--

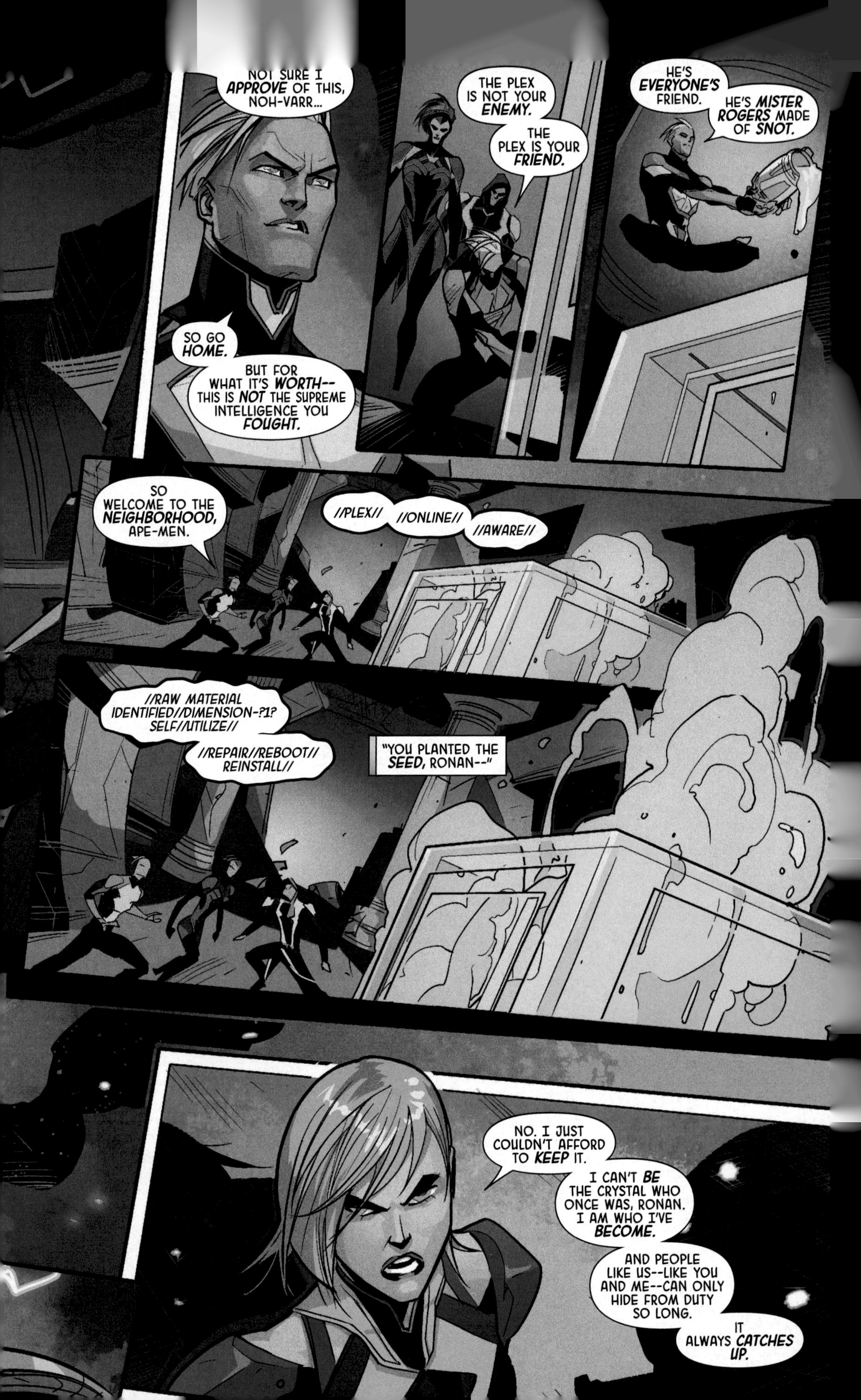
NOT SURE I APPROVE OF THIS, NOH-VARR...
SO GO HOME.
BUT FOR WHAT IT'S WORTH-- THIS IS NOT THE SUPREME INTELLIGENCE YOU FOUGHT.
THE PLEX IS NOT YOUR ENEMY.
THE PLEX IS YOUR FRIEND.
HE'S EVERYONE'S FRIEND.
HE'S MISTER ROGERS MADE OF SNOT.
SO WELCOME TO THE NEIGHBORHOOD, APE-MEN.
//PLEX//
//ONLINE//
//AWARE//
//RAW MATERIAL IDENTIFIED//DIMENSION-?1? SELF//UTILIZE//
//REPAIR//REBOOT// REINSTALL//
"YOU PLANTED THE SEED, RONAN--"
NO. I JUST COULDN'T AFFORD TO KEEP IT.
I CAN'T BE THE CRYSTAL WHO ONCE WAS, RONAN. I AM WHO I'VE BECOME.
AND PEOPLE LIKE US--LIKE YOU AND ME--CAN ONLY HIDE FROM DUTY SO LONG.
IT ALWAYS CATCHES UP.

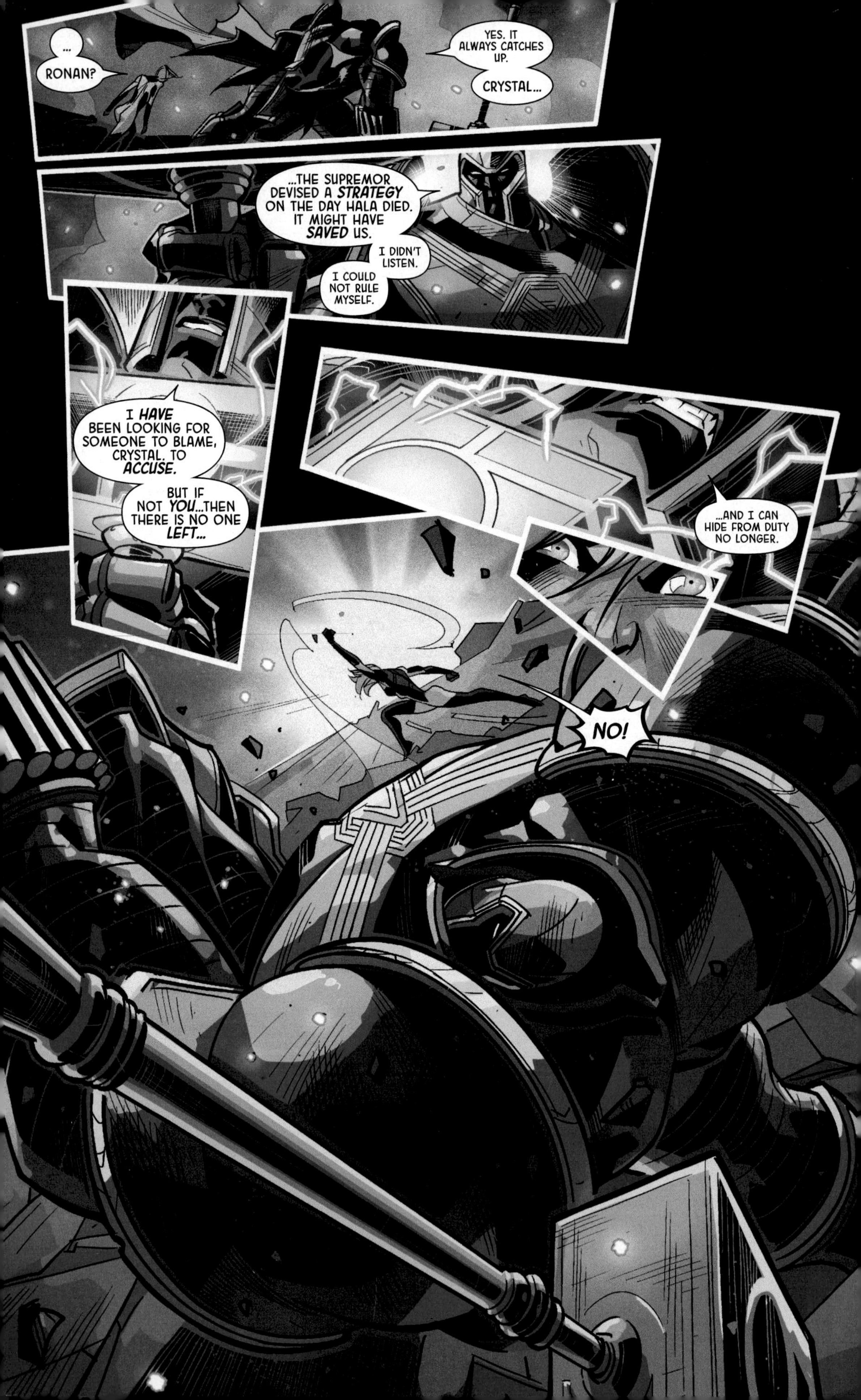
...
RONAN?
YES. IT ALWAYS CATCHES UP.
CRYSTAL...
...THE SUPREMOR DEVISED A STRATEGY ON THE DAY HALA DIED. IT MIGHT HAVE SAVED US.
I DIDN'T LISTEN.
I COULD NOT RULE MYSELF.
I HAVE BEEN LOOKING FOR SOMEONE TO BLAME, CRYSTAL. TO ACCUSE.
BUT IF NOT YOU...THEN THERE IS NO ONE LEFT...
...AND I CAN HIDE FROM DUTY NO LONGER.
NO!

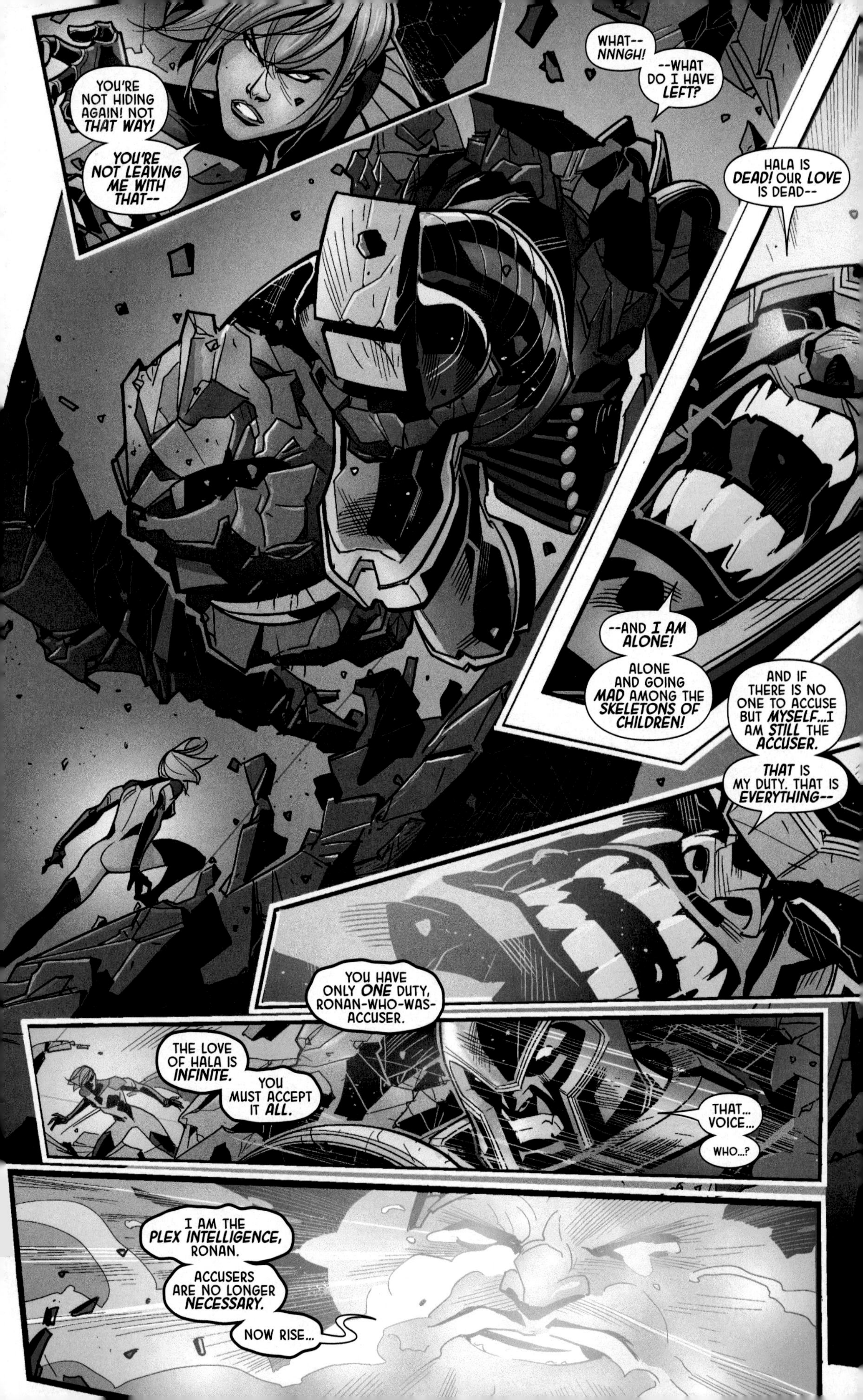
YOU'RE NOT HIDING AGAIN! NOT THAT WAY!
YOU'RE NOT LEAVING ME WITH THAT--
WHAT-- NNNGH!
--WHAT DO I HAVE LEFT?
HALA IS DEAD! OUR LOVE IS DEAD--
--AND I AM ALONE!
ALONE AND GOING MAD AMONG THE SKELETONS OF CHILDREN!
AND IF THERE IS NO ONE TO ACCUSE BUT MYSELF...I AM STILL THE ACCUSER.
THAT IS MY DUTY. THAT IS EVERYTHING--
YOU HAVE ONLY ONE DUTY, RONAN-WHO-WAS-ACCUSER.
THE LOVE OF HALA IS INFINITE.
YOU MUST ACCEPT IT ALL.
THAT... VOICE...
WHO...?
I AM THE PLEX INTELLIGENCE, RONAN.
ACCUSERS ARE NO LONGER NECESSARY.
NOW RISE...

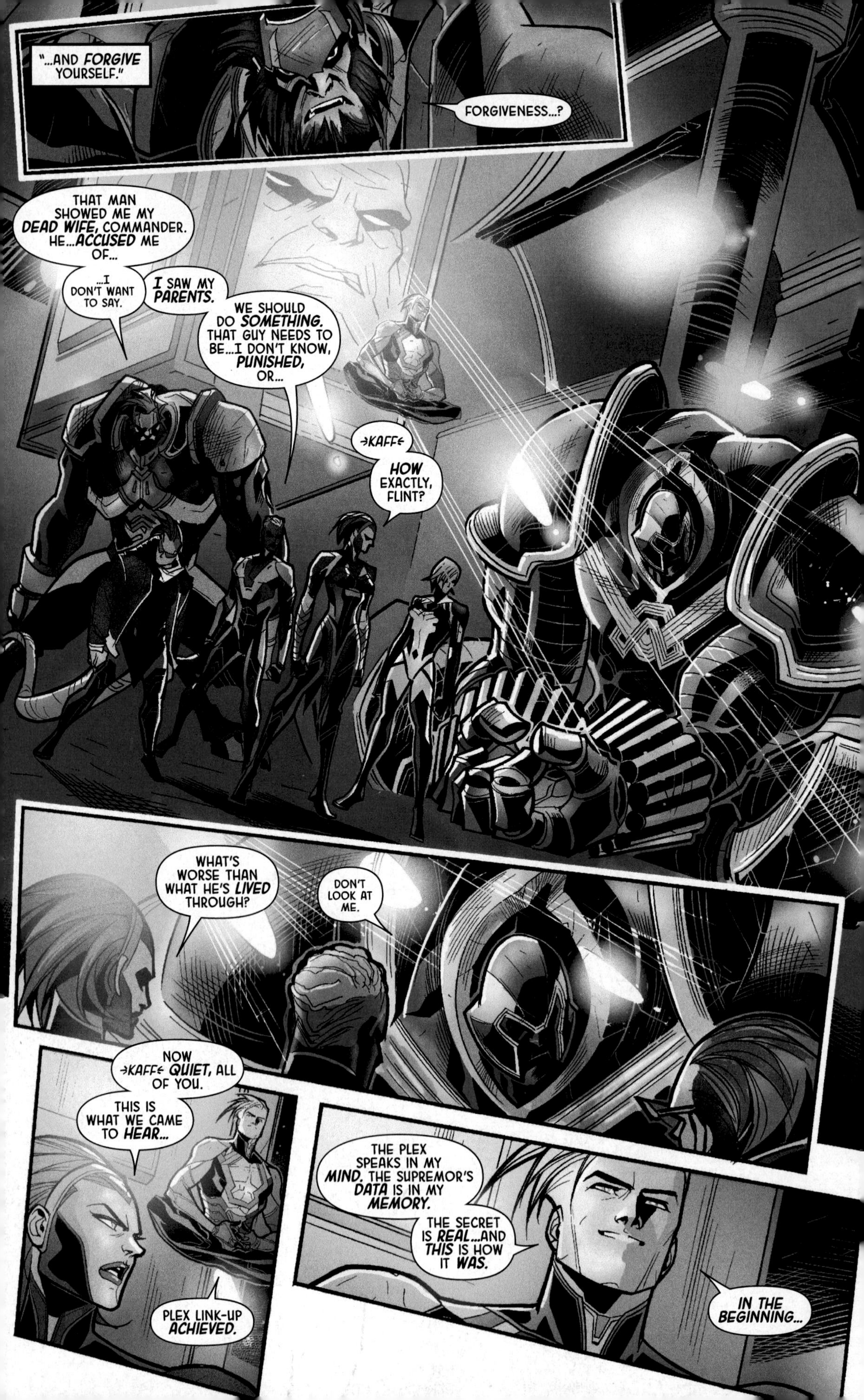
"...AND FORGIVE YOURSELF."
FORGIVENESS...?
THAT MAN SHOWED ME MY DEAD WIFE, COMMANDER. HE...ACCUSED ME OF...
...I DON'T WANT TO SAY.
I SAW MY PARENTS.
WE SHOULD DO SOMETHING. THAT GUY NEEDS TO BE...I DON'T KNOW, PUNISHED, OR...
→KAFF←
HOW EXACTLY, FLINT?
WHAT'S WORSE THAN WHAT HE'S LIVED THROUGH?
DON'T LOOK AT ME.
NOW →KAFF← QUIET, ALL OF YOU.
THIS IS WHAT WE CAME TO HEAR...
PLEX LINK-UP ACHIEVED.
THE PLEX SPEAKS IN MY MIND. THE SUPREMOR'S DATA IS IN MY MEMORY.
THE SECRET IS REAL...AND THIS IS HOW IT WAS.
IN THE BEGINNING...

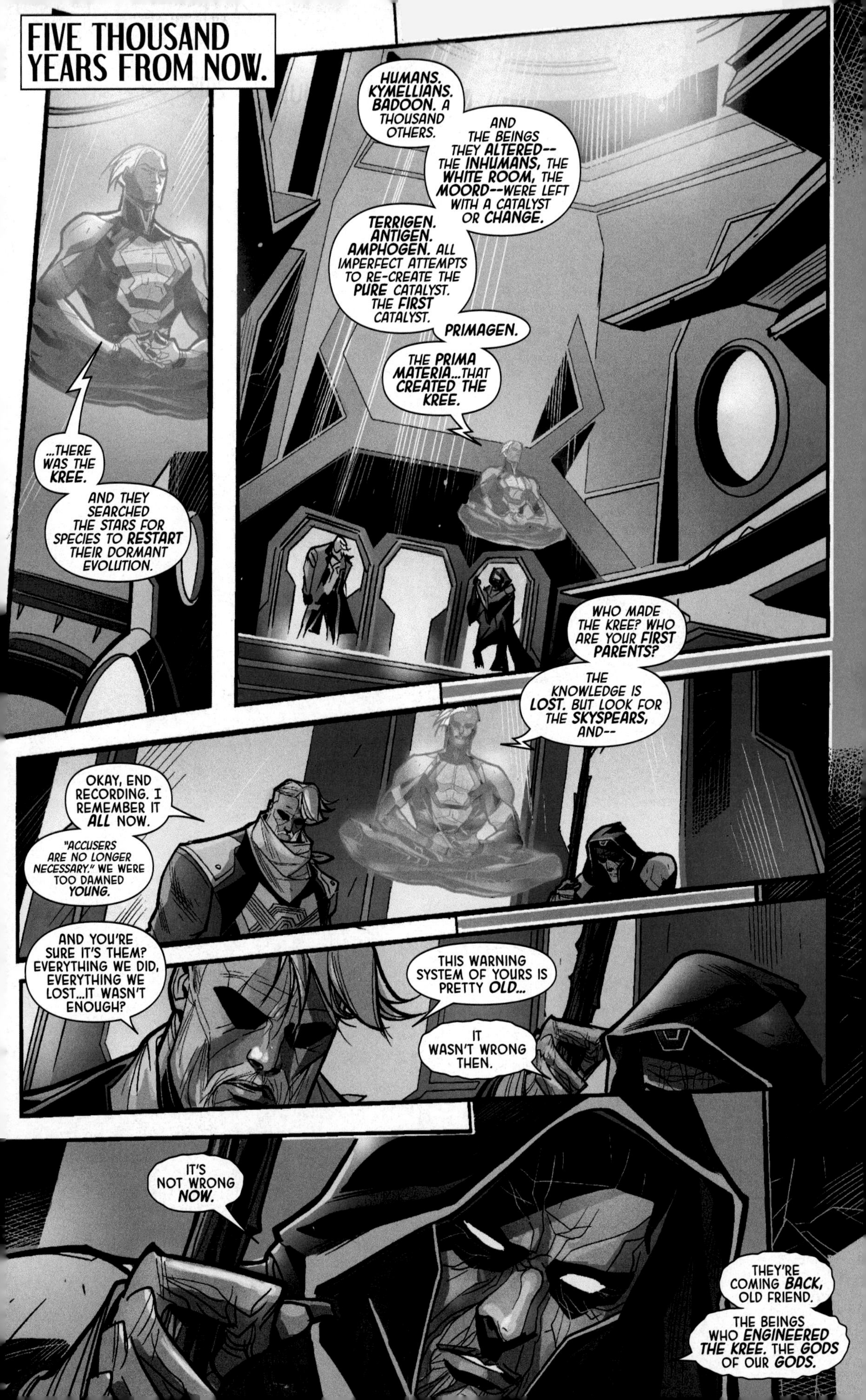
FIVE THOUSAND YEARS FROM NOW.
HUMANS. KYMELLIANS. BADOON. A THOUSAND OTHERS.
AND THE BEINGS THEY ALTERED--THE INHUMANS, THE WHITE ROOM, THE MOORD--WERE LEFT WITH A CATALYST OR CHANGE.
TERRIGEN. ANTIGEN. AMPHOGEN. ALL IMPERFECT ATTEMPTS TO RE-CREATE THE PURE CATALYST. THE FIRST CATALYST.
PRIMAGEN.
THE PRIMA MATERIA...THAT CREATED THE KREE.
...THERE WAS THE KREE.
AND THEY SEARCHED THE STARS FOR SPECIES TO RESTART THEIR DORMANT EVOLUTION.
WHO MADE THE KREE? WHO ARE YOUR FIRST PARENTS?
THE KNOWLEDGE IS LOST. BUT LOOK FOR THE SKYSPEARS, AND--
OKAY, END RECORDING. I REMEMBER IT ALL NOW.
"ACCUSERS ARE NO LONGER NECESSARY." WE WERE TOO DAMNED YOUNG.
AND YOU'RE SURE IT'S THEM? EVERYTHING WE DID, EVERYTHING WE LOST...IT WASN'T ENOUGH?
THIS WARNING SYSTEM OF YOURS IS PRETTY OLD...
IT WASN'T WRONG THEN.
IT'S NOT WRONG NOW.
THEY'RE COMING BACK, OLD FRIEND.
THE BEINGS WHO ENGINEERED THE KREE. THE GODS OF OUR GODS.

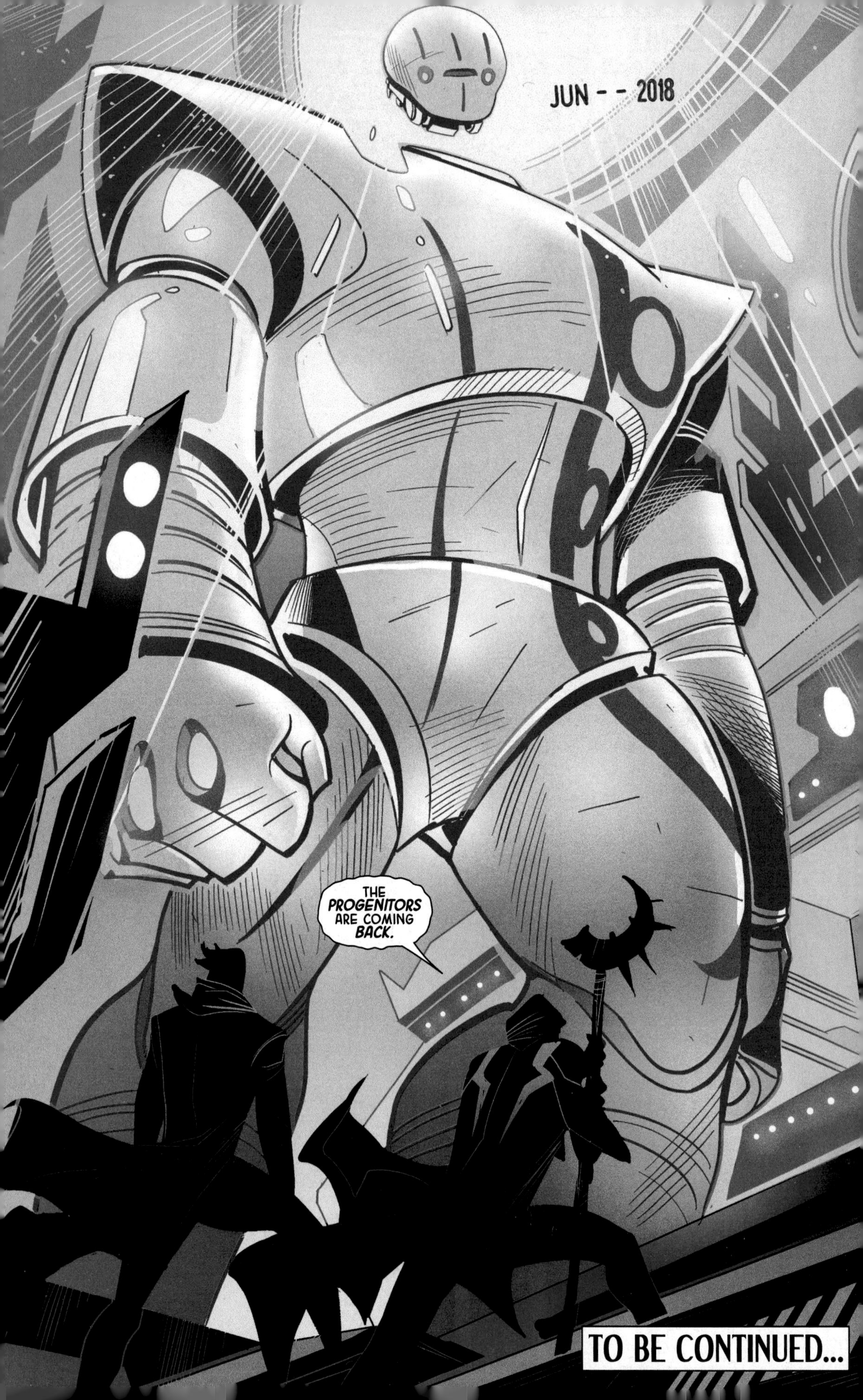
JUN - - 2018
THE PROGENITORS ARE COMING BACK.
TO BE CONTINUED...